Judges
A new translation with commentary

"The Yisra'elites once again did what Yahweh considered the worst thing of all: they gave service to the Ba'als and the Ashtoreths—that is, to Aram's gods, to Tziydon's gods, to Mo'av's gods, to the Ammonites' gods, and to the Philishtines' gods."

Frontispiece: Late Bronze Age figurines of Canaanite gods in the collection of the Metropolitan Museum of Art.

Left: seated deity, accession number 32.161.45, available at:
`https://www.metmuseum.org/art/collection/search/322889`.
Center: nude female figure, accession number 33.47.3, available at
`https://www.metmuseum.org/art/collection/search/322915`.
Right: smiting god, accession number 1986.42, available at
`https://www.metmuseum.org/art/collection/search/327231`.

Judges

A new translation with commentary

Translated with comments by William Whitt

The Cutting Horse Press

Weatherford, Texas

First published in 2024
by The Cutting Horse Press
Weatherford, Texas

Typeset in pdfLaTeX by the author
© 2024 by William Whitt

Print edition: ISBN 978-1-959-4870-3-6
Digital edition: ISBN 978-1-959-4870-2-9

Table of contents

Translator's note to the reader	vii
The book of Judges	1
Notes and comments	51
The composition history of Judges	133
Schema for the composition history of Judges	157
Appendix: The Song of Deborah and the display of songs in the Masoretic tradition	159

Translator's note to the reader

> "Whoever wishes to translate, and purposes to render each word literally, and at the same time adhere slavishly to the order of the words and sentences in the original, will meet with much difficulty; his rendering will be faulty and untrustworthy. This is not the right method. The translator should first try to grasp the sense of the subject thoroughly, and then state the theme with perfect clearness in the other language. This, however, cannot be done without changing the order of words, putting many words for one word, or *vice versa*, and adding or taking away words, so that the subject be perfectly intelligible in the language into which he translates."
> Moses Maimonides, Letter to His Translator Samuel ibn Tibbon
> Cited from *Miscellany of Hebrew Literature*, vol. 1 (1872), p. 222.

This translation of the book of Judges is part of a larger project that I have undertaken to translate the Torah and the Former Prophets—the first nine books of the Tanakh (or what Christians call the Old Testament).[1] These books, which present a history of the people who came to call themselves "Israel" and which begin with the world's creation and end with the destruction of Yahweh's temple in Jerusalem and the exile of the Judean elite to Babylonia, have indisputably had an outsized impact on human history. Through the act of their writing in the centuries spanning the first millennium BCE, their authors laid the groundwork for a new type of religion, one in which study of and adherence to "the book" ultimately displaced animal sacrifice as the primary avenue for humans to access the divine realm. These nine books, as they grew and came to take their current form over a period of centuries, provided a framework out of which the religion of Judaism emerged, and then, centuries later, shaped and inspired Christian theology. Yet despite these books' impact on human history, they are—with the possible exception of Genesis—barely read today.

One reason why they are unread is simply that most people today find them unreadable. This is true not only for the typical university-educated person, but even many devout Jews and Christians view them as such. One of the primary goals I have in this larger transla-

---

[1] This book is the eighth I have translated. The others so far published are my translations of Genesis, Exodus, Leviticus, Numbers, Deuteronomy, Joshua, and Samuel; all are freely available at the Internet Archive and on my webpage at academia.edu.

tion project, then, is to make these books readable—or at least less unreadable—for the modern-day audience.

**

Within this nine-book historical chronicle of the people Israel—that is, the Torah and the Former Prophets—the book of Judges tells stories of an anarchic and unsettled time. These are "the days when there was no king in Israel," the period after the conquest and occupation of the land described in the book of Joshua and before the establishment of the monarchy under Saul—a sort of dark ages when the loosely organized Israelite tribes were repeatedly threatened and oppressed by neighboring kings, when the tribes often warred with one another, and when the people themselves vacillated between loyalty to Yahweh and giving service to the local Ba'als, Ashtoreths, and Asherahs. The stories in the book of Judges are centered on individuals who prove themselves as heroic leaders and champions of the people, who lead the Israelites to victory over their foreign oppressors, bringing peace and order to the land and creating the conditions for the people to return to Yahweh and remain loyal to him. The narrative itself has a highly cyclical structure: the champion rescues the Israelites from their foreign oppressors, following which the Israelites live at peace and are loyal to Yahweh for the remainder of the champion's life; but after the champion's death, they abandon Yahweh for the local gods, and in turn they are punished by Yahweh, who allows neighboring kings to oppress them; the people then cry out to Yahweh for help, and he raises up a new champion for them, and the cycle starts anew.

In seeking to understand the book of Judges and its place within the canon, many scholars have viewed the book's composition as closely connected to the writing of the so-called Deuteronomistic History.[2] Scholars generally agree that this work consists of the books of Deuteronomy, Joshua, Judges, Samuel and Kings. There is also general agreement that this work represents an attempt by individuals asso-

---

[2] The idea of a Deuteronomistic History was first proposed by the German scholar Martin Noth in 1942, and since then has served as a foundation for much scholarship on the Former Prophets. Noth's work devoted to this proposal has been translated into English and published as *The Deuteronomistic History*, Sheffield: JSOT Press, 1981. For a good concise overview of scholarly approaches to the idea of a Deuteronomistic History, see T. Römer, "Deuteronomistic History," EBR 6 (2013), cols. 648-653. For a more detailed discussion of scholarship on the Deuteronomistic History, see S. McKenzie, *The Trouble with Kings: The Composition of the Book of Kings in the Deuteronomistic History*, Leiden: E.J. Brill, 1991.

ciated with the royal court of Judah and/or Yahweh's cult on Mount Zion to explain the history of the Israelite people through the lens of Deuteronomy and the treaty obligations imposed on the people in that book.³ There is, however, a fair amount of disagreement over the specific circumstances behind the composition of the Deuteronomistic History, including when it was written, whether it was the work of one or multiple authors, whether there was more than a single "edition" of it, and to what extent it involved a revision of pre-existing books versus the composition of entirely new books.

In fact, in recent decades, these points of disagreement have led a number of scholars to question the entire concept of a Deuteronomistic History.⁴ At the most general level, the primary problem with such a history is that the books ascribed to it can't really be considered a unified work. The books are only loosely connected by theme and, most importantly, the so-called Deuteronomistic elements differ from book to book—and in some books, these elements barely appear at all. A close reading of the individual books of the history reveals the presence of multiple "Deuteronomistic" authors and editors, to say nothing of the many other "non-Deuteronomistic" authors whose works the so-called Deuteronomists utilized, sometimes revising and editing and other times leaving practically untouched. The messiness of the material in the history, the lack of internal inconsistency both within and across the books of the history, and the absence of Deuteronomic themes in large sections of these books thus create almost insurmountable challenges for the traditional proposal for a Deuteronomistic History represented by Deuteronomy - Kings.

Prior to beginning this translation of Judges, my views about the Deuteronomistic History were by and large within the older mainstream of scholarly thinking. In brief, my views were: that the earliest "edition" of the work was composed in the decades immediately following the destruction of the Jerusalem temple in 586 BCE; that the work as a whole was sponsored by leaders within Yahweh's cult and

---

3   For Deuteronomy's presentation of itself as a treaty document, see the introductory comments to my translation of Deuteronomy.
4   See, for example, K. Noll, "Deuteronomistic History or Deuteronomistic debate? (A thought experiment)," *Journal for the Study of the Old Testament* 31 (2007), pp. 311-345 and G. Knoppers, "Rethinking the relationship between Deuteronomy and the Deuteronomistic History: the case of Kings," *The Catholic Biblical Quarterly* 63 (2001), pp. 393-415. See also K. Schmid, "The Emergence and Disappearance of the Separation between the Pentateuch and the Deuteronomistic History in Biblical Studies," in T. Dozeman, T. Römer, and K. Schmid (eds.), *Pentateuch, Hexateuch, or Enneateuch: Identifying Literary Works in Genesis through Kings* (Atlanta: Society of Biblical Literature, 2011), pp. 11-24.

the royal court of Judah, some of whom also served as lead editors of the work; that these sponsors commissioned a number of individuals to write the books that comprise the history; and that the books' authors drew on and incorporated pre-existing written documents and oral traditions, but shaped these materials in their own individual ways to express the larger themes of their books and of the overall history. The one place where my views differed from those of most other scholars was that I also ascribed the earliest edition of Exodus-Numbers (originally a single book in my view) to the Deuteronomistic History.[5] Over the course of my work on Judges, however, I have come to see that my views on the composition of the books associated with the Deuteronomistic History—and the very idea of a "Deuteronomistic" history itself—would need to be modified significantly to explain the material that we find in Judges. In the sections below, I sketch my thinking on the background of Judges and how it fits into a broader theory about the composition of the earliest "histories" of the Israelite people, and why I have chosen to abandon the "Deuteronomistic" terminology to describe these histories.

**

A close examination of the book of Judges with respect to Deuteronomy and the key concepts in that book helps make clear the problems that Judges poses for the traditional theory of a Deuteronomistic History as a unified work of the sixth century BCE. Most important in my view is that the base narrative of Judges has no fundamental connection to Deuteronomy.[6] For example, Yahweh's treaty with the Israelites—which is a key focus of Exodus and Deuteronomy and which looms in the background throughout Numbers, Joshua, and (to a lesser extent) Kings—appears in Judges only in the summary

---

[5] My rationale for this was that, as I argue in my translation of Joshua, the narratives of the early layers of Numbers and Joshua assume one another and are inextricably linked. Thus, if the earliest edition of Joshua was part of the Deuteronomistic History, then the earliest edition of Numbers must be as well. Likewise, because the early layers of Numbers and Exodus are inextricably linked and in fact seem to comprise a single work, then the earliest version of Exodus must also belong to the Deuteronomistic History. For additional thoughts on Exodus-Numbers as part of the Deuteronomistic History, see the introductions to my translations of Joshua, Exodus, and Numbers.

[6] Judges' tenuous connection to Deuteronomy has been observed by almost all scholars who have studied the book closely. The closest points of connection with Deuteronomy are found in the summary material in chapter 2 that lays out the book's theme and introduces the cyclical narrative structure.

material near the book's beginning, and then is not mentioned again.[7] The treaty chest, which plays an important role in all the other books of the Former Prophets, is absent in Judges except for one reference found in a story that is a very late addition to the text.[8] Moreover, the numerous altars and shrines to Yahweh that appear in Judges are presented without authorial comment or judgement, as though the authors were unaware of Deuteronomy's requirement that there be only one altar to Yahweh and in sharp contrast to the careful treatment of this question in the other books of the Former Prophets. Finally, the base narratives of the stories in Judges show no awareness of the idea that the various tribes of north and south were unified as a single people under the name Israel; yet this idea is an important concept in Deuteronomy and is fundamental to the narrative arc of the history spanning Exodus - Kings. In the few places where we do find comments and material in Judges that are dependent on Deuteronomy, it is always the case that these are secondary and are not intrinsic to the narrative.

The lack of any true fundamental connection to Deuteronomy is, I believe, a strong indication of an early literary layer within Judges that pre-dates the composition during the Babylonian exile of a history that was influenced by Deuteronomy.[9] This quite naturally raises the question of how we can identify such material in Judges. It also raises the question of whether such material exists in the other books of the Former Prophets, and if so, how we can identify that as well. These are important questions, for if we give up the idea of a unified Deuteronomistic History, then any new theory of the composition of these books that we develop in its place must provide a sound explanation of such early material.

**

---

7   The two passages mentioning the treaty are Jud 2.1 and 2.20.
8   See Jud 20.27.
9   My views here are not unique; numerous scholars have argued that the core stories of Judges pre-date Deuteronomy and the so-called Deuteronomistic History. See, for example, Y. Amit, "The Book of Judges: Dating and Meaning," in G. Galil, M. Geller, and A. Millard (eds.), *Homeland and Exile: Biblical and Ancient Near Eastern Studies in Honor of Bustenay Oded* (Leiden: Brill, 2009), pp. 297-322.

In examining the books of the Former Prophets for material that might have served as literary precursors to a history written during the exile and influenced by Deuteronomy (or what I will call the "Israelite History"[10]), I believe there are two simple criteria that one should apply: (1) such material should have neither an awareness of, nor a true dependence on, key themes of Deuteronomy; and (2) such material should show no dependence on concepts and ideas characteristic of either the Persian period (ca. 550 - 330 BCE) or the Hellenistic period (ca. 330 - 30 BCE).

When we apply these two filters to the books of the Former Prophets and remove material clearly dependent on Deuteronomy or showing the influence of late ideas and concepts, what remains is a very diverse set of stories, some set in the tribal areas of the north and/or the transjordan and others set in the tribal areas of the south, some belonging to the written literature of the kingdom of Israel and others to the literature of the kingdom of Judah, some stemming from common folk traditions and others originating in the official records of the royal court. It is within this diverse set of materials that we may identify the literary precursors to the exilic Israelite History. When Joshua is viewed through these filters, there is nothing that can be reliably said to pre-date Deuteronomy and what I call the exilic Israelite History.[11] The other books of the Former Prophets, however, contain a great deal of material that appears to be early and that shows no awareness of Deuteronomy. In Judges, this material consists of the core of the stories of Ehud, Deborah and Baraq, Gideon, Jephthah, and possibly Samson.[12] In Samuel, it consists of the core of the Saul

---

10 Because of the problematic nature of the "Deuteronomistic History" as it is currently conceived, I have decided to abandon that terminology in favor of the term Israelite History. As I use this term, I understand it to mean the books of Exodus-Numbers, Deuteronomy, Joshua, Judges, Samuel, and Kings as they existed in the first half of the sixth century BCE. It is my view that the authors of this history created their work by composing Exodus-Numbers and Joshua and then attaching those books to the pre-existing books of Deuteronomy, Judges, Samuel, and Kings. The authors of the Israelite History added a narrative frame to Deuteronomy, but I believe they made only minor changes to Judges, Samuel, and Kings. The authors of the Israelite History were certainly influenced by Deuteronomy in the works they created (Exodus-Numbers and Joshua), but they introduced few Deuteronomic ideas into Judges, Samuel, and Kings, and they made fewer edits to those books than is generally acknowledged.

11 For Joshua's dependence on Deuteronomy, see the introductory comments to my translation of Joshua.

12 Although it is possible to treat the Samson stories as belonging to the literary precursors of an exilic Israelite History, there are good reasons (as I argue below in the notes and comments) for understanding these stories as late additions to the text, not least of which is that, unlike the other heroes in Judges, Samson

and David narratives, and much of the material about Samuel and Yahweh's "battle-chest."[13] And in Kings, it consists of the core of the "royal chronicles" of Judah and Israel—matter-of-fact depictions of the reigns of those nations' kings, the dates of their ascensions to the throne and of their deaths, and summaries of important events that happened during their reigns—but excludes much of the material about Solomon and Josiah, as well as the stories of Elijah and Elisha.

**

How should we understand these literary precursors to the exilic Israelite History—and, in particular, the stories in Judges that seem to pre-date that work? When we examine the stories in Judges that I suggested above belong to the literary precursors, two things are immediately clear. First, although these stories have many literary elements, they do not read as pure literary inventions. Rather, they read as stories that have their origins in tribal folk traditions—stories about great tribal leaders and heroes that were passed down in folk memory by their descendants and that were only later written down and expanded through the addition of literary features. Second, all of these early stories in Judges are concerned with heroes of tribes associated with the northern kingdom of Israel; stories about heroes from the southern tribes are notably absent. Ehud is from Benjamin, Deborah from Ephraim, Baraq from Naphtali, Gideon from Manasseh, and Jephthah from Gilead.[14] Moreover, when these heroes recruit

---

  does not serve as a great military leader of the Israelite tribes.
    It is worth noting here that the author of 1 Sam 12—who likely was one of the lead editors of the Israelite History—alludes to an early version of the book of Judges, and he specifically mentions Gideon (whom he refers to as Jerubaal) and Jephthah. He also mentions the name Bedan, which many scholars believe is an error for the name Baraq. Among Israel's oppressors, he mentions Sisera (the "villain" in Judges 4-5 who fights Deborah and Baraq), the king of Moab (the villain in Judges 3 who was killed by Ehud), and the Philistines (the villains of both the Samson stories and the Samuel stories). From this passage in 1 Sam 12, we can be reasonably certain that the core of the stories of Ehud, Deborah and Baraq, Gideon, and Jephthah belong to the early literary layer of Judges.

13 In my translation of Samuel completed in 2018, I viewed the book as composed specifically in connection with the creation of the Deuteronomistic History, and I did not identify any pre-Deuteronomistic literary layers in the book. But based on the work I have done over the past several years, I now believe that the composition history of Samuel is more complex and extends both further back and further forward in time than I previously understood.

14 The authors of the stories of Gideon and Jephthah treat Gilead as the name of one of the northern tribes. It was only later, with the composition of what I call the Israelite History, that Gilead as a tribal name is replaced by the tribe of Gad

other tribes to assist in their military adventures, they recruit only from territories inhabited by the northern tribes. Thus, Ehud marshals forces from the Ephraim mountains; Barak summons fighters from Zebulon; Gideon recruits troops from Asher, Zebulon, Naphtali, and Ephraim; and Jephthah collects "all the men from Gilead."

The exclusive emphasis on the northern tribes is a strong indication that these stories were first collected and written down by individuals from the territories of the northern kingdom. But how and why did it happen that these northern stories appear in and play such a prominent role in what I call the Israelite History—a history put together by authors from the south to explain the loss of the land and the exile from it? To answer this question, we must first examine scholars' theories regarding the origin of Deuteronomy.

**

Scholars have long speculated that the ideas and traditions found in Deuteronomy likely originated in one of the numerous locations of Yahweh's cult in the north,[15] and that they were introduced to Judah by northern priests and cult leaders who fled there after the Assyrian

---

and the eastern clans of Manasseh, all of which occupied the region of Gilead. The story of Jephthah does not specify which tribe Jephthah was from, although his hometown was Mitzpah in Gilead. (It should be noted that in Jos 13.26, the authors assigned Mitzpah to the territory of Gad.)

15 The idea that Deuteronomy has a northern origin goes back to the early twentieth century. But for a recent review of the history of scholarship on this proposal, see C. Edenburg and R. Müller, "A Northern Provenance for Deuteronomy? A Critical Review," *Hebrew Bible and Ancient Israel* 4 (2015), pp. 148-161. It should be noted that Edenburg and Müller are critical of the sort of speculations engaged in by myself and other scholars regarding the origins and life setting of Deuteronomy and other biblical books. In their view, rather than speculate on the origins of Deuteronomy, it is more productive to investigate why different audiences found Deuteronomy so significant, how they used the book to reinforce identity, and what characteristics of the book allowed for "multivalent" readings by competing groups.

While I agree that the questions posed by Edenburg and Müller provide productive avenues for research, I firmly believe that there is also much value in addressing questions about the origins and composition history of the different biblical books. For even if we can never move beyond the realm of speculation, there is nonethess value in examining these questions, for such efforts help sharpen our thinking about the complexities and inconsistencies in the material and—most importantly—they can deepen our understanding of the text by offering plausible and historically-grounded explanations for these books' themes, structure, and content.

conquest of Israel in 722 BCE.[16] Scholars who follow this proposal are divided, however, regarding when this group of refugees and their views about the proper conduct of the cult first gained influence in Jerusalem. Some have argued that they quickly became influential in the first years after their arrival, during the reign of Hezekiah, whose rule is traditionally ascribed to the years 715 - 686 BCE.[17] Others, however, argue that these ideas did not gain influence until the reign of Josiah, beginning around 640 BCE; in this scenario, it would have been the refugees' children or grandchildren who rose to positions of power within the royal court.[18] I think the arguments for the latter view—that these families first gained influence at the royal court of Josiah—are more compelling. Most important, in my view, is that the evidence for the "Deuteronomic" cult reforms under Hezekiah is highly questionable. The account of these reforms is given in a single sentence (2 Kings 18.4), and that sentence employs wholly formulaic language that reads as editorial commentary not based on fact. In addition, it is particularly telling that the oracles of Isaiah, who was prominent in the Jerusalem cult during Hezekiah's reign, show no real awareness of Deuteronomic principles, nor of cult reforms based on these principles.

---

16   An early and influential proponent of the idea that northern refugees brought Deuteronomy (or the ideas within it) to Judah was E. W. Nicholson in his book *Deuteronomy and Tradition*, Philadelphia: Fortress Press, 1967. See in particular his discussion on pp. 94-106, especially p. 94 and p. 102. Given the close links between the ideas of Hosea and those of Deuteronomy, it is reasonable to suppose that the individuals responsible for bringing the ideas of Deuteronomy to Jerusalem were associated with the same cult location where Hosea was active, and that these individuals brought a record of Hosea's oracles with them when they relocated to Judah.

17   These scholars base their arguments on Hezekiah's cult reforms described in 2 Kings 18.4, which carry out a program that is consistent with Deuteronomic principles—the abolition of open-air shrines and the destruction of the divine images used for worship in those shrines.

18   These scholars base their arguments on the account of Josiah's reign in 2 Kings 22.1 - 23.30, which describe the "discovery" of the scroll of the Torah (almost certainly a very early version of the book of Deuteronomy) and the subsequent "renewal" of the treaty between Yahweh and his people, including the people's acceptance of their obligations under the treaty. Following the renewal of the treaty, Josiah carried out an especially violent program of religious cleansing instituting the principles espoused in Deuteronomy. This involved the destruction of the cults of the local gods in Judah, the destruction of Yahweh's cult in Samaria and the slaughter of all the priests serving in that cult, the destruction of all altars and shrines in Judah dedicated to Yahweh outside the Jerusalem temple, and the removal and destruction of all cult items within the Jerusalem temple used in the service of Ba'al, Asherah, and other gods.

The origin of what I am calling the Israelite History is best understood against this background of the rising influence of northern families within the royal court at Jerusalem. Numerous scholars have argued for an early version of this history—that is, a version that was the precursor to the history produced after the fall of Jerusalem in 586 BCE. Some scholars propose a single early version connected to the reign of Josiah, while others propose two early versions, one connected to the reign of Hezekiah and then a revision of that version during the reign of Josiah.[19] But if we accept the arguments above that there is no real evidence for cult reforms under Hezekiah inspired by Deuteronomic principles, then there is no reason to think that an early version of the Israelite History (or what others call the Deuteronomistic History) was composed during Hezekiah's reign. For this reason, I follow those scholars who see only one pre-exilic version of this history—a version composed during the reign of Josiah. The primary goal of this Josianic version of the history likely was to legitimize Josiah's implementation of the radical agenda of Deuteronomy.[20] This entailed not only the destruction of the cults of the local gods and the cleansing of Yahweh's cult in Jerusalem, but also the pursuit of an expansionist political policy that aimed to bring the former lands of the northern kingdom under the rule of Judah's king and so "reunite" the peoples of the north and south in accord with the Deuteronomic vision of Yahweh's people.[21] To create a basis for the "reunification" with the

---

19   Frank Moore Cross was the first to propose there was a pre-exilic edition of the Deuteronomistic History that dated to the reign of Josiah; this proposal has proved very popular and is still widely held by scholars today. Cross first published his proposal in "The Structure of the Deuteronomistic History," *Perspectives on Jewish Learning*, Annual of the College of Jewish Studies 3 (Chicago, 1968), pp. 9-24. The idea that there were two pre-exilic editions of the Deuteronomistic History—the first in the reign of Hezekiah and a revision of that during the reign of Josiah—was first proposed by Helga Weippert in 1972; numerous scholars have followed Weippert in this proposal. Weippert's proposal was published in "Die 'deuteronomistischen' Beurteilung der Könige von Israel und Juda und das Problem der Redaktion der Königsbücher," *Biblica* 53, pp. 301-339.

20   Two key features of the Josianic version, as pointed out in the initial proposal of F. M. Cross, were the condemnation of the kingdom of Israel because of the "sin" of Jeroboam (culminating in the destruction of Samaria in 2 Kings 17) and the emphasis on Yahweh's promise to David and his descendants, culminating in the reign of Josiah. Both of these themes were needed to help legitimize the reforms and policies of Josiah, which were intended to bring "all Israel'"—Judah and the former territories of Israel—under a religious system based on Deuteronomy and led by a Davidic king.

21   The idea that Yahweh's adherents living in Judah and in what was then the province of Samaria made up a single people called "Israel" is a core tenet of the authors of Deuteronomy and the exilic Deuteronomistic History (or what I call

peoples of the north, the authors of this history would need to show both that the Davidic dynasty had a legitimate claim on the territories comprising the province of Samaria and that Yahweh had specifically chosen David and his descendants to serve in perpetuity as the leaders of his people. This, in my view, explains the circumstances behind the composition of much of the material about Samuel, Saul, and David in the book of Samuel and much of the material about Solomon, Jeroboam, and Josiah in the book of Kings.

There are good reasons for supposing that the authors of this Josianic precursor to the Israelite History were from the northern families who had brought the ideas of Deuteronomy to Judah and who had found positions within the royal court. First, the history presented Josiah as a great leader who carries out the stipulations of the Torah scroll found in Yahweh's temple, and it promoted some early version of Deuteronomy as the basis of Josiah's reforms. Such a history could only have been written by individuals outside the cult establishment, for the reforms completely obliterated the way the established cult operated, and it dismantled the established leaders' power structure by defiling the local Yahwistic shrines overseen by priests who were allied with the Jerusalem cult establishment.[22] But the use of the history to promote Josiah's reforms and the use of Deuteronomic ideas as the basis of those reforms make perfect sense if the authors of this history were from the northern refugee families who brought these Deuteronomic ideas and principles to Judah. Second, the authors of the history showed a strong interest in the northern kingdom, and the history promoted a political agenda for Josiah that aimed to bring the territories of the former northern kingdom under political control and to subject the citizens in those territories to the same Deuteronomic program carried out in Judah. Again, the interest in the former northern kingdom and the imposition of a Deuteronomic

---

the Israelite History). A number of events described in the accounts of Josiah's reign in 2 Kings 23 and 2 Chr 34-35 make most sense in the context of Josiah's pursuit of a policy to bring the province of Samaria under his control and thus unify Yahweh's adherents as a single people. Such a policy, for example, helps us understand his attack on Yahweh's cult in Samaria in 2 Kings 23.15, 19-20, which describe the destruction of Yahweh's altar in Bethel and the destruction of the Yahwistic shrines in the towns of Samaria. (For, with the destruction of the Samarian shrines and altars to Yahweh, the inhabitants of that province would have no option but to travel to Jerusalem to make offerings to Yahweh and to participate in his festivals.) Equally important, such a policy also helps us understand Josiah's otherwise inexplicable actions in 2 Chr 35.20ff, when he and his army challenge Pharaoh Necho's passage through the Jezreel Valley.

22 For Josiah's actions against these shrines and the priests employed in them, see 2 Kings 23.5, 8-14.

agenda on its former territories make perfect sense if the authors of the history were from these northern refugee families.

In short, the northern refugee families, who were outside the power structure of Yahweh's cult in Jerusalem, used their influence at Josiah's court to accomplish what amounted to a hostile takeover of Yahweh's cult in Judah. This was followed by the obliteration of Yahweh's cult in Samaria, which practiced versions of Yahwism that these families had violently disagreed with since before the fall of the northern kingdom. Their principal tools to convince Josiah to carry out these actions were the composition of two literary documents: an early version of the book of Deuteronomy that tied their program of cult reforms to the authority of the "ancient" scroll of the Torah, and an early version of the Israelite History—or what I will call the Josianic History—that served to legitimate the Davidic dynasty's claim on the territories of Samaria.[23]

**

---

[23] Although this is wholly speculative, one intriguing explanation of the origin of the Josianic History is that these works were initially written in the 630s BCE to educate the young king Josiah about the qualities of a leader and great king and about his obligations to Yahweh, the god of the united people of Israel. The king's curriculum, as it were, would have consisted of Samuel and Kings and an early version of the book of Deuteronomy, as well as stories of the great leaders of the northern tribes—that is, the earliest version of the book of Judges, which at the time was not necessarily connected to the narrative of Samuel. It is interesting to note that the stories in Judges and Samuel seem practically tailored to appeal to a boy in his teenage years, which happened to be Josiah's age in the 630s (he assumed the throne in 640 at the age of nine). This admittedly speculative theory can also help explain the piecemeal nature of Judges, Samuel, and Kings. If they were first written to educate the young king, we could imagine them being written not all at once and then presented to the king, but written over the course of several years, with some parts written before others, and the king given lessons from the books as they were being written. Later, in the 620s, as Josiah's program of reform gets underway, one can imagine the books that had been written for the king's education—the earliest versions of Judges, Samuel, and Kings—being revised and expanded, and then promulgated to a broad audience of Judah's elite in an attempt to gain their support for Josiah's actions.

With respect to Josiah's education, very little is known about the education of royalty in ancient Israel and Judah; a good and concise summary of what is known can be found in "Education, Jewish" in *Encyclopedia Judaica*, 2nd. ed. volume 6 pp. 165f, which argues that royal education principally consisted of three subjects: physical and military training, diplomacy and government, and the national cult. It is worth noting that the early versions of Deuteronomy, Judges, Samuel, and Kings would have provided Josiah with training in all three of these subjects.

What is the relationship between the early stories in Judges and the Josianic History? Were these stories part of that work, or were they only later joined to that work as part of the exilic expansions that transformed the Josianic History into the Israelite History? Cogent arguments can be made for either view, and in fact, over the course of my translation work on the book, I have gone back and forth between the two positions. A key reason for thinking the stories were not part of the Josianic History is that there is no true narrative continuity between the early stories in Judges and the stories in Samuel about the priest and military leader Samuel (which I believe were part of the Josianic History). Moreover, if Judges were part of the Josianic History, we would expect to see some material that could serve as the beginning of that work. But in fact, there is no place in Judges that reads naturally as the beginning of a new work.[24]

Despite these arguments, I lean more toward the view that these early stories were part of the Josianic History.[25] Most telling, in my opinion, is that the treaty between Yahweh and his people—which serves as the lens through which the exilic-period authors of the Israelite History understand the events leading to the loss of the land and the destruction of the Jerusalem temple—is absent from the narrative frame of Judges. If the early stories of Judges were not joined to Samuel until the exile as part of the creation of the Israelite History, we would expect to see the treaty and the people's violation of their treaty obligations as part of the narrative frame. The absence of this theme is most easily explained if we suppose that the early stories of Judges were part of the Josianic History and that the editors of the Israelite History chose to leave these stories largely untouched. The narrative frame in Judges utilizes the idea of the people's forsaking Yahweh for other gods—which the authors call "the worst thing in Yahweh's view"—as the primary structural device within the book. This theme makes sense within the context of a Josianic History, for one of Josiah's main goals was to abolish the practice of giving service to the local gods alongside Yahweh. Moreover, it is plausible that that exilic authors and editors of the Israelite History would have decided to make minimal edits to the Josianic History's narrative frame of Judges, for even though it did not utilize the treaty language, the

---

24 It is worth noting that both these problems—the lack of continuity between Judges and Samuel and the lack of a true beginning to Judges—are explicable if we understand Judges, Samuel, and Kings to have been originally composed to educate the young king Josiah. See note 23 directly above.

25 That is to say, I view the Josianic History as consisting of the early versions of Samuel and Kings plus the early version of Judges.

frame was consistent with that language and with their larger theme about the Israelites' unfaithfulness towards Yahweh. And with respect to the lack of a "beginning" to the Josianic History in Judges, it is possible that the history's beginning was removed from Judges by the authors of the Israelite History when they connected their newly composed book of Joshua to the older book of Judges.

**

Over the course of my work translating Judges, I have identified six broad stages in the book's composition. The earliest stage represents the original written versions of stories about great ancestral heroes of the northern tribes. These stories have their roots in the last centuries of the second millennium, and were passed down orally for several centuries (during which time they would have grown and been embellished) before being written down sometime between the tenth and eighth centuries BCE. I believe that at this stage, the stories remained independent of one another and were not connected in any way.[26]

I understand the second compositional stage of the book as the product of what I call the Josianic History (or what other scholars call the Josianic edition of the Deuteronomistic History). The authors of this stage, which I place in the 630s and 620s BCE, selected stories about six of these ancient heroes—Othniel, Ehud, Deborah and Baraq, Gideon, and Jephthah—and connected them with a narrative frame to create the earliest version of Judges. This version of the book served as the beginning of the Josianic History, and its authors shaped its narrative to support three key themes of that history: the necessity of kingship, the qualities of great leaders and poor leaders, and the unity of the tribes as a single people called Israel.[27] In particular, by presenting the stories within a cyclical "apostasy / oppression / rescue" structure, the authors show the anarchic conditions under which the tribes lived prior to the establishment of kingship, and they show how

---

[26] Many scholars have argued the old stories in Judges were first joined together in a work they call the "Book of Saviors," a theory first proposed by Wolfgang Richter in 1963. However, I do not see a compelling reason to believe these stories of the heroes were connected prior to the composition of the Josianic History. The details for Richter's proposal for a Book of Saviors can be found in his books *Traditionsgeschichtliche Untersuchungen zum Richterbuch*, Bonner Biblische Beiträge 18, Bonn: 1963 and *Die Bearbeitung des 'Retterbuches' in der deuteronomistischen Epoche*, Bonner Biblische Beiträge 21, Bonn: 1964.

[27] It is interesting to note that these three themes would be especially appropriate for a work that was written for the education of a young king, which, as I suggest above in note 23, is one possible explanation for the origin of the Josianic History.

these conditions were conducive to the people abandoning Yahweh to give service to other gods. In this way, they lay the groundwork for the establishment of kingship in the book of Samuel.

The third compositional stage of the book represents the work on Judges done as part of the expansion of the Josianic History and the transformation of it into what I call the Israelite History (or what other scholars call the exilic edition of the Deuteronomistic History). This work took place sometime in the period between the 580s and 550s BCE. The authors of this stage wrote a new beginning to the book in order to connect Judges to the newly composed book of Joshua, but they made few other edits. There was little reason for these authors to make major changes or additions to the book, as the main theme of the Josianic version of the book—that the Israelites repeatedly abandoned Yahweh for other gods despite Yahweh raising "champions" to rescue them from their oppressors—was consistent with the broader message of the exilic Israelite History, which is that Yahweh brought down the treaty curses on his people for their violation of the treaty obligations (in particular the obligation to give service to only him).[28]

The fourth and fifth compositional stages of Judges represent, respectively, early expansions made to the book in the sixth and fifth centuries BCE and late expansions made in the fourth, third, and second centuries BCE. The additions made in these stages were consistent with the types of additions made to the other books of the Former Prophets during these periods. As I discuss in the notes and comments below, the expansions to Judges in these two stages included the stories of Samson, the story of Abimelek's abortive kingship, the material about the conquest of the land at the beginning of Judges, the material about the establishment of the cult of Dan, and at the end of the book, the story of the Levite's concubine and the resulting slaughter of the Benjaminites. The sixth and final compositional stage of Judges, which largely overlapped with the fifth stage, represents editorial activity that took place against the background of the emergence of Judaism, the adoption of a canon of holy scripture, and the recitation and study of the canonical books in an institutional setting (the early synagogue) within the diaspora communities. To support this use of scripture, the authors of this stage added numerous comments, glosses, and harmonizations to Judges, thus giving the book the form it has today.

---

28 The clearest expressions of the overarching message of the Israelite History are Joshua's farewell speech in Jos 23, the Song of Moses in Deut 32, and the lead-in to that song at the conclusion to Deut 31.

**

Modern translation theory speaks of two types of translation—translation that aims for "formal" equivalence and translation that aims for "functional" (or what is sometimes called "dynamic") equivalence. Formal equivalence is concerned with fidelity to the text and aims to produce a translation that accurately reflects the meaning of the source text, preserving wherever possible word order and sentence structure, and seeking to maintain one-for-one correspondences in vocabulary. Robert Alter's translation of the Tanakh, published in 2018, is an example of a translation that emphasizes formal equivalence over functional equivalence. By contrast, functional (or dynamic) equivalence is concerned with fluency; the aim here is to produce a natural-sounding translation that recreates for the reader the same experience of the text as that of a native speaker of the source language. Such a translation by necessity breaks with one-to-one correspondences in vocabulary and word order in order to express a specific thought or idea in the most natural way in the target language.

From antiquity, one of the fundamental debates among translators has been whether translations should strive for formal equivalence or for functional equivalence. The early Church father Jerome, who spent the better part of two decades writing the Vulgate (the first Latin translation of the Christian Old and New Testaments), discusses this issue at length in his "Letter to Pammachius on the Best Method of Translating." Although Jerome believed that Bible translations should aim for formal equivalence (because of the divine inspiration of the text), he argues that for all other texts functional equivalence is the superior method of translation. Thus, he says, he translates "sense for sense and not word for word." He then develops this argument in detail by quoting passages from Cicero and Horace in which they argue in favor of what we today call functional equivalence.[29]

---

29 Cicero's comments are excellent and are worth quoting at length: "I have translated the noblest speeches of the two most eloquent of the Attic orators...I have rendered them not as a translator, but as an orator, keeping the sense but altering the form by adapting the metaphors and the words to suit our own idiom. I have not deemed it necessary to render word for word but I have reproduced the general style and emphasis. I have not supposed myself bound to pay the words out one by one to the reader but only to give him an equivalent in value." And "I shall be well satisfied if my rendering is found, as I trust it will be, true to this standard. In making it I have utilized all the excellences of the originals, I mean the sentiments, the forms of expression and the arrangement of the topics, while I have followed the actual wording only so far as I could do so without offending our notions of taste. If all that I have written is not to be found in the Greek, I have at any rate striven to make it correspond with it."

Today, outside translators of the Bible, the debate has largely been settled in favor of functional equivalence. With translations of the Bible into English, however, it is a different story. Perhaps because of the undue influence of the King James translation (which emphasized formal equivalence), or perhaps out of the (conscious or unconscious) belief that the exact Hebrew and Greek words in the Tanakh and the Christian New Testament are divinely inspired, many English-language translators of the Bible employ approaches that strive for formal equivalence and that reject functional equivalence outright.

I began this note with an epigraph from Moses Maimonides on the translator's task because it sums up succinctly the technique that I believe produces the most successful translations. Along with Maimonides, I come down firmly on the side of functional equivalence. In this and my other translations, I have put special effort into trying to convey the authors' meaning in natural English—in particular, I have written what I imagine the authors would have written had they been native speakers of modern-day English. My priorities are always to try to express the ideas in the text in the most natural way in English, and at the same time to capture the energy and rhythm of the original. When a Hebrew passage is awkwardly phrased, repetitive, or confusing, the English translation should reflect that; likewise, when a passage is written in a fluid or a highly literary style in the original, the English translation should be written that way as well.

Hebrew is very different from English—its vocabulary is limited, it is sparing in its use of particles and adverbs, its sentence structure and verb tenses are simpler, and the logical connections between successive sentences or actions are typically implied and rarely expressed as explicitly as in English. Translations which carry over these features into English—as translations that aim for formal equivalence inevitably must—produce a wooden, lifeless prose (or poetry) that fails to do justice to the energy and vibrancy of the original Hebrew. In this and my other translations, bringing the Hebrew over into natural English and prioritizing functional equivalence have required me to break significantly from literal renderings in nearly every sentence. I have frequently added particles and adverbs, inserted logical connections where lacking, omitted words that are superfluous in translation, introduced word variety consistent with English usage, altered verb tenses and pronouns, changed word order, and, on occasion, added short phrases and clarifying clauses when needed to produce natural English. Following Maimonides' advice to his own translator quoted in the epigraph at the begining of this note, I have relied on my understanding of the text and of what I believed to be the authors' intent to guide my many departures from the literal text. My goal in the translation here was always to be faithful to the ideas that the authors of Judges were expressing in Hebrew—but to express those ideas in English in the most natural way.

One final comment about my approach to translation: in translating names of people and places, I have not employed the traditional anglicized spelling, but have chosen instead to use transliterations that approximate how scholars believe ancient Hebrew was pronounced. Thus, I write Devorah rather than Deborah, Shimshon instead of Samson, and Yisra'el in place of Israel. One other unusual feature of my translation of names is that I have chosen in many places to replicate one of the principal quirks of Hebrew spelling: the consonantal letters *yodh* ("y") and *he* ("h") that are sometimes used to indicate specific vowels. In Judges, this results in my writing Siysera rather than Sisera, and Deliylah instead of Delila. With respect to place names, I sometimes translate the name into an English equivalent if it sounds natural in English rather than simply reproduce the Hebrew name. Thus, I write Pomegranate Rock rather than Sela Rimmon, and Raven Cliff instead of Tzur-Orev. Such an approach to translating personal names and place names, I believe, removes much of the theological baggage that many of the biblical personal names and place names have taken on over the centuries, thus helping modern-day readers look at the text with fresh eyes.

**

One place where I make a major departure from nearly all other present-day English translations of the Tanakh is that I do not follow the familiar chapter divisions, which are based on a scheme introduced by Archbishop of Canterbury Stephen Langton in the thirteenth century CE. Rather, my translations follow the division of the text into literary units—or *parashot*—as preserved in the Masoretic traditions.[30] We know that most of the *parashot* in the Masoretic text reflect very ancient traditions, for they agree broadly with textual divisions found in the biblical texts that were recovered from Qumran and that date between the third century BCE and the first century CE.[31] Moreover, the

---

30 An excellent overview of this system of dividing the biblical text into literary units can be found in Wikipedia in the article "*Parashah*."
31 For detailed discussions of this topic, see the articles by E. Tov: "The Background of the Sense Divisions in the Biblical Texts," in M. Korpel and J. Oesch (eds.), *Delimitation Criticism: A New Tool in Biblical Research*, Pericope 1 (Assen 2001), 312-350 and "Sense divisions in the Qumran texts, the Masoretic text, and ancient translations of the Bible," in J. Krosovec (ed.), *Interpretation of the Bible: International symposium on the interpretation of the Bible* (Sheffield 1998), 121-146.

parashot are marked in an identical fashion in the Masoretic text and in the texts from Qumran—space breaks where the text resumes in the middle of a line are used to indicate the beginning of smaller literary units, and space breaks where the text resumes at the beginning of a new line are used to indicate the beginning of major literary units. The general agreement of the *parashot* in the texts from Qumran with the Masoretic text can be seen in numerous textual fragments from Qumran, but it is most easily and convincingly seen in a simple visual comparison of the *parashot* in the Great Isaiah Scroll from Qumran and the Book of Isaiah in the Aleppo Codex and the Leningrad Codex.

/http://dss.collections.imj.org.il/isaiah

Although the evidence from Qumran clearly demonstrates that the *parashot* have ancient roots, that is of little help in answering the questions of how old they are and whether they might have been part of the earliest "editions" of the books of the Tanakh. It is of course impossible to answer these questions definitively, but it is reasonable to suppose that the ultimate source for most of the *parashot* might indeed be the original composition itself. We know, for example, that textual divisions were regularly employed in ancient texts.[32] And perhaps more important, once the medieval chapter divisions are stripped away and the *parashot* highlighted, it is striking to see how the *parashot* contribute to and enhance the flow of the narrative. I have seen this in all of the translations that I have completed to date—the five books of the Torah, Joshua, Samuel, and now Judges.

Because the *parashot* are sometimes employed in ways that modern-day readers do not expect, it is worth providing some comments on their usage in the Tanakh. There are two types of *parashot*—the *parashah petuhah* (or "open *parashah*") typically marks the beginning of a major literary unit, while the *parashah setumah* (or "closed *parashah*") typically marks the beginning of a smaller literary unit.[33]

In the prose books of the Tanakh, both the *parashah petuhah* and the *parashah setumah* are frequently used to indicate a change in compositional layer, a change in the author's source material, a change of subject matter, or a change of scene. Both types of *parashot* are also used to draw attention to important speeches and to alter the pace of

---

32 For examples predating the biblical texts, see those cited in E. Tov, "Background of the Sense Divisions," pp. 334f.

33 The *parashah petuhah* always begins on a new line and the blank space before it always ends on the previous line. This type of *parashah* gets its name from the fact that the blank space before it is "open" (*petuhah* in Hebrew) and not bounded by text on one side. The *parashah setumah* always begins in the middle of a line; it gets its name from the fact that the blank space in the text placed before it is "closed" (*setumah* in Hebrew) because the blank space is bounded by text on both sides.

the narrative for dramatic effect. In addition, both types of *parashot* are often used to organize related content and to facilitate the reader's navigation of repetitive text. The best example of this in Judges is the material in Jud 1.27-33, which uses *parashot setumot* to break up the repetitive narrative relating the individual tribes' failure to drive out all the local peoples from their territories. Finally, it should be noted that the "closed" blank space associated with the *parashah setumah* has two special uses: to separate items in a list and to separate lines of songs. In the Song of Deborah in Judges 5, for example, there is a "closed" blank space before and after each line of the song.[34]

In my translation, I have indicated the *parashot petuhot* with a triple line break and a double asterisk (**), while I have indicated the *parashot setumot* with a single line break and an em-dash (—). Because I have found the use of *parashot* in the Aleppo Codex to be superior overall to their use in the Leningrad Codex, the *parashot* in my translation follow it and not the Leningrad Codex.[35]

As a convenience to readers, I have noted the Masoretic literary units (the "open" and "closed" *parashot*) and the familiar chapter divisions of the Christian Bible in the margins of my translation. Although the Masoretes did not number the *parashot*, I have taken the liberty of numbering them in order to make it easier for readers to keep track of their place in the text, and to move back and forth between the text and the notes and comments. In the margins of the translation, I indicate the *parashot petuhot* with the prefix "P" followed by a number (P1, P2, P3, etc.). In my numbering system, I treat the *parashot setumot* as subunits of the *parashot petuhot*—thus P5,1 and P5,2, for example, indicate the first and second "closed" *parashot* after P5. In addition, I indicate the more familiar chapter divisions by placing the chapter number within

---

34 In the Masoretic manuscripts, the Song of Deborah is displayed in a special layout unique to it and the Song of the Sea (Exodus 15.1-19); for more details on this special layout, see my comments in the appendix on this topic.

35 It is worth noting here that Maimonides used the Aleppo Codex as his source for the identification of all the *parashot petuhot* and *parashot setumot* within the books of the Torah. His mention of the Aleppo Codex and his listing of the *parashot* in the Torah can be found in chapter eight of the "Laws Governing Torah Scrolls, Tefillin, and Mezuzot" in the Sefer Avahah within the *Mishneh Torah*. Moreover, there is a consensus among scholars of Masoretic studies that the Aleppo Codex is superior to the Leningrad Codex and all other Masoretic manuscripts; in the words of Israel Yeivin in his *Introduction to the Tiberian Masorah* (Scholar's Press: 1980), p. 16f: "A thorough study of the oldest MSS (A, L, B, S, S¹) and their Masorah...shows conclusively that A [that is, the Aleppo Codex] is superior to any other MS in spelling, in the writing of the songs in the Bible, and in its Masorah. Not only this, but A is the only one of these MSS in which the presentation of these features is almost everywhere flawless."

brackets—for example, [Ch. 16] denotes Judges 16. Lastly, I also use the margins to indicate places in the text that are discussed in the notes and comments that follow the translation; for each *parashah*, these are marked in lowercase letters—a, b, c, etc.—and are hyper-linked in the pdf version of this book.

**

Judges contains a diverse assortment of stories and traditions, and the composition of this material spans nearly a millennium. Parts of the Song of Deborah comprise the oldest material in the entire Tanakh and date to perhaps the tenth or eleventh century BCE, whereas the stories at the conclusion of Judges about the Levite's concubine and the search for wives for the Benjaminites are clearly Hellenistic-era compositions that date to the fourth or even third century BCE. The book of Judges thus offers its readers a fascinating window into the growth and development of the books of the Former Prophets. We see early stories about tribal heroes of ancient times—stories that were meant to entertain more than to enlighten. We also see how these stories are initially transformed through the addition of a simple narrative frame and numerous small details to serve as part of a newly composed "history" that promoted a young king's radical agenda of religious reform and his expansionist political policy. Still later, the stories in Judges become part of a different history—a history chronicling the Israelite people's tragic loss of a land to call their own due to their unfaithfulness toward their national god. And finally, as the religion of Judaism emerges in the last centuries before the common era, the book attracts other stories about the days long ago when "there was no king in Israel." These stories filled in gaps and supplemented the old stories; they entertained, they instructed, and they also cautioned, and they added yet more color and life to the rich panoply of Judges. It is my hope that through my work here—both in the translation that strives to express the ancient authors' ideas in natural modern-day English and in the notes and comments that follow—readers may gain a deeper appreciation of this fascinating book, enjoying it and learning from it in equal measure, just as its ancient authors intended.

Judges   שפטים

AFTER YEHOSHUA'S DEATH, the Yisra'elites sought an oracle from Yahweh: "Who should venture out first for us and make war on the Kena'anites?"

"Yehudah should go first," Yahweh answered. "Take note: I've delivered that land into his hands!"

"Come on an expedition with me in the territory I've been given," Yehudah said to his kinsman Shim'on. "We're going to make war on the Kena'anites! Likewise, I'll go with you to fight in the territory you were given." And so Shim'on went with him.

Yehudah commenced the expedition, and Yahweh delivered the Kena'anites and the Perizzites into their hands. They attacked them in the town of Bezeq, killing ten thousand men. When they encountered Adoniy Bezeq in Bezek, they engaged him in battle and defeated the Kena'anites and the Perizzites. Adoniy Bezeq fled, but they chased after him. When they captured him, they cut off his thumbs and his big toes.

"Seventy kings whose thumbs and big toes had been cut off were under my table scrounging for scraps," lamented Adoniy-Bezeq. "Exactly as I did to them God has now done back to me!"

They later took him to Yerushalem, where he died.

P1 [Ch. 1]
a

b

c
Adoniy Bezeq:
'My lord is Bezeq'

∗∗

The Yehudites made war on Yerushalem and captured it—they slaughtered the populace and sent the town up in flames. After that, the Yehudites moved south to make war on the Kena'anites living in the mountains, in the southern desert, and in the lowlands. Yehudah next campaigned against the Kena'anites living in Hevron [*Hevron's name previously was Arba's Town*], where they defeated Sheshay, Ahiyman and Talmay. From there they campaigned against Deviyr's inhabitants [*Deviyr's name previously was Scroll-Town*].

"Whoever attacks Scroll-Town and captures it, I will give him my daughter Aksah for a wife," announced Kalev. So when Othniy'el Qenazsson, a kinsmen of Kalev who was much younger than him,

P2   a   b

c

d

captured the town, he gave him his daughter Aksah for a wife.

When she arrived to see them, she implored him to ask her father for some pasturage. Then, as she slipped off her donkey, Kalev asked her what was bothering her and had prompted her visit. "Give me a gift!" she demanded. "Because you've already given me the Southern Desert region, you also ought to give me some water pools." And so Kalev gave her some of the upper pools and some of the lower pools.

**

The Qeynites [*who are descendants of Mosheh's father-in-law*] made an expedition from Palmville with the Yehudites to the Yehudah wilderness—specifically, to the region south of Arad. But they went and lived with the people there. Then Yehudah went with his kinsman Shim'on and attacked the Kena'anites living in Tzephath. They made a ban devotion of the town and called the town's name Hormah.

Hormah: 'Banned'

Yehudah next captured Azzah and its territory, Ashqelon and its territory, and Eqron and its territory. Yahweh was with Yehudah and so he cleared out the hill country. (However, he wasn't able to drive out the inhabitants of the low country, for they had iron chariots.)

Kalev was given Hevron, exactly as Mosheh promised, and from that place he drove out three Anaqis. The Binyaminites, however, did not drive out the Yevusites (that is, the inhabitants of Yerushalem), and the Yevusites have lived with the Binyaminites in Yerushalem down to the present day.

**

In addition, the nation of Yoseph made an expedition to Beyth-El, and Yahweh was with them. When the nation of Yoseph reconnoitered Beyth-El [*previously the town's name was Luz*], those keeping watch saw a man leaving the town. "Please show us a way to get into the town, and we'll treat you kindly," they said to him.

Once he showed them a way to get into the town, they attacked and put the town to the slaughter. But that man and his entire clan they let go free. The man then went to the Hethites' country and founded a town that he named Luz, which is still its name today.

**

Menashsheh didn't drive the inhabitants from Beyth-She'an and its neighboring villages, nor from Ta'nak and its neighboring villages, nor those living in Dor and its neighboring villages, nor those living in Yivle'am and its neighboring villages, nor those living in Megiddo and its neighboring villages. Rather, the Kena'anites were determined to remain in that land. Now, because Yisra'el was so strong, they made the Kena'anites serve as slave laborers. But they did not actually drive them out.

Ephrayim didn't drive out the Kena'anites living in Gezer; rather the Kena'anites remained living among them in Gezer.

P5,1 a

b

Zevulun didn't drive out the residents of Qitron, nor the residents of Nahelol. The Kena'anites remained living among them, but as slave laborers.

P5,2 a

Asher didn't drive out the residents of Akko, nor the residents of Tziydon, nor Ahlav, nor Akziyv, nor Helbah, nor Aphiyq, nor Rehov. The Asherites lived among the Ken'anites who inhabited that region, for they weren't able to drive them out.

P5,3 a

Naphtaliy didn't drive out the residents of Sun City, nor the residents of Anathville. They lived among the Kena'anites who inhabited that region; however, the inhabitants of Sun City and Anathville served them as slave laborers.

P5,4 a

The Amorites squeezed the Danites into the mountains, for they didn't let them go down into the valleys. The Amorites were determined to remain in Mount Heres, in Ayyalon, and in Sha'alviym. The nation of Yoseph, however, wielded its power harshly, and so the Amorites became slave laborers. [*The Amorites' territory began at Scorpions' Pass, from the cliff northwards.*]

b

c

**

Yahweh's emissary went north from Gilgal to The Cryers.

P6 [Ch. 2] a

**

b

"I took you out of Egypt," it said, "and I brought you to the land that I promised your ancestors. I said that I would never break my treaty with you and that you shouldn't make any treaty with this land's inhabitants but instead must destroy their altars. But you didn't listen to me. What in the world have you done?! Accordingly, I don't intend to drive them out of your way—instead, they'll become traps for you and their gods will become snares for you."

P7 a

As soon as Yahweh's emissary had spoken these words to the Yisra'elites, the people cried out and began wailing. So they named that place "Cryers," and they made sacrifices there to Yahweh.

**

Yehoshua then sent the people off, and the Yisra'elites left to take possession of the land, each one going to his property. The people gave service to Yahweh for Yehoshua's entire life and for the entire lives of the elders who lived long after Yehoshua, who had seen every great thing that Yahweh had done for Yisra'el.

Yehoshua Nunsson Yahwehservant died at one hundred and ten years of age; he was buried within his property's borders in Timnath-Heres, in the Ephrayim mountains to the north of Mount Ga'ash. That entire generation as well joined its ancestors in death, and a new generation after them arose which didn't know Yahweh, nor moreover what he had done for Yisra'el.

**

Then the Yisra'elites did what Yahweh considered the worst thing of all—they gave service to the Ba'als and abandoned their ancestors' god Yahweh who had brought them out of Egypt. They followed some of the different gods of the surrounding peoples, worshipping them and thus enraging Yahweh. They abandoned Yahweh and gave service to Ba'al and to the Ashtoreths. And so Yahweh was inflamed with anger at Yisra'el: he delivered them up into the hands of bandits who robbed them, and he sold them into the hands of their enemies all around them, with the result that they were no longer able to hold their ground against their enemies. In every campaign they undertook, Yahweh's hand was against them to do them harm, exactly as Yahweh had said [*and exactly as Yahweh had sworn to them*], and so they suffered mightily.

Yahweh then raised up champions who saved them from those terrorizing them. However, they didn't obey their champions either; rather, they whored after different gods and worshipped them, turning quickly from the path that their ancestors trod. As for obeying Yahweh's commandments—they did nothing like that.

When Yahweh raised up champions for them, Yahweh would be with the champion and he would save them from their enemies for the champion's entire life, for Yahweh felt pity on account of how they groaned and suffered at the hands of their tormentors and oppressors. But whenever the champion died, they would revert to acting more despicably than their ancestors, following after different gods, doing service to them, and worshipping them. They abandoned none of their practices, nor any part of their obnoxious way of life.

And so Yahweh's anger burned against Yisra'el. "Because this damnable nation has violated the terms of my treaty which I commanded their ancestors to follow and because they haven't obeyed me," he thought, "in turn, I won't drive away anyone anymore who belongs to the nations that Yehoshua left behind when he died." (This was in order to test Yisra'el through them, to see whether or not they would keep to Yahweh's path by walking in his precepts, just as their ancestors did. Yahweh thus left those peoples alone, so as not to drive them out quickly—he didn't deliver them into Yehoshua's hands.)

**

These are the nations which Yahweh left alone, in order that through them he might test Yisra'el (none of whom had any experience of the wars for Kena'an) [*It was only so that future generations of Yisra'elites might have knowledge, to teach them the ways of war (only, however, the ways which they didn't know previously).*]:
 —The five archonships of the Philishtines
 —All the Kena'anites, Tziydonians, and Hiwwites living in the Levanon mountains, from Mount Ba'al Hermon to the entrance to Hamath.

They were to test Yisra'el by them, in order to know whether they would obey Yahweh's commandments, which he transmitted to their ancestors through Mosheh.

Now the Yisra'elites were living among the Kena'anites, Hethites, Amorites, Perizzites, Hiwwites and Yevusites. They took their daughters for themselves as wives, and gave their own daughters to the those peoples' sons, and so they did service to those peoples' gods.

**

The Yisra'elites did what Yahweh considered the worst thing—they forgot their god Yahweh and did service to the Ba'als and the Asherahs. And so Yahweh was inflamed with anger against Yisra'el. He sold the Yisra'elites into the possession of Kushan Doublywicked, the king of Aram of the Two Rivers, and they were subjects of Kushan Doublywicked for eight years.

But then the Yisra'elites cried out to Yahweh, and he raised up a liberator for them who liberated them—Othniy'el Qenazsson, a kinsman of Kalev who was much younger than him. Yahweh's power was on him, and he championed Yisra'el. When he marched out to war, Yahweh delivered Aram's king Kushan Doublywicked into his hands, and his power was firm against Kushan Doublywicked. The land remained tranquil for forty years and then Othniy'el Qenazsson died.

**

The Yisra'elites again did what Yahweh considered the worst thing, whereupon Yahweh emboldened Mo'av's king Eglon against Yisra'el, because they had done what Yahweh considered the worst thing. He gathered the Ammonites and Amaleq as his allies and then went and attacked Yisra'el, driving them out of Palmville. And so the Yisra'elites were subjects of Mo'av's king Eglon for eighteen years.

But then the Yisra'elites cried out to Yahweh, and he raised up a liberator for them—Ehud Gerasson the Binyaminite, a man who didn't use his right hand. The Yisra'elites sent him with a tribute to Mo'av's king Eglon. (Now Ehud had made a dagger for himself that was sharp on both edges, about a *gomed* in length, and he had strapped it onto his right thigh beneath his clothes.)

Ehud presented the tribute to Eglon King of Mo'av (now Eglon was an obese man), and as soon as he had finished presenting the tribute, he dismissed the people who were carrying it. Then, once he had returned from the gods' statues at the Circle district, he said, "I have a secret message for you, your highness."

"Quiet!" he replied. All those attending him then left his presence.

Now Ehud had come to see him when he was sitting by himself in the breezy roof-chamber that belonged to him.

"I have a message for you from God," Ehud said.

When Eglon rose from his seat, Ehud grabbed the dagger hidden under his clothes with his left hand and plunged it into his belly. The hilt went in right after the blade. The fat closed up behind the blade (for he didn't slip the dagger back out from his belly) and his feces began oozing out.

Ehud went out to the colonnade, shutting the doors to the roof-chamber behind him and then bolting them. He had already made his exit when Eglon's officials arrived. They noticed right away that the doors were bolted and thus presumed he was having a sit in the breeze room.

They waited so long it became embarrassing. When they realized no one was going to open the doors to the roof-chamber, they fetched the key and opened them. And there was their lord, lying dead on the ground!

Ehud meanwhile had slipped away during all their dithering about. He passed by the gods' statues as he left and made his escape to Se'iyrah. As soon as he arrived, he sounded the ram's horn throughout the Ephrayim mountains. The Yisra'elites accompanied him out of the mountains, with him leading the way.

"Follow me," he cried, "for Yahweh has delivered your enemies [*that is, Mo'av*] into your hands!"

Swooping down behind him, they captured the fords of the Yarden belonging to Mo'av and didn't allow anyone to cross. At that time they attacked Mo'av and killed around ten thousand men—all of them stout and able warriors, with none escaping.

Mo'av was humbled that day, crushed under Yisra'el's grip, and the land remained tranquil for eighty years.

**

After Ehud was Shamgar Anathsson. He killed six hundred Philishtines with a cattle-prod, and he too rescued Yisra'el.

**

Once Ehud was dead, the Yisra'elites once again did what Yahweh considered the worst thing. So he sold them into the hands of Yaviyn King of Kena'an, who ruled in Hatzor. The head of his army was Siysera, who himself resided in the town Harosheth-of-the-Nations.

The Yisra'elites cried out to Yahweh, for Yaviyn had nine hundred iron chariots and he severely oppressed the Yisra'elites for twenty years.

**

Devorah was a prophetess, the wife of Lapiydoth—she was championing Yisra'el at that time. She would hold court beneath Devorah's Pillar (between Ramah and Beyth-El in the Ephrayim mountains), and the Yisra'elites went to see her to settle their legal disputes.

She sent messengers to summon Baraq Aviyno'amsson from the town of Qedesh in Naphtaliy. "You should know," she informed him when he arrived, "that Yisra'el's god Yahweh has given the following order: 'Go and proceed at once to Mount Tavor, taking with you ten thousand men from the Naphtalites and the Zevulunites. I will lead the head of Yaviyn's army Siysera to you, along with his chariotry and his battalions, to the Wadi Qiyshon and then deliver him into your hands.'"

"I'll go if you come with me," Baraq replied. "But I won't go if you don't come with me."

"Certainly I'll go with you," she said. "However, you'll get no glory from the mission you're going on, for Yahweh is going to sell Siysera into the hands of a woman!"

Devorah then went straight away with Baraq to Qedesh. Baraq marshaled Zevulun and Naphtaliy to Qedesh. He then led ten thousand men on foot, and Devorah went with him.

(Now Hever the Qeynite had separated from Qayin—that is from the descendants of Mosheh's father-in-law Hovav—and he had made his home beside a terebrinth in Tza'ananniym, which is near Qedesh.)

When Siysera was informed that Baraq Aviyno'amsson had gone to Mount Tavor, he marshaled all nine hundred of his iron chariots and the military forces that accompanied them and proceeded from Harosheth-of-the-Nations to the Wadi Qiyshon.

"Get going!" Devorah said to Baraq. "For today's the day that Yahweh delivers Siysera into your hands. Know that Yahweh goes out in front of you!"

Then Baraq descended Mount Tavor followed by ten thousand men. Yahweh confused Siysera, his entire chariotry, and his entire army as the battle raged on Baraq's front, causing Siysera to dismount his chariot and flee on foot. Meanwhile Baraq chased the chariotry and the army all the way back to Harosheth-of-the-Nations. Siysera's entire army fell in battle—not a single man remained.

Now Siysera had fled on foot to the tent of Ya'el Hever-the-Qeyniteswife, for Yaviyn King of Hatzor and Hever the Qeynite's family were on friendly terms. Ya'el went out to greet Siysera. "Stop here, my lord," she said to him. "Stop here with me. Don't be afraid." And so he stopped there and entered her tent, whereupon she covered him with a blanket.

"Please let me have a little water to drink," he said to her, "for I'm thirsty."

She opened a skin of milk and gave him some to drink, and then covered him back up.

"Stand at the entrance to the tent," he said to her. "If a man happens to come by and question you, asking if there's a man here, tell him there's not."

But Ya'el Heverswife instead took a tent stake and, placing a hammer in her hand, snuck over to where he was. She then drove the stake into the side of his head with such force that it slid right into the ground. (He was fast asleep at the time.) His body convulsed and then he was dead.

And then Baraq, who had been chasing Siysera, showed up. Ya'el went out to greet him. "Come," she said. "Let me show you the man you're looking for."

He went inside with her, and there Siysera was, lying dead on the ground with a tent stake through the side of his head.

And so that day God humiliated Yaviyn King of Kena'an at the hands of the Yisra'elites. The Yisra'elites' power grew more and more oppressive against Yaviyn King of Kena'an, and they eventually destroyed Yaviyn King of Kena'an.

**

On that day, Devorah and Baraq Aviyno'amsson sang "When in Yisra'el commanders commanded—when men joined up for war (give praise to Yahweh!)."

"Listen here, kings and viziers, and to me turn your ears—
    A song I shall sing, a song to Yahweh—
    plucking the lyre for Yahweh, god of Yisra'el!

[*When you, Yahweh, march from Se'iyr—*
    when from Edom's fields you stride forth—
the earth shudders and shakes, the sky bursts and spurts—
    clouds let loose great floods of water.
Mountains judder and quake at Yahweh's approach—
    (that is, Siynai) yes, *at the approach of Yahweh, god of Yisra'el!*]

"Back in the days of Shamgar Anathsson—
    yes, back in Ya'el's time, the highways had vanished—
    and wayfarers traveled tortuous roads.
Country folk had disappeared from Yisra'el, had vanished—
    until Devorah appeared, until a great mother rose in Yisra'el!

"God chose new things: food was bought and sold—
    but neither shields were seen, nor lances—
    among the forty thousand living in Yisra'el.

"Sing of the plans of Yisra'el's commanders—
    of men joining up for war (give praise to Yahweh!)—
    of men astride tawny jenny-asses—
    sitting atop saddle-blankets, and traveling down the road!

	"Arrows whizzed to and fro, twixt the watering holes—
m	(where later were recounted Yahweh's victories—
	the victories of Yisra'el's country-dwellers)—
	and then Yahweh's forces swooped, attacking the gates!

n " 'Get up, Devorah, get going!
       Get up, get going and recite this song!
    Quickly, Baraq! Take captive those you captured, Aviyno'amsson!'

o p " 'But then arrived a fugitive, one of the nobles—[*Yahweh's*
           people] a valiant one among warriors, seeking refuge with me—
q   someone from Ephrayim, whose ancestors lived in Amaleq.'

r " 'After you, Binyamin, right there with your troops!'

s "From Makiyr the generals marched down—
       from Zevulun those who wielded the officer's baton.
    Yissakar's commanders took position with Devorah—
t u   as Yissakar, so too Baraq—deployed into the valley on foot.
    Meanwhile in Re'uven's brigades, leaders planned their attack.

v " 'Why do you sit amongst desolate encampments—
       listening to the bleatings of goats—
    while for Re'uven's brigades, great men mull over their plans?'
w [*Across the Yarden, Gil'ad stays put.*]

x y [*As for Dan, why does he tarry back by the ships?*
    Or Asher, why does he stay at the edge of the sea,
       settling in where he disembarked?
    Zevulun—a people belittling life to the point of death.
    And Naphtaliy—up in the heights of the countryside.]

z "Kings arrived, they entered battle—
       'twas then the kings of Kena'an waged war—
aa   at Ta'nak, alongside Megiddo's watercourses—
ab   while plunder of silver they forswore.

   "Swooping down from the sky, they attacked—
ac   yes, from their tracks the stars at Siysera struck.

ad "The Wadi Qiyshon swept them away—
       that most ancient of wadis, the Wadi Qiyshon—
       its mighty stream stamping them under.

"Then the horses' hooves hammered down—   ae
    their warriors charging at a furious gallop.
['Damn Meroz!' Yahweh's envoy cried. 'Its denizens be damned!   af
For they came not to Yahweh's aid—
*   went not with the valiant to Yahweh's support!*']   ag

"Most bless'd of women: Ya'el Hever-the-Qeynites-wife—   ah
    most bless'd of women living in tents!
He asked for water, she gave him milk—
    yes, she proffered clotted cream in the finest of bowls!
She reaches with her hand for a tent spike—   ai
    with her right hand, grasps a workman's hammer.
She hammers Siysera, she obliterates his head—
    smashing and slicing through his temple!
At her feet he crumpled, fell and lay—
    at her feet he crumpled and fell!
Where he crumpled, there he fell—destroyed!

"Siysera's mother gazed out the window, squealed thru the lattice: aj
    'Why is his chariot so bashful about arriving?
    Why are the hoof-beats of his chariotry still slow to sound?'
Her ladies-at-court shrewdly responded—
    (to her own question she too posed an answer):
'Surely they found and are divvying the spoils—   ak
    a lass, maybe two lasses for each of the men!
For Siysera, great piles of finely dyed cloth—
    yes, great piles of intricate finery—
    intricate weavings brilliantly dyed, borne on captives' backs!'

"Thus may all your enemies, O Yahweh, perish!" [*And may all those*   al am
who love him stay strong as the rising sun!]
                                              —   an
And so the land was tranquil for forty years.   P16,1

**

But then the Yisra'elites did what Yahweh considered the worst thing.   P17 [Ch. 6] a
So he delivered them into Midyan's hands for seven years, and Midyan dealt harshly with Yisra'el.

Because of Midyan, the Yisra'elites made signal towers for themselves located in the mountains, as well as caves and forts. And whenever Yisra'el would plant crops, Midyan would come up along

		with Amaleq and the Qedemites and attack them, engaging in hostilities and ruining the land's crops as far west as Azzah. They didn't
	b	leave any form of sustenance in Yisra'el—nor any sheep, nor cattle, nor asses. For when they and their livestock would come up (not to mention their tents), they would arrive in multitudes, like swarms of
	c	locusts. It was impossible to count either them or their camels. They came to the land in order to destroy it, and so Yisra'el was greatly weakened because of Midyan. But then the Yisra'elites cried out to Yahweh…

**

P18	a	Now when the Yisra'elites cried out to Yahweh on account of Midyan, Yahweh sent a prophet to them.
		"Thus says Yisra'el's god Yahweh," he said to them. " 'I brought you up from Egypt, freeing you from your condition of servitude. I
b	c	rescued you from Egypt and from all those oppressing you, driving
	d	them out of your path and giving you their land. 'I am your god Yahweh,' I said to you. 'Don't give reverence to the gods of the Amorites, in whose land you're living.' But you didn't obey me.' "

**

P19	a	An envoy from Yahweh arrived and sat under the terebrinth tree in
	b	Ophrah (the town settled by the Ezrites' ancestor Yo'ash). At the time,
	c	his son Gid'on was beating wheat in a wine-press in order to hide it from Midyan.
		Then Yahweh's envoy showed itself to him. "May Yahweh be with you, great warrior!" it said.
		"If I may, my lord," Gid'on replied, "supposing Yahweh is with us,
	d	why has all this happened to us? Where are all those amazing things he did that our ancestors told us about? 'Indeed,' they said, 'Yahweh brought us up from Egypt!' But now Yahweh has abandoned us and delivered us into Midyan's clutches!"
		Yahweh then turned to face him. "Go with the strength you possess
	e	and rescue Yisra'el from Midyan's grasp. Be assured, I have sent you!"
		"If I may, my lord," he replied, "how will I rescue Yisra'el? My
	f	clan is the weakest in Menashsheh, and I'm the youngest one in my family."
		"Because I will be with you," Yahweh assured him, "you will defeat Midyan as though it were a single man."
		"Please, if I've found favor with you," he said, "give me a sign of what you're speaking about with me. Please don't leave here until I

come back to see you—I'm going to bring out a gift and present it to you."

"I'll stay here until you return."

Gid'on then left and prepared a buckling and some flat bread made from an *eyphah* of flour. He put the meat in a basket and the broth in a pot and then brought it out to him beneath the terebrinth and placed it in front of him.

**

"Take the meat and the bread," God's envoy said, "and lay them on that rock. Then pour out the broth."

And so he did.

Then Yahweh's envoy stretched out the tip of the staff that was in its hand. When it touched the meat and the bread, a flame leapt up from the rock and consumed both the meat and the bread. At the same time, Yahweh's envoy disappeared from his sight, and Gid'on immediately realized that the being was an envoy from Yahweh.

"Oh no, Yahweh my lord!" Gid'on cried. "Oh no! For now I've seen Yahweh's envoy face to face!"

"It's okay," Yahweh said to him. "Don't be afraid—you won't die."

Gid'on built an altar to Yahweh at that place and named it 'Yahweh-It's-Okay.' Even today it can still be seen in the Ophrah founded by the Ezrites' ancestor.

—

Now that very night Yahweh spoke to him: "Get one of your father's bulls, and a second bull seven years. Tear down your father's altar to the Ba'al, and also chop down the Asherah pole that's next to it. Then build an altar to your god Yahweh in the proper arrangement at the summit of that refuge. Take the second bull and make a whole offering of it with the wood of the Asherah pole that you're going to cut down."

Gid'on then summoned ten of his servants and did just as Yahweh had told him. Now as he was too afraid of his family and of the men in town to do this during the day, he did it at night. When the men in town began their work in the morning, they noticed right away that the altar to the Ba'al had been demolished and the Asherah pole next to it cut down, and that the second bull had been offered up as a whole offering on the new altar that had been built.

"Who could have done such a thing?" they asked one another. After examining and investigating the matter, they determined that Gid'on Yo'ashsson was the culprit.

"Make your son come out here so that he can die!" the townsmen demanded of Yo'ash. "Because he tore down the altar to the Ba'al, and because he also chopped down the Asherah next to it!"

f "Are you prosecuting this case on behalf of the Ba'al," Yo'ash said to all those opposing him, "or do you expect to win it for him? May anyone who contends on his behalf be put to death by morning! Surely it's the god who should contend for himself if he tore down his altar!"

g Yerubba'al: Ba'al contends

And so from that day they called him Yerubba'al, saying "Let the Ba'al prosecute him if he tore down his altar."

h

—

P20,2   a

Now all Midyan, Amaleq, and the Qedemites had united their forces and had gone and established a position in the Yizre'el Valley.

b

Yahweh's spirit, meanwhile, had enveloped Gid'on. He blew the ram's horn and Aviy'ezer marshaled its forces behind him. Then he sent messengers into all parts of Menashsheh, and it too marshaled its forces behind him. At the same time he sent messengers into Asher, Zevulun, and Naphtaliy, and they marched out to meet them.

c

"Are you really going to rescue Yisra'el through me like you said?" Gid'on asked God. "Here's what I'm going to do: I'll lay out some sheared wool on the threshing floor. If there's dew only on the shearings and it's dry everywhere on the ground, then I'll know for sure that you're going to rescue Yisra'el through me like you said."

And so it happened: he got up early the next day and when he squeezed the shearings, some dew drained out from them—enough water, in fact, to fill a large bowl.

"Don't be mad at me," Gid'on said to God. "However, I'd like to speak one more time. Please let me make just one more test with the shearings—let it be dry only on the shearings while there's dew everywhere on the ground."

That night God did exactly that: it was dry only on the shearings, whereas there was dew everywhere on the ground.

**

P21   [Ch. 7]
a

Yerubba'al (that is, Gid'on) made an early start, as did all the forces with him, and they established a position at Quaking Spring. Midyan's camp was to the north of them, in the lowland beside Teacher's Hill.

b

—

P21,1

"The forces with you are too many for me to deliver Midyan into their hands," Yahweh said to Gid'on. "Otherwise Yisra'el might give themselves the glory instead of me, thinking that it was their own ability that made them victorious. So then, please announce the following to

a

your forces: 'Whoever is afraid or scared ought to go back and chirp away from Mount Gil'ad.'"

Twenty-two thousand men from his forces went back, while ten thousand remained.

"Your forces are still too numerous," Yahweh said to Gid'on. "Have them go down to the water so that I can make a test of them for you there. Then, whichever ones I say to you, 'He should go with you,' those ones must go with you. And all those who I say to you, 'He shouldn't go with you,' those ones mustn't go with you."

So Gid'on had his forces go down to the water, and then Yahweh said to him, "Anyone who slurps water with his tongue like a dog, set him aside. And anyone who crouches down on his knees to drink."

Those who slurped water out of their hands into their mouths numbered three hundred; all the rest of the men crouched down on their knees to drink water.

"With the three hundred men who slurped water I will make you victorious and deliver Midyan into your hands," Yahweh said to Gid'on. "Everyone else ought to leave and go back to their homes."

Once the forces had taken their provisions in hand along with their rams' horns, Gid'on sent all the Yisra'elites back home, keeping back only the three hundred men.

Now Midyan's army was camped below him, in the lowland…

**

"Go attack their camp right away, for I've delivered them into your hands!" Yahweh said to Gid'on after night had fallen. "But if you're afraid to go attack, then you and your adjutant Phurah ought to go to their camp and listen to what they're saying. After that you'll gain your courage—then you can go attack their camp."

So Gid'on and his adjutant Phurah went down to the edge of the battalions that were in the camp. (Now Midyan, Amaleq, and all the Qedemites had spread themselves out in the lowland like swarms of locusts. And they had countless numbers of camels, as numerous as the sand on the seashore.)

When Gid'on arrived, there was a man telling his buddy about a dream. "Hey, I just had a dream," he said. "There was a loaf of barley bread tumbling through Midyan's camp. When it came upon a tent, it struck it. It collapsed, and the bread flipped it over. And so the tents would fall."

"That can't be anything except the sword of Gid'on Yo'ashsson the Yisra'elite," his buddy replied. "God has delivered Midyan and all its army into his hands!"

∗∗

P23 a As soon as Gid'on heard the dream being recounted and how it was interpreted, he prostrated himself on the ground and then returned to Yisra'el's camp.

"Get up!" he cried. "For Yahweh has delivered Midyan's army into your hands!"

He divided the three hundred men into three companies and put rams' horns into everyone's hands, along with empty jars and torches to go inside the jars.

"Observe me closely and do exactly what I do," he said to them. "Take note: I'm going to go to the edge of camp, and then in the way that I do, so you must do. I'm going to sound the ram's horn—me and everyone with me. You also should sound your rams' horns on all sides of the camp and then shout out, "For Yahweh and for Gid'on!"

b
c

∗∗

P24 a Gid'on and the hundred men with him arrived at the edge of the camp at the beginning of the night's middle watch. They did, however, wake up the guards. They sounded the rams' horns and broke the jars that were in their hands. All three companies sounded the rams' horns and then, upon breaking their jars, grabbed hold of their torches with their left hands while continuing to blow the rams' horns in their right hands.

b "The battle is Yahweh's and Gid'on's!" they cried. Each man remained standing in place all around the edge of the camp while the entire camp ran and shouted and took flight. As the three hundred men blew their rams' horns, Yahweh pitted one man's sword against another's—everywhere in the camp. The camp fled all the way to Acacia Town, to Tzererah, as far as the edge of Dancing Meadow near Tabbath.

c

d Yisra'elites were marshaled from Naphtaliy, from Asher, and from all of Menashsheh, and they went in pursuit of Midyan. Meanwhile, Gid'on sent messengers throughout the Ephrayim mountains telling men to come down and engage Midyan, and to take control of the Yarden River for them and the watercourses as far as Beyth Barah.

And so every man in Ephrayim was marshaled to help fight. They captured the Yarden River and the watercourses all the way to Beyth Barah, and they captured Midyan's two generals—Orev and Ze'ev. They killed Orev at Raven Cliff while Ze'ev they killed at Wolf Wine-

Orev: *Raven*
Ze'ev: *Wolf*

Vat. They continued in pursuit of Midyan, but in the meantime, they took the heads of Orev and Ze'ev to Gid'on back on the other side of the Yarden.

"What in the hell is this thing you did to us?" complained the Ephrayimites to Gid'on. "Not summoning us to join you when you went to fight against Midyan!" They argued with him vehemently.

"How does what I did justify what you're doing now?" Gid'on asked. "Aren't the leftover grapes Ephrayim gleaned better than those Aviy'ezer harvested? It was into your hands that God delivered Midyan's generals, Orev and Ze'ev. I couldn't have captured them if I'd wanted to!"

Their anger at him abated when he spoke those words. Gid'on then proceeded to the Yarden, crossing over along with the three hundred men with him, all of them exhausted but still in pursuit.

"Please give some loaves of bread to the men following me," he said to the leaders of Sukkoth, "for they're exhausted, and we're chasing after Midyan's kings Zevah and Tzalmuna."

"Are Zevah and Tzalmuna in your custody right now," Sukkoth's chiefs asked, "that we should give your army some food?"

"So be it," Gid'on replied. "But when Yahweh delivers Zevah and Tzalmuna into my hands, I'm going to tread all over your bodies with desert brambles and thorns!"

From there he proceeded to Penu'el and made a similar request of them, but Penu'el's leaders answered him just as Sukkoth's had. So he also threatened Penu'el's leaders: "When this war is over, I'm going to come back and demolish this tower!"

**

Now Zevah and Tzalmuna were at Qarqor, and the armies with them numbered about fifteen thousand men—all the remaining forces from the Qedemites' entire army. (One hundred twenty thousand soldiers had fallen in combat.) Gid'on proceeded north along the Occupied-Tents Highway, to the east of Novah and Yogbehah, and attacked the army when it was at rest. Zevah and Tzalmunah fled and he went after them. And so he captured Midyan's two kings, Zevah and Tzalmunah, while also routing their entire army.

Gid'on Yo'ashsson turned back from the battle at Heres Pass, at which time he captured an attendant of one of Sukkoth's leaders. At Gid'on's request, the attendant wrote down for him the names of Sukkoth's chiefs and its elders—seventy-seven men in all. Then he went to pay a visit to Sukkoth's leaders.

"Here are Zevah and Tzalmuna," he said to them, "about whom you insulted me when you said, 'Are Zevah and Tzalmuna in your custody right now that we should give your exhausted men some food?'"

Gid'on then took the town's elders and some desert brambles and thorns, and with them he taught a lesson to the leaders Sukkoth. (At the same time he also demolished Penu'el's tower.) After he had killed the town's leaders, he addressed Zevah and Tzalmuna: "Where are the men you killed in Tavor?"

"May your fate be the same as theirs!" they replied. "One of them even looked like royalty!"

"They were my brothers—my mother's sons," he answered. "As Yahweh lives, if you had let them live, I wouldn't have killed you."

Then he turned to his oldest son Yether and said, "Kill them at once!"

But the boy didn't draw his sword, for he was afraid, as he was still just a boy.

"'At once,' you coward! Come at us like a real man!" shouted Zevah and Tzalmuna.

Straight away, Gid'on killed Zevah and Tzalmuna, and then he took the moon-shaped ornaments that were on their camels' necks.

**

"Rule over us!" the Yisra'elites said to Gid'on. "You and then your son and grandson in turn, for you've rescued us from Midyan's clutches!"

"I certainly will not rule over you," Gid'on replied. "Nor shall my son rule over you. Rather, Yahweh is the one who rules over you. However," Gid'on continued, "I do have a request to make of you: each of you give me an earring from the spoils you took." (Now, the earrings they had were gold because they were taken from the Yishma'elites.)

"Of course we'll do that," they said. Then they spread out a blanket and on it each of them threw an earring from the spoils he had taken. The gold earrings given in response to his request amounted to seventeen hundred sheqels of gold; this was separate from the moon-shaped ornaments, the pendants, and the purple garments worn by Midyan's kings, and separate from the ornamental gear on their camels' necks. Gid'on made these things into a priest's shoulder-vest and kept it in his home town, in Ophrah. (But all Yisra'el whored after it there, and it became a trap for Gid'on and his family.)

And so Midyan was subjected by the Yisra'elites and they didn't regain power. During Gid'on's days, there was tranquility in the land for forty years.

**

Yerubba'al Yo'ashsson went on his way and thereafter lived at his home. (Now Gid'on had seventy children whom he had fathered, for he had numerous wives.) The concubine of his who was in Shekem also bore him a son, whom he named Aviymelek. Gid'on Yo'ashsson died at a ripe old age and was buried in his father Yo'ash's grave in Ophrah [*the one founded by the Ezrites' ancestor*].

P27 a

b

**

As soon as Gid'on died, the Yisra'elites again went whoring after the Ba'als and they adopted Ba'al Beriyth as their god. The Yisra'elites no longer honored their god Yahweh, who had saved them from all their enemies in the surrounding regions, nor did they treat Yerubba'al's [*that is, Gid'on's*] family with the favor appropriate to all the good things he had done for Yisra'el.

P28
a
b

**

Aviymelek Yerubba'alsson went to Shekem to see his mother's kinspeople. "Please speak to the citizens of Shekem," he said to his kinspeople and to his mother's ancestral clan, "and ask them, 'What's better for you—that seventy men (all Yerubba'al's sons) rule over you, or that a single man rule over you?' Keep in mind that I'm your flesh and blood."

P29 [Ch. 9]

So his mother's relatives spoke about him to all Shekem's citizens, saying exactly those things. Thus they were persuaded to follow Aviymelek, for they reasoned that he was their kinsman. They gave him seventy sheqels of silver from the temple of Ba'al Beriyth, which he used to hire some good-for-nothing ruffians as his followers. Then he paid a visit to his father's family at Ophrah and murdered his brothers, the seventy Yerubba'alsssons, killing each of them with a single stone. However, Yerubba'al's youngest son Yotham survived, because he had hidden himself.

a

b c

d

All Shekem's citizens and all Beyth Millo joined together, and then they went and made Aviymelek king beside the terebrinth post that was in Shekem. When Yotham was told the news, he went to Mount Gerizim, stood on the summit, and made this proclamation to them:

"Listen to me, citizens of Shekem, so that God may hear about you! Once upon a time the trees decided to anoint a king over themselves.

P29,1
a
b

c

'Be king over us!' they said to the olive tree. 'Could I stop the oil which through me both gods and men are honored,' the olive tree replied, 'that I could go and wield it over the trees?' So the trees spoke to the fig tree: 'Come, madam, you be queen over us!' But the fig tree's answer was no different. 'Could I stop my sweetness and my luscious fruit,' she asked, 'that I could go and wield it over the trees?' Next the trees spoke to the grapevine: 'Come, madam, you be queen over us!' But the grapevine too refused. 'Could I stop my newly made wine that gladdens both gods and men,' she responded, 'that I could go and wield it over the trees?' Finally, all the trees spoke to the thornbush: 'Come, dear sir, you be king over us!' The thornbush answered, 'If you're truly going to anoint me as king over you, then come and take shelter in my shade! But if you don't: 'A fire sparked from a thornbush consumes mighty cedars!'

"So now, have you acted honestly and forthrightly in making Aviymelek king? Have you treated Yerubba'al and his family fairly, or have you dealt with him as he did with you? For my father went to war for you, boldly risking his life and saving you from Midyan's harsh rule. But now today you've risen up against my father's family: you murdered his seventy children, each with a single stone, and you've made Aviymelek—the offspring of his maidservant!—king over the citizens of Shekem just because he's your kinsman.

"So if today you've dealt honestly and forthrightly with Yerubba'al and his family, then be happy with Aviymelek, and let him also be happy with you. And if that's not possible, 'a fire will spark' from Aviymelek and consume Shekem's citizens and Beyth Millo! Likewise 'a fire will spark' from Shekem's citizens and from Beyth Millo and consume Aviymelek!"

Then Yotham took flight, fleeing and going to Be'er, where he lived out of the reach of his brother Aviymelek.

**

Aviymelek ruled over Yisra'el for three years. But God sent a spirit of ill-will between Aviymelek and the citizens of Shekem, as a result of which the citizens of Shekem betrayed Aviymelek, in order that retribution for the violence done to Yerubba'al's seventy children might come to pass, and in order to put their blood-guilt on their brother Aviymelek who murdered them, and to put it on the citizens of Shekem, who gave him the courage to murder his brothers. Thus to undermine Aviymelek, Shekem's citizens stationed bandit gangs atop the mountains, and they robbed all those who crossed over them on their journeys.

Now after Aviymelek had been informed of this...

**

Ga'al Evedsson and his kinsmen showed up, and as they made their way through Shekem, the citizens of Shekem put their trust in him. They went out into the countryside and harvested their vineyards, crushing their grapes and celebrating the vintage. Then they proceeded to their god's temple, where they ate and drank and insulted Aviymelek.

"Who is Aviymelek and who the Shekemites," Ga'al Evedsson argued, "that we should be his subjects? Isn't he Yerubba'al's son and Zevul just his henchman? Go serve instead those loyal to Shekem's founder Hemor. Why really should we be subject to him? How I wish the people were under my control—then I would depose Aviymelek!"

Then, speaking about Aviymelek, he said: "Make your army even larger, and then go and shit yourself!"

When the town chief Zevul heard what Ga'al Evedsson had said, he became enraged. So he surreptitiously sent messengers to Aviymelek with the following message: "Attention: Ga'al Evedsson and his kinsmen showed up in Shekem, and now they're securing the town against you. So you and your men ought to get going tonight and set an ambush out in the countryside. Then in the morning around sunrise, you should start in right away and make a raid on the town. That way, when he and his men come out to engage you, you can bring the full brunt of your power against him."

Aviymelek and all his men went into action that night and set an ambush against Shekem, separating into four gangs. When Ga'al Evedsson stepped outside the town wall and stood at the town gate's entrance, Aviymelek and his men jumped up from their hiding places. Catching sight of the men, Ga'al turned to Zevul and exclaimed, "Look—some troops are coming down from the hilltops!"

"Those are shadows on the hills that you're seeing," Zevul replied. "They just look like men."

"Look!" repeated Ga'al. "Some troops are coming down from the elevation over there, and another group is coming from the direction of the Soothsayers' Terebrinth!"

"So where are your big words now?" Zevul asked. "You know, when you were saying—'Who's Aviymelek that we should be his subjects?' Aren't those the troops that you mocked? So please, get out there now and fight them!"

And so Ga'al marched out at the head of the citizens of Shekem and engaged Aviymelek in battle. But Aviymelek put him to flight, and he ran away from him, with large numbers of dead strewn all the way back to the entrance to the town gate.

Aviymelek stayed back in Arumah, Zevul having driven Ga'al and his kinsmen out and preventing them from remaining in Shekem.

—

On the following day, the people went out into fields as was their normal practice, and this was reported to Aviymelek. Taking his own men, he divided them into three gangs and then lay in hiding in the fields. He kept watch, and when he noticed people leaving town, he attacked and killed them. And so Aviymelek and his gangs carried out their raids—they stood outside the entrance to the town gate while two of the gangs carried out raids against everyone in the fields and killed them.

Aviymelek fought against the town that entire day. He captured the town and murdered the people in it, and then demolished the town and sowed it with salt.

**

When the citizens of Shekem Tower heard what had happened, they went to the *tzeriah* of Beyth El Beriyth. When Aviymelek was informed that all the citizens of Shekem Tower had gathered in one place, he proceeded up to the top of Mount Tzalmon, accompanied by all his men. Taking axes in hand, Aviymelek cut off a branch of a tree and then picked it up and put it on his shoulder.

"What you saw me do," Aviymelek said to his men, "be quick and do just as I did!"

After his men had each also cut off a branch for himself, they followed Aviymelek and placed the branches on the *tzeriah*. They then used them to set fire to the *tzeriah*, and so all the people of Shekem Tower also died—about one thousand men and women in all.

**

Aviymelek next went to Tevetz, established a position against it, and then captured it. There was a well-fortified tower in the middle of the town where all the men and women—all the town's citizens—had fled. They locked the entry behind them and went up to the tower's roof. When Aviymelek arrived at the tower, he attacked it, going right up to the tower's entry to set fire to it. But a woman on the roof, acting alone, threw a mill stone on Aviymelek's head and it crushed his skull.

He quickly called to the ensign serving as his equipment-bearer. "Take out your sword and finish me off," he begged. "Otherwise they'll say a woman killed me!" And so his ensign ran him through and he died.

When the Yisra'elites saw that Aviymelek was dead, they all returned home. And so God repaid Aviymelek's wickedness which he had perpetrated against his father by killing his seventy brothers. Likewise, God brought punishment upon Shekem's citizens for all their wickedness, and Yotham Yerubba'alsson's curse about them came to pass.

d

e
f

**

Tola Pu'ahsson Dodosson, a Yissakarite who lived in Shamiyr in the Ephrayim mountains, succeeded Aviymelek to rescue Yisra'el from its enemies. He championed Yisra'el for twenty-three years, and then died and was buried in Shamiyr.

P34 [Ch. 10]
a

**

Succeeding him was Ya'iyr the Gil'adite, who championed Yisra'el for twenty-two years. He had thirty sons who rode thirty jackasses. [*That is, they owned thirty jackasses.*] They were called 'Ya'iyr's Hamlets,' as they still are today, which are in the Gil'ad region. Ya'iyr died and was buried in Qamon.

P35 a

b c

**

The Yisra'elites once again did what Yahweh considered the worst thing of all: they gave service to the Ba'als and the Ashtoreths—that is, to Aram's gods, to Tziydon's gods, to Mo'av's gods, to the Ammonites' gods, and to the Philishtines' gods. They forsook Yahweh and didn't give service to him.

And so Yahweh became enraged with Yisra'el and made them subjects of the Philishtines and the Ammonites. They crushed and oppressed the Yisra'elites that year—doing so for a total of eighteen years to all the Yisra'elites in the region across the Yarden, in the Amorites' country in the Gil'ad region. Then the Ammonites crossed the Yarden to go to war also with Yehudah, Binyamin, and the people of Ephrayim, putting Yisra'el in great distress.

The Yisra'elites in turn cried out to Yahweh. "We've wronged you," they said, "for we've forsaken our god and given service to the Ba'als."

P36 a

b Midpoint of the book

c

**

P37	a b	"Didn't from Egypt and from the Amorites [*and from the Ammonites and the Philishtines*]?" Yahweh replied to the Yisra'elites. "And when the Tziydonians and Amaleq and Ma'on oppressed you, you cried out to me and I rescued you from them. Nevertheless you forsook me and gave service to other gods. Therefore I won't rescue you again! Go on, cry for help to the gods you've chosen—let them save you whenever you're in trouble!"
	c	
	d	"We've done wrong!" the Yisra'elites said to Yahweh. "Do to us as you think is best. Only, please, save us this time!" Then the Yisra'elites removed the foreigners' gods from their communities and they gave service to Yahweh—and so he grew aggravated over Yisra'el's suffering.
	e	

**

P38		The Ammonites marshaled their forces and made camp in the Gil'ad region. In turn the Yisra'elite forces gathered and made camp in Mitzpah.
		"Who's the man that will start the fight against the Ammonites?" the Yisra'elite forces [*that is, Gil'ad's chieftains*] were saying to one another. "Let him be the leader for everyone who lives in Gil'ad!"
	a	

**

P39 [Ch. 11]		Now Yiphtah the Gil'adite was an accomplished warrior; he was, however, also the son of a prostitute. Although Gil'ad had fathered Yiphtah, Gil'ad's wife bore him a number of sons and when that woman's sons grew up, they drove Yiphtah out of the family. "You're not going to inherit any of our father's wealth," they told him, "because your mother's a foreigner!"
	a	
	b	
Tov: *Pleasant*		So Yiphtah ran away from his kinspeople and settled in the Tov region. Some good-for-nothing men joined up with him there and went out on missions with him.
	c	
	d	

**

P40		Now some years had passed, and the Ammonites were at war with Yisra'el. It so happened that when the Ammonites went to war with Yisra'el, Gil'ad's elders went to summon Yiphtah from the Tov region.
	a	
		"Come and serve as the leader of our army," they said to him, "so that we might fight the Ammonites."
	b	"Didn't you in fact oppose my lawsuit and drive me away from my family?" asked Yiphtah. "So why have you come to see me now, just as you're in trouble?"

"Be that as it may, we've come back to you now," Gil'ad's elders replied. "You must come with us and fight the Ammonites. Then you'll become our leader—the leader of everyone in Gil'ad!"

"If you're going to take me back to fight against the Ammonites, and if Yahweh delivers them up to me, then you must accept me as your leader," Yiphtah demanded.

"Let Yahweh be the judge if we don't do as you say," the elders vowed.

And so Yiphtah travelled back with Gil'ad's elders, and the people made him their leader and head of the army, whereupon Yiphtah repeated all his demands in front of Yahweh there in Mitzpah.

**

Yiphtah sent envoys to the Ammonites' king with the following message: "What exactly is the quarrel between you and me that you've come here to make war in my land?"

"It's because Yisra'el took my land when they came up from Egypt," the Ammonites' king told Yiphtah's envoys. "The lands between the Arnon, the Yabboq and the Yarden. So now, I demand that you return them peacefully!"

Yiphtah sent envoys to the Ammonites' king a second time with this message: "Thus says Yiphtah: 'Yisra'el took neither Mo'av nor the Ammonites' country. Rather, after the Yisra'elites left Egypt, they travelled in the desert wilderness as far as the Reed Sea, and then they went to Qadesh. When Yisra'el sent envoys to Edom's king kindly requesting to cross through his land, he refused them. Likewise, they sent envoys to Mo'av's king and he wasn't willing to let them pass through his land either. So Yisra'el remained in Qadesh.

"'Then they resumed their travels through the wilderness, going around Edom and Mo'av, arriving at a place east of Mo'av and making camp in the region north of the Arnon. They didn't enter Mo'av's borders, for the Arnon was Mo'av's border. Then Yisra'el sent envoys to the Amorites' king Siyhon King of Heshbon kindly requesting to cross through his land in order to arrive at their destination. But Siyhon didn't trust Yisra'el to cross through his territory. So he mustered all his forces and, after making camp in Yahtzah, went to war with Yisra'el. And Yisra'el's god Yahweh delivered Siyhon and his entire army into Yisra'el's hands—Yisra'el defeated them and took possession of all the land belonging to the Amorites who lived in that region. They took possession of the entire territory of the Amorites between the Arnon and the Yabboq and between the desert and the Yarden.

"'So then, Yisra'el's god Yahweh drove the Amorites away from his people Yisra'el and dispossessed them, and now you want to drive out Yisra'el? Isn't it true that whatever your god Kemosh gives you possession of, that's what you'll possess? And that whomever our god Yahweh has driven from our path, that's whose land we'll take possession of? So now, are you really going to be more successful than Mo'av's king Balaq Tzipporsson? Did he in fact engage Yisra'el in battle, or did he actually go to war with them? For three hundred years Yisra'el has lived in Heshbon and the nearby villages, in Ar'or and the nearby villages, and in all the towns along the Arnon's tributaries. So why didn't you steal them back during that time? I personally haven't wronged you, yet you're harming me by going to war against me. May Yahweh the Judge today decide between the Yisra'elites and the Ammonites!'"

But the Ammonites' king didn't heed the message which Yiphtah sent to him.

**

Yahweh's power filled Yiphtah, and so he passed through the Gil'ad region and Menashsheh and proceeded to Mitzpah in Gil'ad. When he crossed into the Ammonites' territory from Mitzpah in Gil'ad, Yiphtah made a vow to Yahweh. "If you really do deliver the Ammonites into my hands," he said, "then whoever is the one who opens the door and comes out of my house to greet me when I safely return from fighting the Ammonites, that person will be given over to Yahweh—I will offer him up to Yahweh as a whole offering."

**

Yiphtah crossed into the Ammonites' territory to fight against them, and Yahweh delivered them into his hands. He struck them hard, first at Aro'er and continuing all the way to Minniyth—twenty towns in all—and then continuing on to Vineyard Meadow, achieving an overwhelming victory. And so the Ammonites were humiliated by the Yisra'elites.

**

Yiphtah arrived at his house in Mitzpah—and there was his daughter, coming out to greet him, beating a tambourine and dancing. Indeed, she was his only child—apart from her, he had no sons or daughters. As soon as he saw her, he tore his clothes in anguish. "Oh no, my daughter, no! Seeing you has ruined me! You're not to blame, but you're why I'm in such agony! For I vowed something to Yahweh, and I can't take it back!"

"Father," she said to him, "you vowed something to Yahweh. Do to me exactly as the vow that came from your lips, for Yahweh has carried out vengeance for you against your enemies, the Ammonites! So let this thing be done to me," she continued, "but leave me alone for two months, so that I might go and clamber on the mountains and mourn over my youth, me and my girlfriends."

"Go and do that," he said.

And so he sent her away for two months. She went with her girlfriends, and she mourned her youth in the mountains. Then at the end of two months, she returned to her father, and he carried out the vow on her that he had made. She never knew a man sexually, and it became a custom in Yisra'el that each year for four days the young women of Yisra'el would go off to share stories in honor of Yiphtah the Gil'adite's daughter.

**

The men of Ephrayim took up arms and went north. "Why did you go to fight the Ammonites," they asked Yiphtah, "without inviting us to go with you? We ought to burn down your house with you in it!"

"I like a good fight!" Yiphtah retorted. "Me and my people—and even the Ammonites! Quite so! Anyway, if I had summoned you, you wouldn't have saved me from them! When I realized that you couldn't save me, I took my life into my own hands, and went to the Ammonites without you. And Yahweh did deliver them into my hands! So why have you come to me today to attack me?"

Yiphtah then collected all the men of Gil'ad and went to war with Ephrayim. The men of Gil'ad attacked Ephrayim because Ephrayim had called them "Ephrayim's trash" to their face. [*Now Gil'ad was located between Ephrayim and Menashsheh.*] The Gil'adites captured the fords of the Yarden that belonged to Ephrayim, and whenever some "trash" fleeing Ephrayim would ask to cross, the men of Gil'ad would ask if they were from Ephrayim. If someone said "no," then they would say to him, "Please say *shibboleth*." When someone said "*sibboleth*" (because he wasn't able to speak the correct sound), then they would grab him and slaughter him beside the Yarden's fords. During that conflict, some forty-two thousand people from Ephrayim were killed.

Yiphtah championed Yisra'el for six years. Yiphtah the Gil'adite died and was buried somewhere in Gil'ad.

**

P46 a   After him Ivtzan from Beyth Lehem championed Yisra'el. He had
    b   thirty sons and thirty daughters. he married off to foreigners, and at the same time he brought in thirty foreign wives for his sons.

            Ivtzan championed Yisra'el for seven years. He died and was buried in Beyth Lehem.

**

P47   After him Eylon the Zevulunite championed Yisra'el. He championed Yisra'el for ten years.

Ayyalon: Eylon the Zevulunite died and was buried in Ayyalon in the terri-
Deerfield   tory of Zevulun.

**

P48   After him Avdon Hillelsson the Pir'athonite championed Yisra'el. He had forty sons and thirty grandsons who rode seventy jackasses.

            He championed Yisra'el for eight years. Avdon Hillelsson the Pir'athonite died and was buried in Pir'athon in the territory of Eph-
a   rayim in the Amaleqite mountains.

**

P49   [Ch. 13]   The Yisra'elites once again did what Yahweh considered the worst
          a   thing, and so Yahweh delivered them into the hands of the Philishtines for forty years.

**

P50   a   There was a certain man from the town of Tzor'ah from the Danites'
        b   tribe whose name was Manoah. His wife was barren and had not borne any children.

            An emissary of Yahweh showed itself to the woman. "You should know," it said, "that although you're barren and haven't borne any children, you're going to conceive and give birth to a boy. So now, please be very careful—don't drink any wine or beer, and don't eat anything unclean. Because, you should know, you're going to conceive
        c   and give birth to a boy. Don't let a razor touch his head, for the boy
        d   will be a *naziyr* dedicated to God from the time he's in the womb,
        e   and he's the one who will begin to free Yisra'el from the Philishtines' clutches."

The woman immediately went and spoke to her husband. "A holy man came to see me," she told him, "and he looked like a divine being—it was terrifying. I didn't ask him where he was from, and he didn't tell me his name. He told me I was going to conceive and give birth to a boy, and that therefore I shouldn't drink any wine or beer, or eat anything unclean. Because the boy's going to be a *naziyr* dedicated to God, from the time he's in the womb until the day he dies!"

∗∗

So Manoah made supplication to Yahweh. "I beg you, my lord," he said, "please let the holy man you sent come see us again, so that he might show us what we should do for the boy who's going to be born!" P51

God heeded Manoah's request, and so God's emissary went to see the woman again. At the time she was sitting out in the fields and her husband Manoah wasn't with her. The woman quickly ran and told her husband what had happened. "Guess what!?" she declared. "The man who came to see me the other day just showed up!" a

Manoah followed his wife back right away to see the man. "Are you the man who spoke to my wife?" he asked. b

"Yes I am."

"Then may what you said come true!" exclaimed Manoah. "What will the boy be like and what will he do?"

"Everything that I told your wife she must take care to do," Yahweh's emissary said to Manoah. "She mustn't eat anything made from wine grapes, and she mustn't drink any wine or beer. Nor may she eat anything unclean. She must follow everything that I instructed her to do." c

— d

"Please allow us to detain you," Manoah said to Yahweh's emissary, "so that we may prepare a kid goat for you." P51,1 a

"If you do detain me, I won't eat any of your food," Yahweh's emissary replied. "But if you wish to prepare a whole offering for Yahweh, I won't object." (For Manoah didn't realize that the man was an emissary from Yahweh.) b

"What's your name?" Manoah asked Yahweh's emissary. "For when your prediction comes true, we'd like to honor you." c

"Why in the world do you want to know my name?" replied Yahweh's emissary. (Now it was Pil'iy.)

Pil'iy: Amazing
d
e

∗∗

P52   Manoah fetched a kid goat and grain for the grain offering and placed them on a rocky outcrop to be offered to Yahweh. As Manoah and his
a   wife looked on, they were being prepared with amazing skill. And then when the flames leapt from the altar toward the sky, Yahweh's
b   emissary vanished into the altar's flames. Manoah and his wife were still looking on, and at once they threw themselves flat on the ground.
c   [*Yahweh's emissary didn't show itself again to Manoah and his wife.*] That's when Manoah realized that the man was Yahweh's emissary.

"We're surely going to die!" Manoah exclaimed to his wife. "For we've seen God!"

"If Yahweh had wanted to kill us, he wouldn't have taken a whole offering and grain offering from us," his wife replied. "Also, he wouldn't have shown us any of these things, and he wouldn't have
d   earlier let us hear anything like this."

Shimshon: 'Little Sun'   The woman gave birth to a boy and she named him Shimshon. When the boy grew up, Yahweh blessed him.

e   The first time Yahweh's spirit struck him was at the place called Dan's Camp between Tzor'ah and Eshta'ol...

**

P53 [Ch. 14]   Shimshon went down to Timnathah and noticed a woman there who
a   was a Philishtine. When he went back home he told his father and mother about her. "I saw a woman in Timnathah who's a Philishtine," he said. "I want you to get her for me to be my wife!"

b   "Are you telling us there isn't one woman from all the Danite girls—or from anywhere in Yisra'el for that matter—that you have
c   to go and get a wife from those dickhead Philishtines?!" objected his father and mother.

d   "Get her for me!" Shimshon insisted to his father. "For I really like her!"

Now, neither his father nor his mother knew that this was Yahweh's doing, for he was looking for an opportunity against the Philish-
e   tines. (At that time, the Philishtines ruled Yisra'el.) So Shimshon went down to Timnathah with his father and mother. They had gotten as far as the vineyards outside Timnathah when a young lion suddenly roared and came at him. Yahweh's spirit rushed into him and he dismembered it like he was dismembering a kid goat, even though there
f   was nothing in his hands. But he didn't tell his father and mother what he had done. And so Shimshon went down to Timnathah. He spoke to the woman, and he really liked her.

g   He returned some days later to get her. On the way, he turned off to have a look at the dead lion and noticed there was a swarm of bees in the lion's carcass and some honey as well. He scraped some into his hand and continued on his way, eating as he went. When he went back to his father and mother, he gave them some of the honey, which they ate, but he didn't tell them that he had scraped it from a lion carcass.

When his father went down to get the woman, Shimshon held a party there, for that's what young men would do back then. When they saw the festivities, they fetched thirty of their acquaintances and they joined in the fun with him.

"I'd like to pose a riddle to all of you," Shimshon said to the thirty fellows. "If you actually tell me the answer during the seven days of festivities and find the solution, then I'll give each of you a linen cloak and a change of clothes. But if you're not able to tell me the solution, then each of you must give me a linen cloak and a change of clothes!"

"Tell us your riddle!" they cried. "Let's hear it!"

"From the eater comes something to eat," he said, "and from something strong comes something sweet."

For three days they couldn't solve the riddle. Then on the seventh day of the party, they went to Shimshon's wife and threatened her. "Trick your husband so that he tells us the answer," they demanded. "Or else we're going to burn you and your family to death! Did you all invite us here simply to take our money, or what?!"

Shimshon's wife went to see him and was crying. "You must really hate me," she sobbed. "You don't love me. You gave a riddle to these Philishtine fellows, but you haven't told me the answer."

"Look," he said, "I haven't even told my father and mother the answer, but now I'm going to tell you?"

She cried like this with him on each of the seven days that they were having the party. But then on the seventh day, he told her the answer, for she had pressed him so much. And so she told the answer to the Philishtine fellows.

As a result, on the seventh day—just before the sun was to set—the fellows from town announced to Shimshon: "What's sweeter than honey, and what's stronger than a lion?"

"If you hadn't schemed with my heifer calf, you wouldn't have found the answer to my riddle!" he raged at them.

Yahweh's spirit rushed into him, whereupon he went down to Ashqelon and killed thirty men among its citizenry. He stripped them of their belongings and gave the clothes to the men who answered his riddle. But he was enraged, and so he went back home to his family. Shimshon's wife meanwhile was given to a friend of his who had been especially close to him.

*

P54 [Ch. 15] Some time later during the wheat harvest, Shimshon went to give his wife a fine buckling, thinking that he would then consummate the marriage at her house. But her father wouldn't let him go to her. "I truly thought you'd rejected her," her father told him, "so I gave her to your friend. But her youngest sister is better than her, don't you think? Please, you can have her instead!"

"I wasn't to blame last time for what I did to the Philishtines," Shimshon said to them, "but I'm going to do wreak havoc on them now!"

Shimshon then went and caught three hundred foxes. He got hold of some torches and, after turning the foxes tail to tail, he placed one torch between every two tails. He then set the torches on fire and released the foxes into the Philishtines' grain fields: he burned all of it down—the standing grain as well as sheaves from the harvest—and even vineyards and olive groves.

"Who could have done this?" wondered the Philishtines. And then it dawned on them: "The Timnite's son-in-law, Shimshon—that's who! Because he took his wife and gave her to his friend." So the Philishtines went to Timnathah and immolated both the woman and her father.

"I'll be damned," Shimshon cried, "if you do a thing like this and I don't take revenge on you until I'm done!" Whereupon he killed them all, striking them from head to toe and carrying out a great slaughter. He then went down to Eytam and took up residence in a hollow on the bluff there.

*

P55 The Philishtines made a foray into Yehudah, establishing camp and conducting raids near the town of Lehiy.

"Why did you come up here to attack us?" the Yehudites asked.

"We've come to capture Shimshon," they answered. "To do to him exactly as he did to us!"

Three thousand men from Yehudah went down to the hollow in the bluff at Eytam. "Don't you know the Philishtines are ruling us now?" they asked Shimshon. "What in the world have you done to us?"

"Exactly as they did to me," replied Shimshon, "I did back to them!"

"We've come here to tie you up," they said to him, "to turn you over to the Philishtines."

"Swear it to me," demanded Shimshon, "so I know you've not come to do me harm."

"No," they assured him. "We're only going to tie you up and turn you over to them. We're certainly not going to kill you."

They then bound him with two newly-made ropes and hoisted him up the rock face. He had gotten as far as Lehiy when the Philishtines gave out a war cry to attack him.

But Yahweh's spirit rushed into him. The ropes tied around his arms were like flax consumed in a fire, and the restraints simply dissolved from his hands. Then, finding a jawbone from a freshly-killed ass, he reached out and picked it up, and proceeded to kill a thousand men with it.

"With an ass's jawbone—one heap, then two heaps!" Shimshon exulted. "With an ass's jawbone, I killed a thousand men!" Once he had finished his boasting, he threw the jawbone from his hand. (That's why that place is called Lehiy Height.)

Lehiy: jawbone

But then he was extremely thirsty and so he called out to Yahweh. "You granted your servant this great victory," he complained, "but now I'm about to die of thirst and fall back into the dickheads' hands!"

So God broke open the pothole that was in Lehiy and water flowed forth from it. When Shimshon drank, his energy returned and he recovered. This is the reason that place is still today known as Caller's Spring which is in Lehiy.

He championed Yisra'el during Philishtine times for twenty years.

**

Once when Shimshon went to Azzah, a prostitute there caught his eye and he had intercourse with her. to the Azzathites that Shimshon had come there, they surrounded his location and lay in wait all night long at the town gate, plotting during the night to murder him as soon as day broke. But Shimshon only slept until midnight. When he got up at midnight, he grabbed hold of the town gate's doors and the two door-posts and dislodged them with the bar of the gate. Then he put them on his shoulders and took them up to the top of the mountain facing Hevron.

P56 [Ch. 16]

**

Some time afterwards, he became enamored with a woman in the Red Vine Wadi region whose name was Deliylah. The Philishtines' archons went to see her. "Trick him," they said to her, "and find out why he's so strong and how we can get the best of him. Then we'll tie him

P57

up and torture him. We'll each give you eleven hundred sheqels of silver."

"Please tell me how you're so strong," Deliylah said to Shimshon, "and how you could be tied up if someone wanted to hurt you."

"If I was tied up with seven fresh cords of catgut that haven't been dried," he replied, "then I would grow weak and be like a normal man."

So the Philishtines' archons brought her seven fresh cords of catgut that hadn't been dried, and she tied him up with them. Once the ambush was positioned for her in a back room, she cried, "The Philishtines are coming for you, Shimshon!" But he snapped the cords like a strand of flax snapping when exposed to a flame, and the source of his strength remained a mystery.

"Hey now, you're playing with me," Deliylah said to Shimshon. "You told me a bunch of lies! Now please, tell me how can you be tied up!"

"Actually," he replied, "if I was tied up with new ropes that haven't yet been used for anything, then I would grow weak and be like a normal man."

So Deliylah got some new ropes and tied him up with them. "The Philishtines are coming for you!" she cried. (Now at the time the ambush was waiting in the back room.) But he snapped them from his arms like thread.

"All this time you've been toying with me!" Deliylah exclaimed. "You told me a bunch of lies! Tell me how you can be tied up!"

"Try weaving a net into the seven braids on my head," he answered.

So she beat netting into his hair with a weaving peg. When she cried, "The Philishtines are coming for you, Shimshon," he awoke from his nap and removed both the weaving peg and the netting.

"How can you say that you love me when your heart clearly isn't with me?" she asked. "That's three times now you've toyed with me! You still haven't told me how you're so strong." And so it happened that she pressured him relentlessly, day after day, and pushed him so much that he became dreadfully frustrated. That's when he revealed to her his innermost secret.

"A razor has never touched my head," he told her at last, "for I've been a *naziyr* dedicated to God from the time I was in my mother's womb. But if I'm shaved bald, my strength will leave me—I'll become weak and be like everyone else."

Deliylah realized at once that he had told her his innermost secret. She sent off a messenger and summoned the Philishtines' archons with this message: "This time you must come, for he's revealed his innermost secret to me!"

The Philishtines' archons went to see her, bringing the silver with them. Once she had lured him to sleep in her lap, she summoned a man and she shaved the seven braids from his head. And so she commenced his torture, his strength having left him.

"The Philishtines are coming for you, Shimshon!" she cried. When he awoke from his nap, he thought he would go outside as he had done previously and shake himself free of his bonds, for he didn't realize that Yahweh had left him. The Philishtines seized him and gouged out his eyes, and then they took him down to Azzah. They bound him in two sets of bronze shackles and set him to work milling grain in the prison.

But the hair on his head began growing back the moment that he was shaved bald...

**

The archons of the Philishtines convened to make a great sacrificial offering to their god Dagan and to celebrate, proclaiming "Our god has delivered our enemy Shimshon into our hands!"

When the people saw him, they gave praise to their god, for they thought, "Our god has delivered our enemy into our hands—the man who laid waste to our land and who caused so many deaths among us!" And as they were in such good spirits, they cried, "Summon Shimshon so that he might entertain us!" So they summoned Shimshon from the prison and he made sport in front of them. Then they called for him to stand between the pillars.

"Let me rest a minute," Shimshon said to the attendant who was holding his hand. "Let me touch the pillars supporting the building so that I might lean against them." (Now the building was full of men and women, and all the Philishtines' archons were there; moreover, about three thousand men and women were on the roof watching Shimshon's antics.)

That's when Shimshon called out to Yahweh: "O Yahweh, my lord," he cried, "please remember me! Please God, give me strength just one more time, so that I can avenge myself against the Philishtines once and for all for what they did to my two eyes!" Then Shimshon got a firm grip on the middle part of the two columns supporting the building and braced himself against them, setting his right hand against one and his left hand against the other. "Now let me die along with the Philishtines!" said Shimshon to himself. Then he extended his arms with all his might, and the building fell down on the archons and everyone inside it. The number of deaths that he caused with his own death was greater than all the deaths he caused when he was alive.

f   His kinsmen and all his family went to retrieve his body. They picked him up and then brought him back and buried him in his father Manoah's grave, between Tzor'ah and Eshta'ol.

g   He championed Yisra'el for twenty years.

**

P59 [Ch. 17]
a b   There once was a man from the Ephrayim mountains whose name was Miykayehu. "Remember the eleven hundred sheqels of silver which were taken from you," he said to his mother, "and which you swore a curse over and spoke to me about? Well, the silver is with me. I'm the one who took it."

"May you be blessed to Yahweh, my son!" his mother exclaimed as
c   he returned all eleven hundred sheqels of silver to her. (*"It's decided—I*
d   *shall dedicate this silver to Yahweh,"* she thought, *"to have an icon of the god cast for my son."*)

e   "And now I'm giving it back to you."
f   So he returned the silver to his mother, and then she took two
g   hundred sheqels and gave them to a silversmith. He cast the silver into an icon, and the icon was kept in Miykayehu's house. Now this man Miykah owned property on which there was a shrine to God. He
h   made a priest's shoulder-cape and some *teraphim*; then he installed one of his sons to serve as priest for him.

i   Back in those days, there was no king who ruled over Yisra'el—each man did as he thought was right...

**

P60   There was a young man from Beyth Lehem in Yehudah, from Yehudah's tribe, although he himself was a Lewite and he was only temporarily residing there. This man moved on from his town, from Beyth Lehem in Yehudah, staying for a while in whatever place he happened upon. Along the way, he entered the Ephrayim mountains, making his way as far as Miykah's house.

"Where are you coming from?" Miykah asked him.
a   "I'm a Lewite from Beyth Lehem in Yehudah," he replied, "and
b   I'm currently travelling, staying awhile in whatever place I happen upon."

"Stay here with me," Miykah said to him. "I'd like you to serve as
c   an advisor and priest to me. I'll pay you ten sheqels per year, as well

as provide you with a full set of clothes and room and board."

The Lewite agreed. And so he was willing to stay with the man—and in fact the young man became like a son to him. Miykah performed the priestly installation rite for the Lewite and made the young man his priest.

He stayed in Miykah's house. "Now I know," thought Miykah to himself, "that Yahweh is going to make things go well for me, because I have this Lewite as my priest."

**

Back in those days, there was no king who ruled over Yisra'el. Also back in those days, the Danites' tribe was looking for territory to occupy, for up until that time it had not been allotted any territory among Yisra'el's tribes.

**

The Danites sent five men from their tribe—some of the most capable men in their entire tribe—giving them orders to go investigate the land. And so they departed from the towns of Tzor'ah and Eshta'ol to explore the land and investigate it.

They journeyed into the Ephrayim mountains as far as Miykah's house, where they spent the night. While they were at Miykah's house, they noticed the young Lewite's Yehudite accent. Turning aside, they spoke to him there in private. "Who brought you here?" they asked. "And what are you doing in this place? What's your business here?"

When he told them exactly what Miykah had done for him—that he had hired him, and that he was serving as his priest—they said to him, "Please request an oracle from God, so that we might learn whether the mission we're going on will be successful."

"Be on your way and don't worry," the priest said to them. "The mission you're going on has Yahweh's approval."

**

The five men travelled on and came to the town of Layish. They observed that the people there were living peacefully—similar in behavior to the Tzidonians, in peace and quiet, and no one in the region being obnoxious about anything—a model of restraint. But the citizens of Layish lived quite far from the Tzidonians, and they had no regular business with other people.

When the men arrived back at Tzor'ah and Eshta'ol and met their kinspeople, their kinspeople asked them how they had fared.

"Quick," they replied, "let's go and attack them, for we observed the region and have concluded it's an excellent place. We can see you're being quiet—don't hesitate to make the move and go and take possession of that land! When you go, you'll come to a people living peacefully and a land that is spacious (for God has delivered it into your possession)—a place where there's no scarcity of anything in the world!"

So some of the Danites' tribe departed there, leaving Tzor'ah and Eshta'ol—six hundred men in all, outfitted in their battle gear. Travelling up into the hills, they made camp at Forest Village in Yehudah. (That's why that place has been called Dan's Camp down to the present day—it's just west of Forest Village.) From there they crossed into the Ephrayim mountains, going as far as Miykah's house. In light of the circumstances, the five men who had gone to explore the Layish region addressed their kinsmen. "Did you all know that among these houses here there's a priest's shoulder-cape and some *teraphim*, as well as a sacred icon? So now, consider what you should do!"

So they turned off there and went to the young Lewite's house—that is, Miykah's house—and greeted him warmly. Now the six hundred men who were outfitted in their battle gear were standing in front of the gate [*that is, the men who were from the Danites*] when the five men who had gone to explore the land went up to the house. Upon arriving there, they took the icon, the priest's shoulder-cape, the *teraphim*, and the icon. At the time the priest was standing in front of the gate along with the six hundred men dressed in their battle gear.

Now when these men entered Miykah's house and took the icon of the priest's shoulder-cape, the *teraphim*, and the icon, the priest cried to them, "What are you doing?!"

"Be quiet!" they demanded. "Shut your mouth and come with us. You're going to serve as our advisor and priest! Really now, would you rather be priest to the family of a single man, or priest to an entire tribe in Yisra'el?"

The priest cheered up when he heard this. He took the priest's shoulder-cape, the *teraphim*, and the icon, and joined the Danites' entourage. They turned back on the road and proceeded on their way, putting the children and livestock and their most precious possessions in the front. They had travelled a fair distance from Miykah's house when the men in the houses next to Miykah's marshaled their forces and went after the Danites, hot on their heels. They called out to the Danites, who turned to face them.

"What's your problem?" the Danites asked Miykah. "Why have

you called your men to arms?"

"You took the god that I made, and the priest as well, and then left! What do I still possess?! Why the hell are you asking me what my problem is?!"

"Don't let us hear a peep from you again!" the Danites snarled. "Otherwise, some rough fellows might chance upon you and your friends here, and then you'd lose your life—and your family too!"

The Danites then proceeded on their way. Seeing that they were stronger than him, Miykah turned around and went back home.

After they had taken the things Miykah had made and the priest who had served him, they went to attack Layish, striking a people who were living quietly and peacefully. They slaughtered them all and burned the town to the ground. There was no one who could come to the town's rescue, for it was far from Tziydon and they had no regular business with other people. [*It's located in the valley that is under Beyth-Rehov's control.*] The Danites then rebuilt the town and lived there. They gave the town the name Dan after the name of their ancestor Dan, who was one of Yisra'el's children, although previously the town's name was Layish.

The Danites set up the icon for their own use, and Yehonathan Gershomsson Me^{n}ashshehsson along with his sons served as priests to the Danites' tribe until the time of the land's exile. They installed for their own use the icon that Miykah had made for the entire time that a temple to God stood in Shiloh.

**

Back in the days when Yisra'el didn't have a king, there was a certain Lewite who was living for a time in a remote part of the Ephrayim mountains. He acquired a concubine for himself from Beyth Lehem in Yehudah. But his concubine played the harlot on him, leaving him and going back to her family in Beyth Lehem in Yehudah. She had been there for a period of four months when her man decided to go after her, to sweet-talk her and get her to come back. With him were his valet and a pair of donkeys. And so she caused him to go visit her family.

When the young woman's father saw him, he was thrilled to meet him. At the insistence of his father-in-law (the young woman's father), he stayed with him for three days, eating and drinking and spending the night there. He got up early in the morning of the fourth day and made ready to go.

"Fortify yourself with a little food," the young woman's father said to his son-in-law, "and then you all may be on your way!"

So they stayed, the two of them eating and drinking together. "Please consider staying the night and enjoying yourself!" the young woman's father said to the man. But when the man made preparations to leave, his father-in-law was insistent, and so he relented and spent the night there.

When on the fifth day he got up early in the morning to leave, the young woman's father waylaid him: "Please have some refreshments and take it easy until the afternoon!" And so the two of them ate. When the man made ready to be on his way—he along with his concubine and his valet—his father-in-law (the young woman's father) said, "Look here now, the day has slipped away and it's almost evening. Please spend the night. As you can see, the day's nearly gone. So spend the night here and enjoy yourself! Then tomorrow you can get an early start on your journey and travel back to thine abode."

But the man wasn't willing to spend another night there, and he left right away. He had gone as far as the outskirts of Yevus (to wit, Yerushalem); with him were the pair of donkeys that had been saddled, and his concubine was with him too. They were close to Yevus and the daylight was quickly disappearing. "Come now," the valet said to his lord, "let's turn off to the Yevusites' town right here and spend the night there."

"We're not going to turn off to a town of foreigners where there aren't any Yisra'elites," his lord replied. "We'll continue on to Giv'ah."

Some time later, he again spoke to his valet: "Come, we're getting close to one of the places. We'll spend the night in either Giv'ah or Ramah." They continued on their way. The sun set when they were near Giv'ah in Binyamin, so they turned off there to go and spend the night in Giv'ah. Once they entered town, they settled down in the town plaza, as there was no one who took them into his house for the night.

Now there was an old man coming back into town that evening from his work out in the countryside. This man was from the Ephrayim mountain region, but he was living at the time in Giv'ah (a place whose inhabitants were Binyaminites). From a distance, he espied the traveller in the town plaza.

"Where are you headed?" the old man asked. "And where are you coming from?"

"We're travelling from Beyth-Lehem in Yehudah," he replied, "and heading to a remote part of the Ephrayim mountains, where I'm from. I travelled to Beyth Lehem in Yehudah, and now I'm going to visit Yahweh's shrine. I'm here in the plaza because there wasn't anyone who took me in for the night. There's straw bedding and hay for our donkeys, and there's also food and wine for me and your maidservant and for the valet who's with us. There's really nothing we lack."

"I wish you well," the old man said. "However, anything that you lack I'm happy to provide. But you really mustn't spend the night in the plaza." Then he took him into his home. He gave the donkeys some hay while they washed their feet, and then they ate and drank. They were enjoying themselves in this fashion when suddenly some men from town—some worthless scoundrels, actually—surrounded the house and began beating violently against the door.

"Make that man who went into your house come out here—we're going to have our way with him!" they shouted to the old man who owned the house.

The man who owned the house went outside to speak to them. "Brothers, no! Please don't do such a wicked thing after this man has come into my house as my guest! Don't do such an immoral thing! Look, my teenage daughter and his concubine are inside—please, let me bring them out to you. Rape and abuse them, and do whatever you want to them! But to this man, don't do such an immoral thing!"

But the men had no intention of listening to him. So the man grabbed hold of his concubine and brought her outside to them. They had their way with her and ruthlessly abused her all night long until morning, finally letting her go when light dawned. She came back as it turned morning and fell down in front of the man's house where her master had planned to be until first light.

Her master rose in the morning, and when he opened the doors of the house and went out to resume his journey, he was surprised to see a woman there—it was his concubine!—sprawled in front of the house with her hands touching the threshold.

"Get up. Let's get going," he said to her. But there was no response. The man picked her up and laid her atop one of the donkeys and then left at once to go back home. Once he got to his house, he took a knife, grabbed hold of his concubine, and butchered her limb by limb into twelve pieces.

He sent the pieces of her into every part of Yisra'el, and whenever anyone saw one of them, he would say to them, "Nothing like this has ever happened or been seen from the time the Yisra'elites came here from Egypt down to the present day! Consider her closely—please advise and speak!"

**

All the Yisra'elites came out: from all ends of the land—from Dan to Be'er Sheva to Gil'ad—the community convened in a single body at

c   Yahweh's shrine in Mitzpah, and the grandees of the people—of all Yisra'el's tribes—took their places in the assembly of God's people,
d   along with four hundred thousand infantrymen armed with swords.

**

P66   (Now the Binyaminites heard that the Yisra'elites had gone to Mitzpah.)

"Tell us how this abominable thing happened," the Yisrae'lites demanded.

"I had come to Giv'ah in Binyamin—me and my concubine—in order to spend the night," replied the Lewite man (the husband of the woman who had been murdered). "The citizens of Giv'ah attacked me—during the night they surrounded the house where I was staying,
a   intending to kill me. Then they raped my concubine and she died. So I took hold of my concubine's body and I cut it into pieces. Then I sent them into every part of the territory in Yisra'el's possession, for they had committed an evil and depraved act in Yisra'el. Give this your attention, fellow Yisra'elites—come up with a response and a plan here and now!"

The people rose in unison: "Not a single one of us will go back to
b   his abode or return home. So then, here's what we're going to do to
c   Giv'ah: cast lots for who will attack it. We're going to take ten men out of every hundred for all the tribes of Yisra'el—a hundred men out of a thousand, and a thousand men out of ten thousand—to procure provisions for the fighting forces and to prepare them for when they
d   go to Giv'ah in Binyamin, as appropriate for the act of depravity which they committed in Yisra'el." Then all the men of Yisra'el gathered together at the town, united as a single force.

**

P67 a   Yisra'el's tribes sent men among all Binyamin's tribes with the following message: "What is this horrendous thing that happened among you? We demand that you turn over the worthless scoundrels in
b   Giv'ah so that we may put them to death and thoroughly cleanse such wrongdoing from Yisra'el."

But the Binyaminites were unwilling to heed their kinsmen the Yisrae'lites. So the Binyaminites left their towns and gathered at Giv'ah, in order to march out to war with the Yisra'elites. At that time the Binyaminites mustered twenty-six thousand armed men from their towns, separate from the seven hundred valiant men they had mustered from the citizens of Giv'ah. (Out of this entire fighting force there were seven hundred valiant men who were left-handed; each one of them could sling a stone at a strand of hair and not miss.)

**

Separate from Binyamin, the Yisra'elites mustered four hundred thousand armed men—all of them able warriors. Straight away they went to Beyth-El and sought an oracle from God. "Who should go first," asked the Yisra'elites, "to fight for us against the Binyaminites?"

"Yehudah should go first," answered Yahweh.

The Yisra'elites rose the next morning and established a position against Giv'ah. The Yisra'elites then marched out to battle with Binyamin, organizing their battle lines with them at Giv'ah. The Binyaminites marched out from Giv'ah and on that day they laid low twenty-two thousand men from Yisra'el.

The forces [*the Yisra'elites*] regrouped and reestablished their battle lines in the same place they had established them the previous day. The Yisra'elites then went to Beyth-El and bewailed their situation in front of Yahweh until evening. Then they sought an oracle from Yahweh. "Should we engage our kinsman Binyamin again in battle?" they asked.

"Go and attack him!" Yahweh answered.

**

The Yisra'elites approached the Binyaminites on the second day. When Binyamin marched out from Giv'ah to engage them that same day, this time they laid low from the Yisra'elites eighteen thousand men, warriors one and all.

All the Yisra'elites—their entire forces—headed north and went to Beyth-El, where they sat and bewailed their situation in front of Yahweh. They fasted that day until evening and offered up whole offerings and welfare offerings in front of Yahweh. The Yisra'elites then sought an oracle from Yahweh [*Now God's treaty chest was located there in those days, and also in those days Phiynehas El'azarsson Aharonsson was stationed in front of it as priest.*]: "Should we march out again to battle with our kinsman Binyamin, or should we hold off?"

"Attack them," Yahweh answered, "for tomorrow I'm going to deliver them into your hands!"

Yisra'el then set ambushes all around Giv'ah…

**

P70 On the following day the Yisra'elites went back to the Binyaminites, organizing their battle lines at Giv'ah as they had done previously. The Binyaminites marched out to engage Yisra'el's forces, having been drawn away from the town. They began inflicting casualties on Yisra'el's forces as they had previously done—this time on two highways, one of which leads to Beyth-El and the other of which goes through the countryside to Giv'ah—about thirty men total out of the Yisra'elites.

"They're losing to us like they did previously!" the Binyaminites thought, whereas the Yisra'elites were thinking, "Let's run away and draw them out from town onto the highways!"

a All the Yisra'elites then stood up from their hiding places and set their battle lines at Ba'al Tamar; meanwhile, Yisra'el's ambuscades
b burst forth from their hiding places in the caves around Geva, ten thousand of the most valiant warriors in Yisra'el moving to the front
c of Giv'ah. But the battle was heavy, and they didn't know that a great harm was about to befall them.

**

P71 a Then Yahweh let Binyamin be routed by Yisra'el—that day the Yisra'el-
b ites wiped out twenty-five thousand one hundred men in Binyamin,
c warriors one and all. Once the Binyaminites saw that they had been routed, the Yisra'elites gave Binyamin some breathing space, for they
d were confident in the ambush that they had set for Giv'ah. The ambush forces quickly went into action and raided Giv'ah, proceeding into the town and putting it to the slaughter. The Yisra'elites had agreed a signal with the ambush force—that they would make a gigantic column of smoke rise from the town.

When the Yisra'elites reengaged in the battle, the Binyaminites began inflicting casualties on them—about thirty men in all—thinking to themselves that Yisra'el was certainly being defeated by them as in the previous battles. That's when a cloud started rising from the town—a gigantic column of smoke. Binyamin turned around and saw at once that the entire town was burning, its flames rising into the sky. The Yisra'elites then went on the offensive, and the Binyaminites grew terrified, for they saw that a great harm had befallen them. They
e retreated from the Yisra'elites down Wilderness Road, but the fighting
f g was hot on their heels, and in the midst of it all, the forces who had emerged from the towns were ravaging them.
h They surrounded the Binyaminites and then gave chase, smashing them at Menuhah all the way back to the eastern side of Giv'ah. Eighteen thousand men from Binyamin fell in the fighting, able sol-

diers one and all. The remaining Binyaminites turned and fled to the wilderness, to Pomegranate Rock. In the mopping up operations on the highways, the Yisra'elites inflicted five thousand more casualties; they pursued closely after them as far as Gid'om and killed two thousand additional men among them. The total number of soldiers from Binyamin who fell in battle that day was twenty-five thousand, able warriors one and all.

Six hundred men turned and fled to the wilderness, to Pomegranate Rock, and stayed at Pomegranate Rock for four months. The Yisra'elites meanwhile returned to the Binyaminites and slaughtered them all—people in the towns, livestock, and anything else that was found; in addition, all the towns they happened upon they burned to the ground.

**

(Now the Yisra'elites had sworn at Mitzpah that no one among them would give his daughter to a Binyaminite for a wife.)

The people went to Beyth-El and sat there in front of God until evening, crying loudly and weeping great volumes of tears. "Why, O Yahweh god of Yisra'el," they wailed, "has such a thing happened here in Yisra'el—for one whole tribe now to go missing from Yisra'el?" The next day, the people rose early and built an altar there and then offered up whole offerings and welfare offerings.

**

"Who's the one out of all Yisra'el's tribes who didn't come to the assembly at Yahweh's shrine?" the Yisra'elites asked, for anyone who hadn't come to Yahweh's shrine at Mitzpah was subject to a severe curse that he be put to death.

(For the Yisra'elites had changed their mind about their kinsman Binyamin. "Now that one whole tribe has been cut out of Yisra'el," they thought, "what can we do for them—for those who are left—with respect to wives? For we swore by Yahweh that we wouldn't give them any of our daughters for wives.")

When they asked which one of Yisra'el's tribes was the one that hadn't come to Yahweh's shine at Mitzpah, it was determined that no one had come to the camp from Yaveysh Gil'ad [*to the assembly*]. After the people had made an accounting of themselves and had determined that none of the inhabitants of Yavesh Gil'ad had been present, the community sent twelve thousand men there from their very capable forces. "Go and slaughter the inhabitants of Yavesh Gil'ad, including women and children," they ordered them. "This is what you must do: all males and all women who have had sexual intercourse with a male you must make a ban devotion of."

Out of all Yaveysh Gil'ad's inhabitants, they found four hundred young women who had never had sexual intercourse with a male, and they brought them back to the camp at Shiloh, which is in Kena'an.

**

P74 The community sent messengers to the Binyaminites who were at Pomegranate Rock and offered them terms of peace. When Binyamin returned at that time, the Yisra'elites gave them the women whom they had spared from Yavesh Gil'ad, but the numbers they found were insufficient.

Now the people were feeling sorry for Binyamin, for Yahweh had caused a breach among Yisra'el's tribes. "What should we do to find wives for those who remain?" wondered the community's elders. (For all the women in Binyamin had been wiped out.) "But Binyamin does have in its possession some escapees," they reasoned, "and no tribe should be erased from Yisra'el. Unfortunately we're unable to give them any of our daughters as wives." (For the Yisra'elites had sworn a curse on anyone who would give a woman to Binyamin.)

———

P74,1 Then it dawned on them. "That's it!" they exclaimed. "Yahweh's annual festival in Shiloh!" [*which is north of Beyth-El, east of the highway going from Beyth-El to Shekem, and south of Levonah*]

"Go and lie in wait in the vineyards," they told the Binyaminites. "Keep a close watch: when you notice Shiloh's females coming out to perform their dances, come out from the vineyards and each one of you grab yourself one of Shiloh's females to be your wife, and then go back to Binyamin. If their fathers or brothers happen to bring a legal action against us, we'll tell them, 'Show some kindness to us about them, for none of us acquired a wife in the war, for you wouldn't have given women to them when you would be the ones in the wrong.'"

———

P74,2 The Binyaminites did exactly that: they carried off the requisite number of women from those who were dancing (that is, those whom they had kidnapped). They then went and returned to their property, rebuilt their towns, and took up residence in them. At that time, the Yisra'elites went their separate ways from there, each person going back to his tribe and clan. And so each man departed there for his own property.

**

In those days, there was no king who ruled over Yisra'el, and each man would do whatever he thought was right.

Total sentences in the book:
Six hundred and eighteen

Notes and comments

This book, like the others I have written, is first and foremost a translation. Because I am employed outside the academy and have access only to resources freely available on the internet, I have consulted few sources apart from the Masoretic text and online versions of the standard Hebrew-English lexicon and Hebrew grammar. As I discuss in my introductory note, I have focused principally on how best to bring the prose of the authors of Judges over into English, striving to produce a fluent translation that is also faithful to the meaning of the Hebrew. My approach here is similar to that taken in my other translations. As with those translations, my intention was not to write a traditional Biblical commentary, nor a work of literary or historical criticism. Because my personal circumstances practically forced me to engage with the text solely on my own, I did not consult other translations or make use of commentaries in writing this translation, and I relied on only a small number of academic studies and scholarly papers in developing my understanding of the book and its background.

As with the notes in my other translations, I focus many of my comments below on passages that will give readers some understanding of how I employed "functional equivalence" in crafting this translation and how it departs from a more literal rendering of the text. Although biblical scholars might find such notes of little interest, the notes can help those who don't know Hebrew understand what is involved in producing a translation that is functionally equivalent to the source text. In addition, I frequently use the notes to comment on my translation choices when dealing with unusual, idiomatic, or difficult prose. While my comments on these topics are relatively extensive, I have not aimed to be comprehensive and have not necessarily commented on every idiomatic, unusual or difficult passage. Finally, because the act of translation often required me to consider the composition history of Judges and its relationship to the so-called Deuteronomistic History—and because there is such scholarly interest in these topics—I comment extensively in the notes on places where I see indications of different authors and different dates. As I discuss in my essay at the end of the book, my comments on composition history are, by necessity, speculative; their value lies primarily in helping the reader appreciate the complexities in the text and in presenting a plausible scenario that explains those complexities.

With respect to the language of Judges, the Hebrew prose is relatively straightforward and presents few real difficulties. In addition, the text appears to have suffered little in its transmission history. As a result, there are only a few places in the book where the meaning of the Hebrew is unclear or where the text is obviously corrupt. That said, where there do appear to be errors, I typically reflect the error in my translation and I do not attempt to correct the Hebrew that has been transmitted to us. Consequently, there is no place in this translation where I have intentionally emended the Masoretic consonantal text.

As mentioned in the notes to my previous translations, I did not consult the Biblia Hebraica Stuttgartensia in my translation work, but instead relied on the excellent iPhone app Tanakh for All as my main source for the Masoretic text. In general, I find the Tanakh for All app superior for the purposes of translation, as the line lengths are similar to those in the Aleppo Codex and the Leningrad Codex, and the *parashot petuhot* are prominently marked in the text. Because of the excellent state of preservation of Judges in the Aleppo Codex, I translated large portions of the text directly from the photographic copy of that codex, which can be found on the Internet Archive. And when I used the Tanakh for All app as my source for the Masoretic text, I regularly checked my translation against the photographic copies of the Aleppo Codex and the Leningrad Codex. Because I have generally found the Aleppo Codex superior to the Leningrad Codex, the placement of the *parashot* in my translation follow the former and not the latter.

The lexicon and grammar that I used were the 1906 edition of Wilhelm Gesenius' *Hebrew and English Lexicon of the Old Testament*, as edited and updated by Francis Brown, S.R. Driver, and Charles Briggs and the 2nd English edition of *Gesenius' Hebrew Grammar*, as edited and enlarged by E. Kautsch and A.E. Cowley (abbreviated below, respectively, as BDB and GKC).

**

Notes to P1 **1a Who should venture out first for us and make war on the Kena'anites:** Note that the author's view of the occupation of the land is consistent with a Persian period or Hellenistic period date for this *parashah*. In the early material in Joshua, which dates to the early sixth century BCE, Joshua and the Yisra'elites kill all the native inhabitants of the land, in keeping with the command given in Deut P19,4 to subject the native peoples of Kena'an to the ban devotion. In the Persian period layers of Joshua, however, the authors did not adhere to such a strict view regarding the conquest of Kena'an, and they added much material to Joshua that presumed the continued presence of some native peoples in the land.

This view of the occupation of the land here in P1 is one of several indications that this *parashah* along with P2-P7 are not part of the earliest version of Judges, but represent later additions made during the Persian period and/or Hellenistic period. I understand P1-P5,4 to represent traditions related to the conquest that the Persian period editors of Judges wished to preserve but that didn't fit easily into Joshua (perhaps because the Samarian editors of Joshua did not approve their insertion into that book). It is interesting to note that P1-P5,4 includes material about each of the tribes living west of the Yarden with the exception of Yissakar: traditions about Yehudah, Shim'on, and the Binyaminites are preserved in P1-P3; traditions about the nation of Yoseph (i.e. Ephrayim and Menashsheh) are found in P4-P5,1; Zevulun's failure to drive out all the native peoples from its territory is the subject of P5,2; the failure of Asher to drive out all the native peoples from its territory is the subject of P5,3; and finally, traditions about Naphtaliy's and Dan's occupation of their respective territories are treated in P5,4. Given that the authors of these *parashot* seem to have made a concerted effort to include all the tribes west of the Yarden, I think it is very likely that originally there was a short *parashah* about Yissakar that has fallen out of the text. The authors of P1-P5,4 did not feel any obligation to mention the tribes living east of the Yarden—Re'uven, Gad, and the eastern Menashshehites—presumably because this territory was not part of the land promised to the ancestors.

The phrase that I translate as "venture out" reflects the verb עלה ("go up, ascend"); this verb is often used in Judges and other books in an idiomatic sense meaning "go on a military campaign, expedition." See BDB, p. 748, def. 2c for citations.

1b "Come on an expedition with me...," Yehudah said to his kinsman Shim'on: Recall from Jos P38 that the territory allotted to Shim'on was part of the territory originally allotted to Yehudah. As both tribes occupy the same territorial allotment, it is natural that they should assist each other in clearing the native peoples from the land they have been given.

1c Bezeq: This town is probably a different town than the Bezeq mentioned in Sam P22. In Samuel, Bezeq is the place where Sha'ul musters forces for the battle against Nahash the Ammonite at Yavesh-Gil'ad. That Bezeq is likely in Binyamin, where Sha'ul is from, whereas the Bezeq here in Judges must be in Yehudah. Bezeq likely was the name of a local Kena'anite god, as is suggested by the name Adoniy Bezeq, which means "my lord is Bezeq."

2a The Yehudites made war on Yerushalem and captured it: In the earliest layer of the book of Joshua, the Yisra'elites defeat and kill the king of Yerushalem, but there is no explicit mention of the capture of Yerushalem. In Jos P18, Yerushalem's king Adoniy-Tzedeq forms an alliance with four other Amorite kings against the Yisra'elites. Yehoshua himself kills the five kings in Jos P19,2. The narrative mentions the capture of the towns ruled by three of these kings—Lakiysh (Jos P19,5), Eglon (Jos P20), and Hevron (Jos P21)—but does not mention the capture of the towns ruled by the other two kings (Yerushalem and Yarmuth).

2b they slaughtered the populace and sent the town up in flames: This language implies that in this tradition, Yerushalem was put to the ban devotion. On the ban devotion, see note 3c below.

Notes to P2

2c they defeated Sheshay, Ahiyman, and Talmay: In Jos P30, it is Kalev who kills Sheshay, Ahiyman, and Talmay. I believe the reference in Joshua reflects the original tradition; the author of this *parashah* in Judges has altered this tradition because his central focus is explaining Yehudah's efforts to eradicate the native peoples from its territory.

2d "Whoever defeats Scroll-Town...: I understand the material from here to the end of the *parashah* to be an addition to the material that precedes it. Both the first half and the second half of P2 belong to the large body of material from what I call Judges' fifth compositional stage (ca. 425 - ca. 150 BCE), but the material in the second half (which concerns Kalev) was clearly added after the material in the first half (which concerns Yehudah).

The material in the second half of the *parashah* about Aksah and Othniy'el also appears at the conclusion to Jos P30. Although this material in Judges is late, I believe that it is the older version and that the authors of Joshua's final compositional stage (who were active in the late Persian period and in the Hellenistic period) used it as the source for their version of this event.

The relationship between the material here in Jud P2 and the book of Joshua provides a good illustration of the extremely complex composition history of parts of the books of the Former Prophets. The authors of the first half of Jud P2, who likely were writing in the fifth century BCE as part of Judges' fifth compositional stage, have chosen to present an alternative narrative about the conquest of southern Kena'an than the one presented in Jos P18 - P21, which is a product of the early sixth century BCE; this alternative conquest narrative reflects the evolution of ideas about the occupation of the land during Persian period, which acknowledged the continued presence of the native peoples. Some years later, the authors of Judges' fifth compositional stage expanded P2 by adding the material about Kalev, Othniy'el and Aksah in order to preserve a related ancient tradition about the settlement of the territory of Judah. At the time this addition was made, the book of Joshua was still attached to the books of the Torah and was part of the cult library at Mount Gerizim. It was during this period, when Joshua was still attached to the books of the Torah, that the material about Kalev, Othniy'el and Aksah must have been added to Jos P30, to ensure that Joshua contained a complete record of the settlement of the land. Thus we see that traditions in one book influenced additions in a second book, with subsequent additions in the second book then being reflected back into the first book; we also see these additions motivated by the evolution of ideas about important concepts and events, and by the dynamics of the collaboration between Samaria and Yehud on the composition of the book of Joshua.

As I discuss in the notes to the following *parashot*, there is a similar dynamic between Jud P3 - P5,4 and the book of Joshua, with Judges showing dependence on Joshua but presenting alternative traditions to those preserved in Joshua.

2e Kalev asked her what was bothering her and had prompted her visit: I have added language to express the nuance of the Hebrew in natural sounding English. More literally, "Kalev said to her, 'What concerns you [that you've come here]?'"

2f Give me a gift: The word for blessing (ברכה) was often used colloquially by ancient Hebrew speakers to mean what English-speakers would call a gift. I believe that is the usage here, and I have translated accordingly. It's worth noting how the author has characterized Aksah in this short passage—she comes across as impatient and demanding. She presses her husband to ask her father for pasture land (presumably to supplement her dowry), but in her impatience doesn't wait for him to act. Her father notices she is perturbed as soon as she slips off her donkey, whereupon she immediately takes the opportunity to demand that he give her a gift (again, presumably to supplement her dowry). However, rather than ask for pasture land, she is even bolder and asks for secure sources of water.

3a The Qeynites (who are the descendants of Mosheh's father-in-law)...: This *parashah* is a mish-mash of old traditions that the author has somewhat clumsily combined. Some of the traditions are unknown elsewhere in the Tanakh; for the comment about Kalev, however, the author has clearly used Jos P29 and Jos P30 as his sources.

Notes to P3

3b They went and lived with the people there: The text is ambiguous because the author has not expressed himself very clearly. I believe this sentence and the previous sentence refer to a tradition known by the author regarding a group of Qeynites who joined the Yehudites on a military campaign in the southern desert and then decided to abandon the campaign and settle in the area instead.

3c They made a ban devotion... called the town's name Hormah: The ban devotion of a town required the slaughter of all the town's inhabitants—including women and children and the elderly—and the destruction of all their personal property. The ban devotion was directed at people who were hostile to Yahweh or had offended him in some way. In the conquest narrative in Joshua, Yahweh required the Yisra'elites to put all towns in Kena'an to the ban devotion. On the concept of the ban devotion, see the detailed discussion in my introductory note to the book of Joshua.

The king of Hormah is listed in Jos P24,10 as one of the kings whom Yehoshua defeated in Kena'an. The material preserved here in Judges represents an alternative tradition about the conquest, in which Yehoshua did not subdue all of Kena'an, and the tribes continued fighting the native peoples after his death. The town Hormah is mentioned in Joshua P31 and P38. In P31, it is said to belong to the Yehudites, but in P38, it is said to belong to the Shim'onites.

3d he cleared out the hill country... they had iron chariots.): The author may have modeled this passage on the passage in Jos P34,1 that describes the Yosephites' difficulties in occupying the Ephrayim mountain region.

3e Kalev was given Hevron... he drove out three Anaqis: This sentence is an addition to Judges that is based on the tradition about Kalev appearing in Jos P30. We know this sentence in Judges must be based on the passage in Joshua because of the presence of the phrase "exactly as Mosheh promised," which is common in Joshua but is absent from Judges. The author has likely placed this material about Kalev here in P3 and not with the material about Kalev in the previous *parashah* in order to avoid drawing attention to conflicting traditions about the Anaqis in these *parashot*. (The author of Jos P30 identifies the three Anaqis as Sheshay, Ahiyman, and Talmay, and Jud P2 states that it was the Yehudites, not Kalev alone, who defeated these three individuals.) The Kalev traditions in Judges P2 and P3 and in Jos P29 have interacted with each other in multiple stages, and there are several plausible ways that one may reconstruct their composition history. A similar dynamic exists between the Kalev traditions in Jud P2 and Jos P30; see note 2d above.

A literal translation of the beginning of this sentence is "They gave Hevron to Kalev." It was not common to conjugate verbs in ancient Hebrew in the passive voice; authors often avoided passive constructions and instead used an active verb with an indefinite subject when they wished to express the passive voice. I believe that is the case with the sentence here, and I have accordingly translated as the passive, "Kalev was given Hevron." On this usage of an active verb with an indefinite subject to represent the passive, see notes 9b and 31c in my translation to Leviticus.

3f The Binyaminites, however, did not drive out the Yevusites...: This last sentence of the *parashah* represents a separate addition to the text that preserves an alternate tradition about Yerushalem—note in particular that it is at odds with the tradition preserved in P2, in which it is the Yehudites who capture Yerushalem and in which it is implied that all the inhabitants are slaughtered. It's worth noting here that Jos P32,1 (which is a late addition to the text) preserves a tradition about the Yehudeans (not the Binyaminites) being unable to drive out the Yevusites from Yerushalem. In the traditions preserved in Joshua and Judges, there were alternative views as to whether Yerushalem was a Yehudean town or a Binyaminite town.

3g **: The Leningrad Codex has a *parashah setumah* here.

Notes to P4

4a the nation of Yoseph: That is, the tribes of Ephrayim and Menashsheh. The material about the division of the land in Joshua refers several times to "the nation of Yoseph," and this short *parashah* here in Judges preserves a tradition that likely was rejected for the book of Joshua (perhaps because the Samarian editors of Joshua objected to the idea of the slaughter of the Beyth-El's inhabitants). The material in Judges P1 - P5,4 preserves several alternative traditions that appear to have been rejected from Joshua. There are two likely reasons why such material might have been rejected from Joshua: either the Samarian editors objected to its inclusion in Joshua, or the material did not fit into the overall structure of Joshua's conquest narrative, which presents the conquest as a unified effort of the Yisra'elites under the leadership of Yehoshua (as opposed to piece-meal efforts by individual tribes, as we see here in Judges). But by the late Persian period and the Hellenistic period the books of the Former Prophets had come to be viewed as authoritative, and there was great interest in making these books more comprehensive by adding to them traditions thought to be ancient.

4b we'll treat you kindly: The exchange between the Yosephites and the man and the promise to spare him and his family because of the assistance he has rendered is reminiscent of the exchange between the spies and the prostitute in the story of Yeriyho in Jos P4.

Note to P5

5a Menashsheh didn't drive out...: This *parashah* is a variant of the last paragraph of Jos P34, which is a late addition to the material in Joshua about the allotment of land to Menashsheh. The *parashah* here in Judges utilizes language that is common in Joshua—in particular the phrase "and its neighboring villages." There would be no reason for the author of this *parashah* to use this language here in Judges unless he based his passage on the *parashah* in Joshua. For that reason, I view the addition in Jos P34 as older, and Judges P5 as derivative of that.

Notes to P5,1

5,1a Ephrayim didn't drive out the Kena'anites...: This *parashah* is a variant of the final sentence of Jos P33, the subject of which is the land allotted to Ephrayim. I understand that sentence from Jos P33 to be a very late addition to the text, and I understand this *parashah* in Judges to be borrowed from Joshua.

5,1b —: The Leningrad Codex has a *parashah petuhah* here.

Note to P5,2

5,2a The Kena'anites remained living among them, but as slave laborers: This comment employs a theme that appears a number of times in the later compositional layers of Joshua, when the authors made alterations to the conquest narrative to indicate that some native peoples escaped the ban devotion and instead served as slave laborers to the Yisra'elites. However, in Joshua, there is no mention of Kena'anites in Zevulun serving as slave laborers. Rather, we should view this *parashah* here in Judges as a later correction to the traditions about the occupation of the land preserved in Joshua.

5,3a Asher didn't drive out…: There is no parallel passage in Joshua to this *parashah*. It seems clear to me that in the material in P5-P5,4 about the failure of six of the northern tribes to drive out the Kena'anites from all parts of their territories, the authors borrowed material from Joshua for Ephrayim and Menashsheh and then composed material with this same theme for Zevulun, Asher, Naphtaliy, and Dan based on independent traditions about these tribes.

It should be noted that there is no mention of Yissakar in the material about the northern tribes in P5-P5,4. I think it likely that originally there was a brief *parashah* about Yissakar's failure to drive out the Kena'anites, but that this *parashah* has fallen out of the text.

5,4a Sun City: This is a different town than the Sun City (Beyth Shemesh) mentioned in Jos P30 and Jos P43. The Sun City here is located in the north in the territory of Naphtaliy; the other Sun City is located to the south, on the border between Yehudah and Dan.

5,4b The Amorites sqeezed the Danites…: The Leningrad Codex has a "closed" blank space before this sentence to indicate the beginning of a new *parashah setumah*.

The material here in Judges provides an alternate tradition about the Danites that is at odds with the treatment in Joshua. In Joshua, the Danites' allotted territory is on the coastal plain bordering Menashsheh, Ephrayim, Binyamin, and Yehudah, but—in keeping with Joshua's treatment of the conquest and occupation as a complete eradication of the native peoples—there is no mention of the Danites' inability to occupy their land and being squeezed into the mountains.

5,4c [*The Amorites' territory…northwards.*]: This sentence reads as a later addition to the text, but its purpose is similar to the other material in P1-P5,4—to correct and supplement material in Joshua about the occupation of Kena'an and the territory controlled by each of the tribes living west of the Yarden.

6a Yahweh's emissary went north…: The material in P6-P7 is another late addition to Judges, likely made in the Hellenistic period after the mostly Persian period additions in P1-P5,4, in my opinion. The story was added by an author who wished to connect the narrative of Judges more closely to Deuteronomy and the demand to destroy the altars of the Kena'anites' gods (see Deut P12,5). Note also the presence of Yahweh's emissary as the one who leads the Yisra'elites to Kena'an (known from Exod P40) and the language of "traps" and "snares," which the author has borrowed from Num P88,2 (and which also appears in Yehoshua's farewell speech in Jos P53, a passage that was deeply influenced by Deuteronomy).

6b **: Both the Aleppo Codex and the Leningrad Codex very clearly show a *parashah petuhah* here. It is unclear to me why the editors of *Biblica Hebraica Stuttgartensia* do not show a *parashah* here but simply show a blank space in the text. As discussed in my introductory note, it was common for the Biblical authors to mark the beginning of an important speech by beginning a new *parashah petuhah* or a new *parashah setumah*; in this instance they have chosen the former.

7a I took you out of Egypt…: The speech of Yahweh's emissary here in P7 makes several indirect allusions to Deut P6,4 and P7. It seems clear that the author of this addition in Judges was familiar with that material in Deuteronomy and that he has based his composition here in P7 in large part on that material. In Deut P6,4, there is a mention of Yahweh bringing the Yisra'elites to the land followed by commandments not to make treaties with the natives and to tear down their altars; and in Deut P7,

Note to P5,3

Notes to P5,4

Notes to P6

Notes to P7

Mosheh warns the Yisra'elites that making offerings to the local gods would be a "trap."

7b they made sacrifices to Yahweh there: It's worth noting that no altar is mentioned here. Given that the author of this *parashah* was clearly influenced by Deuteronomy, he may have avoided mention of any altar, as one of the key principles of Deuteronomy is that there is only one legitimate altar to Yahweh.

Notes to P8

8a Yehoshua then sent the people off...: In the version of Judges composed for the Josianic History, I believe the book began with the material in P9. When Judges was edited by the authors of the Israelite History, they composed P8 in order to connect the old book of Judges to their newly composed book of Joshua. In the Israelite History, Jud P8 followed directly from Joshua's farewell speech in Jos P53, which was the original ending to Joshua. (As an aside, during the Persian period, the priestly authors from Samaria and Yehud collaborated on a new ending to Joshua, and as part of that work, they lifted much of the language here in P8 and used it as the basis for the new conclusion to Joshua in Jos P57.)

As I discuss in the essay on the Judges' composition history, the authors of the Israelite History made very few edits and additions to Judges. Apart from the addition of P8 and four small additions to P9, they left the Josianic History's version of Judges untouched.

8b who had seen every great thing that Yahweh had done for Yisra'el: This clause provides a good example of how one must depart from a literal translation to express the idea in natural English. Literally, "who had seen every great deed of Yahweh which he had done for Yisra'el."

8c Yehoshua Nunsson Yahwehsservant: It is noteworthy that the authors of the Israelite History here give Yehoshua the honorific surname Yahwehsservant in their account of Yehoshua's death. I believe these same authors were responsible for what I call the second compositional stage of Deuteronomy, and as part of their work on that book, they also gave this surname to Mosheh when he died (see Deut P35,7). On the significance of this surname, see my comments in note 57b to my translation of Joshua.

8d he was buried: Literally, "they buried him." Ancient Hebrew frequently used an active verb with an indefinite subject where it would be most natural in English to use the passive. My translation reflects the most natural way to express the idea in this passage in English. On the use of the active verb with indefinite subject in place of the passive, see note 3e above and notes 9b and 31c in my translation of Leviticus.

8e a new generation arose after them which didn't know Yahweh: With this clause, the author sets up the plot for the book of Judges as it functioned within the Israelite History—the generations of Yisra'elites after Yehoshua did not know Yahweh, nor what he had done for their ancestors, and accordingly they gave service to other gods and not Yahweh alone, as is required by the treaty recorded in the book of Deuteronomy.

8f **: The Leningrad Codex has a *parashah setumah* here.

Notes to P9

9a Then the Yisra'elites did what Yahweh considered the worst thing...: This *parashah* belongs to the earliest compositional layer of Judges, which I believe was first composed in the 630s BCE as part of what I call the Josianic History. (There likely was a short *parashah* preceding P9 that served as the beginning of the Josianic History, but that *parashah*, I believe, was removed by the authors of the Israelite History when they added P8.) Here in P9, the Josianic historians establish the key themes of their book and laid out the cyclical apostasy / punishment / repentance / rescue structure behind the stories that follow. This *parashah* is especially noteworthy as it is the most extensive material in Judges by the authors of the Josianic History. Outside of this *parashah*, the authors of the Josianic History mostly confined their work to adding the narrative frames to the old stories of the heroes of the northern tribes and adding references to "Yisra'el" and "the Yisra'elites" with the meaning of all the tribes from the north and the south.

When the leaders of Yahweh's cult on Mount Zion edited Judges as part of their work to turn the Josianic History into the Israelite History, they connected Judges to the newly composed book of Joshua by writing Jud P8. In their history, Jud P8 followed directly from Jos P53, which was the original ending to that book. As I discuss below in the essay on Judges' composition history, there is very little material in Judges that seems clearly to have been composed by the authors of the Israelite History. One reason why they may not have made many changes to Judges is that the themes of the Josianic History's version of Judges supported the broader themes that they wished to develop in their own history. In this regard, it is interesting to read Jud P9 in the context in which it appeared in the Israelite History, in which Jud P8 and P9 followed directly from Jos P53, which is the original version of Yehoshua's farewell speech that was composed for the Israelite History. In that speech, Yehoshua specifically tells the Yisra'elites to "stay close to your god Yahweh," and he warns them that if they "do service to other gods and worship them," then Yahweh's anger "will burn against" them and they will lose possession of the land he has given them. Similarly, if they "violate the terms of the treaty" with Yahweh, he will bring down upon them "every harmful thing" until he wipes them off "the face of this excellent land" that he has given them. The speech in Jos P53 thus looks forward to all the events that follow—the stories in Judges, Samuel, and especially Kings. By providing a lens through which to view these future events, the authors of the Israelite History succeed in transforming the Josianic History without needing to make substantial revisions or expansions to that work.

Going directly from Jos P53 to Jud P8 - P9 allows us to see how the authors of the Israelite History must have read Judges: we see that immediately after Yehoshua's death, the Yisra'elites did not stay close to Yahweh as Yehoshua had told them to—instead they "gave service to the Ba'als and abandoned their ancestors' god Yahweh." And as a result, "Yahweh was inflamed with anger at Yisra'el." The most significant addition that the authors of the Israelite History made to P9 is at the end of the *parashah*, which refers back to Jos P53. In that addition, they specifically state that "this damnable nation" has violated the terms of its treaty with Yahweh, which they connect to the requirement not to give service to other gods. This does not yet result in a permanent loss of the land—that will take another eight hundred years in the schema of these authors. Instead, Yahweh won't protect the Yisra'elites from "the nations that Yehoshua left behind when he died" (a reference to the nations that surround Kena'an, not to the native peoples of Kena'an).

9b the worst thing: For the authors of the Josianic History, who composed this *parashah*, the "worst thing" (הרע) was giving service to other gods. The authors of the Josianic History in their work regularly pass judgement on the Yisrae'lites and on the kings of Yisra'el and Yehudah with the phrase 'עשה את־הרע בעיני יה ("to do what Yahweh considered the worst thing of all"). The phrase occurs eight times in Judges, and thirty times in Kings. The editors of the Israelite History later used this phrase as well, most notably in the conclusion to Deut P30, which introduces the Song of Mosheh. In that conclusion, Mosheh uses the exact phrasing found here in Judges—'עשה את־הרע בעיני יה ("to do what Yahweh considered the worst thing of all").

And Mosheh then specifically equates the "worst possible thing" with "enraging [Yahweh] with the idols that you made."

9c they gave service to the Ba'als: These are the local gods of Kena'an. The term *ba'al* means "lord, master, owner" in Hebrew. It was used to refer to a god because it is more respectful than referring to the god by name. Over time, it also came to be used as a term for gods in general, which is how it is used here in P9.

9d different gods: The phrase used here—אלהים אחרים—is common in both the Josianic History and in the later literature that was influenced by Deuteronomy. A literal translation of the phrase is "other gods," but the adjective אחר ("other") is very often used with the sense of "different, alien, strange," and that is how the adjective is used in this particular phrase.

9e the Ashtoreths: Ashtoreth was an ancient Near Eastern goddess of war. She was known as Ishtar in Mesopotamia and as Ashtoreth (and various permutations of that name) in the Levant. The biblical authors often used the name Ashtoreth as a general term for all the local goddesses, including Asherah. Here in P9, the author is clearly using the name as a general term for goddess. For a discussion of this goddess, see "Astarte" in K. van der Toorn, B. Becking, and P. van der Horst (eds.), *Dictionary of deities and demons in the Bible*, 2nd ed. (Leiden: Brill, 1999), pp. 109-114.

9f with the result that they were no longer able to hold their ground against their enemies: The language "hold their ground against their enemies" (לעמד לפני אויביהם, literally "stand in front of their enemies") is characteristic of the authors of the Israelite History, and I believe the clause here is an addition made by them. By inserting the clause here, the authors allude to one of the key themes of Joshua, which is that if the Yisra'elites follow Yahweh's commands, their enemies will not be able to "confront them." See Joshua P47,11, which represents a summary statement written by the lead editor of the earliest edition of Joshua: "Not a single one of their enemies dared to confront them" (ולא־עמד איש בפניהם מכל־אויביהם). This theme is also present in Deuteronomy; see Deut P12,3: "No man will dare oppose you" (לא־יתיצב איש בפניכם).

9g In every campaign they undertook: The author here uses idiomatic language. The verb יצא ("go out, come out") when used in a military context has the specific meaning "embark on a military campaign, go on a military mission," and I believe that is the meaning here. For interesting examples of this idiomatic usage of יצא, see Sam P41,1 and P41,2, where Dawid is said to be "carrying out missions" (וַיֵּצֵא וָיָבֹא and יוֹצֵא וָבָא).

9h Yahweh's hand was against them to do them harm, exactly as Yahweh had said: When biblical authors use the phrase "as Yahweh said," they always have a specific *parashah* or passage in a *parashah* in mind. I believe that the phrase "as Yahweh had said" here is an addition by the authors of the Israelite History. It is not entirely clear which *parashah* these authors are alluding to here in P9. It is almost certainly a text from Deuteronomy. Although the allusion could possibly be to the treaty curses in Deut P26, I think it is most likely that the allusion is to Deut P30. In that *parashah*, Yahweh tells Mosheh that the Yisra'elites will "go whoring after foreign gods" immediately upon taking possession of the land, that Yahweh "will blaze with anger against them," and that as a result, "a multitude of harmful and distressful things will find them."

Both the Josianic historians and their successors, the authors of the Israelite History, were deeply influenced by the versions of Deuteronomy known to them and by the theology of those versions. In Judges, this influence is seen most clearly in this *parashah*, P9. The Josianic historians' exposition of the cycle of apostasy and retribution here in their introduction to Judges is quite consistent with the theology of their version of Deuteronomy, which emphasized the obligation to give service to Yahweh alone, but which likely lacked the treaty structure and which made no mention of Mosheh. The version of Deuteronomy known to the authors of the Israelite History, however, did utilize the treaty structure, and thus we see later in the *parashah* that these authors state clearly that it was the Yisra'elites' violation of their treaty with Yahweh that is the reason they are being punished.

9i [*and exactly as Yahweh had sworn to them*]: I believe the clause that I have placed in brackets is an addition to the text, made sometime in the Persian or Hellenistic period. With this addition, the author wishes to tell the reader that the preceding sentence in Judges alludes not to Deut P30, but instead to Deut P31 (the Song of Mosheh). Specifically, in the original conclusion to Deut P31, Yahweh raises his hand to the sky and swears that he will "deal out vengeance" on his foes (that is, the Yisra'elites who have forsaken him) and "repay" his enemies in full.

9j champions: The term that the author uses here is שֹׁפְטִים. The term is traditionally translated as "judges" and gives the book of Judges its name. However, the term had a broad range of meanings. In Judges, it specifically is used to describe an individual who combines the qualities of military leader and governor, with a strong emphasis on the former quality. For this reason, I believe the term "champion" is a more accurate reflection of how the meaning of the word would have been perceived by a native speaker of ancient Hebrew who was reading this passage of Judges.

It is worth noting here that the theme of "leadership" (both good and bad) runs throughout the three books of the Josianic History—Judges, Samuel, and Kings. The material about the individual champions in the following *parashot* in Judges is best understood against the background of this theme. Here in P9, the summary material written by the Josianic historians expresses a theme that runs throughout their history, which is that the people need a strong leader who keeps true to Yahweh's ways. When the people have such a leader, they are loyal to Yahweh and do not give service to other gods. But in the absence of such a leader, the people abandon Yahweh for other gods. At its core, the Josianic History is a justification of the monarchy and the role of the king in ensuring both that Yahweh's cult is properly practiced and that cults to all other gods are abolished.

9k they whored after different gods: The language of "whoring" is characteristic of the Josianic Historians as well as later authors who, like them, were influenced by the versions of Deuteronomy known to them. The earliest use of this language is by the northern prophet Hosea. If, as I suggest in my introductory note, the authors of the Josianic History were from northern families who were sympathetic to Hosea's ideas about the obligations owed to Yahweh, it is not surprising to see these authors adopt Hosea's language in their own work. This language was later adopted by the authors of the Israelite History, and it is not always possible to tell in the books of the Former Prophets where this language is from the Josianic historians and where it is from the Israelite History's authors.

9l As for obeying Yahweh's commandments—they did nothing like that: That is, they did not obey the treaty obligations. The treaty obligations are absent from the Josianic History, whereas they are central to the Israelite History. For that reason, I believe this sentence is an addition by the authors of the Israelite History.

9m Yahweh felt pity on account of how they groaned and suffered: The presence of the rare word נאקה, which I translate here as "groaned and suffered," is noteworthy. This is the word that the author of Exodus P4 uses to describe the Yisra'elites' plight in Egypt, and it is this word that prompts Yahweh to action and sets in motion the events of the exodus and of the entire Israelite History. I argue in my translations of Exodus and Numbers that the original beginning of Exodus (and thus the original beginning of the Israelite History) was removed when Exodus was connected to the Samarian book of Genesis, but that Exodus P4 preserves a kernel of the original beginning of the book. (See notes 4a and 4,1a in my translation of Exodus and note 69,2a in my translation of Numbers.) I believe that the authors' choice of the word נאקה at the beginning of Exodus was influenced by the use of the word here in Jud P9. By using the word in Exodus, the authors of the Israelite History make an implicit connection between Mosheh and the champions: Yahweh's calling Mosheh to save the Yisra'elites from their suffering at the hands of the Egyptians is similar to his calling "champions" to save the Yisra'elites prior to the establishment of the monarchy.

9n acting more despicably than their ancestors: The implication that the ancestors were "despicable" is odd, as in the preceding paragraph the author praises the ancestors for their loyalty to Yahweh ("the path that their ancestors trod"). The tension between the two statements provides a good example of the loose attitude that the authors of the Tanakh often had toward narrative logic. In their writing, these authors typically sought to maximize the emotional impact of their work, even when doing so created inconsistencies and breaks in logic within the narrative. Writing in this way must have been second nature to them, and I do not believe the author of this passage, for example, would have even realized there was a logical inconsistency in his text. And if he had realized that there was a break in the logic, I do not believe it is something he would have been particularly bothered by.

9o They abandoned none of their practices, nor any part of their obnoxious way of life: I believe this was the concluding sentence to the earliest version of P9.

9p And so Yahweh's anger burned against Yisra'el: I believe that this sentence and the following sentence were added by the authors of the Israelite History as part of the work on Judges' third stage. This addition contains the only reference in the entire book of Judges to Yahweh's treaty with the Yisra'elites. As mentioned above, the idea of a treaty between Yahweh and his people is absent from the Josianic History—this treaty first appears in the work of the authors of the Israelite History, who were writing several decades later. In the Josianic History, Yahweh's treaty (or "binding agreement") is with the Davidic king, not with the people.

9q this damnable nation: Literally, "this nation." In ancient Hebrew, the demonstrative particle זה ("this") is often used to express contempt or disparagement, which is how it is used here. In these situations, the functionally equivalent word in English is a mild term of profanity, such as "damn" or "damnable." I have commented frequently on this usage of the demonstrative particle in my other translations. See, for example, notes 15e and 27,2c in my translation of Exodus.

9r the terms of my treaty which I commanded their ancestors to follow: It is unclear whether this is a reference to the treaty at Mo'av or the treaty at Siynai. Both require that the Yisra'elites acknowledge and give service to only Yahweh—it is this requirement of the treaty that the Yisra'elites have violated.

9s the nations Yehoshua left behind when he died: This is a reference to the nations bordering Kena'an—it is not a reference to the native peoples who inhabited Kena'an before the Yisra'elites dispossessed them and took their land. In the original version of the Israelite History, Yehoshua and the Yisra'elites slaughtered all Kena'an's native peoples, not sparing "any living soul" in fulfillment of the commandment to put the native peoples to the ban devotion. (They spared only the citizens of Giv'on, who tricked the Yisra'elites into making a treaty with them.)

In the Josianic History's version of Judges, all the nations that oppress the Yisra'elites with one exception live outside Kena'an. These nations were: Aram of the Two Rivers (P11); Mo'av (P12); Midyan plus Amaleq and the Qedemites (P17 - P26); and the Ammonites (P36 - P43). The exception is Yaviyn King of Hatzor (P14 - P16,1). (The oppression of the Yisra'elites by the Philistines in P36 and in P50 - P58 are the result of later additions to Judges.) The statement by the Israelite History's authors that Yahweh "won't drive away" peoples left behind by Yehoshua is their way of providing a theological justification for the events narrated in Judges—they are a consequence of the Yisra'elites violating the terms of their treaty with Yahweh.

9t (This was in order... into Yehoshua's hands): I believe these two sentences, which I have placed within parentheses, are a very late addition and are not original to either the Josianic or the Israelite History. In this addition, the author is commenting on the previous statement (from the authors of the Israelite History) that Yahweh "won't drive away" anyone from the nations that Yehoshua left behind.

The author's reference to not delivering other peoples "into Yehoshua's hands" presumes these people are Kena'anites. This supports the view that this passage is an addition, as it is at odds with the original version of the Israelite History in which Yehoshua puts all of Kena'an to the ban devotion with the exception of the Giv'onites. Moreover, the idea of Yahweh "testing" Yisra'el is a late idea that also supports the view that this sentence is a late addition. Note, for example, the presence of Yahweh "testing" Yisra'el in Judges P10, which is clearly a late addition to Judges, and in Deut P8, which I view as a Persian period addition to Deuteronomy. I suspect this addition in Jud P9 is earlier than the addition of Jud P10, but it is certainly possible to understand P10 as being added earlier, or to see both additions as contemporaneous.

9u by walking in his precepts: This phrase provides a good example of the departures from the literal text one must make in producing a functionally equivalent translation. The phrase literally reads, "by walking in them." The pronoun has no antecedent; this is not that unusual in Hebrew, especially if the language is formulaic and the author would expect the reader to be familiar with the language and so understand the reference without the antecedent being made explicit. Translating this phrase literally does not reproduce the original reader's experience, as the modern-day English language reader typically doesn't have a similar familiarity with all the formulas the ancient authors of Tanakh regularly used.

10a These are the nations which Yahweh left alone...: This *parashah* is an addition to the text. It likely dates to the late Persian period or the Hellenistic period, as it utilizes information given in the first half of Jos P25, which in my translation of Joshua I attributed to late in the second compositional stage of that book (ca. 400 BCE).

Notes to P10

In the addition by the authors of the Israelite History near the end of P9, "the nations that Yehoshua left behind" refers to the nations surrounding Kena'an (see note 9s above). The author of P10 has a different understanding of the occupation of the land than the Israelite History's authors; his conception is consistent with the view of the occupation that developed during the Persian period, which is that the Yisra'elites did not slaughter every human being in Kena'an, but some local peoples remained in parts of the land granted to the Yisra'elites. The author of P10 explains the presence of these peoples as Yahweh's way of "testing" his own people, a concept that is absent in the earliest layers of Judges.

NOTES AND COMMENTS 63

10b the wars for Kena'an: This is a reference to the battles the Yisra'elites fought to take possession of Kena'an, which are the subject of Jos P11,2 - P23,2.

10c [*It was only so that... didn't know previously*).]: The text that I have translated within brackets represents two separate additions to this *parashah*, both made very late in the editorial process in the sixth compositional stage.

10d The five archonships of the Philistines: The word סרן is a Philishtine loan-word. It means either "ruler" or "territory under a ruler's control," depending on the context, and the word is used only in reference to the Philishtines. To reflect the fact that ancient Hebrew speakers would have perceived the word as foreign-sounding, I translate with a loan-word meaning "ruler" that has come over into English and that English speakers perceive as foreign-sounding: "archon." For the area ruled by the archon, I have chosen an ugly neologism: "archonship." In Sam P11,6 - P11,10, there is a list of the five "archonships" of the Philishtines; they are the towns of Ashdod, Azzah, Ashqelon, Gath, and Eqron. It's worth noting that in Joshua, the towns of Ashod, Azzah and Eqron are allotted to Yehudah (Jos P31,4 and P31,5), and the town of Gath is part of Zevulun (P39); oddly, the town of Ashqelon is not mentioned in the allotment to the tribes in the book of Joshua.

10e They were to test Yisra'el by them: The clause is nonsensical, and the subject of the verb is unclear. I believe the text is corrupt. A minor emendation—removing the final *waw* from the first word of the clause, so that it reads ויהי instead of ויהיו—produces the appropriate idea in fluid Hebrew. With this emendation the functionally equivalent English translation would be, "This was in order to test Yisra'el by them."

10f which he transmitted to their ancestors through Mosheh: Note that for the author of P10, "the ancestors" are the generation of Yisra'elites who left Egypt with Mosheh, and not the patriarchs. Although this *parashah* is a late addition, the view its author expresses is consistent with the original version of the Israelite History. In that version, the patriarchs Avraham, Yitzhaq, and Ya'aqov are entirely absent and the "ancestors" are the Yisra'elites who left Egypt. The patriarchs are from the Samarian book of Genesis, and that book and its traditions were only joined to the books of the Israelite History in the late sixth century or early fifth century BCE, nearly a century after the authors of the Israelite History wrote their work.

10g Now the Yisra'elites were living among the Kena'anites...: I understand the final two sentences of P10 to be a separate addition from the rest of P10. I assign both additions to the fifth stage, but view this one as being part of a later edition of that stage. The mention of foreign marriage, and attributing the Yisra'elites' apostasy to that practice is suggestive of a date in the Persian period or Hellenistic period.

10h and so they did service to those peoples' gods: The author wishes the reader to understand that it was the practice of marrying foreigners that led the Yisra'elites to acknowledge the foreigners' gods and to participate in their cults.

Notes to P11

11a The Yisra'elites did what Yahweh considered the worst thing: On the phrase "the worst thing," see note 9b above. This *parashah* is a brief record of the first "champion" (or liberator) of Yisra'el, Othniy'el Qenazsson and his defeat of Aram's king Kushan Doublywicked. This *parashah* gives us some insight into the composition techniques of the authors of the Josianic History. The author of this particular *parashah* seems to have had a single (written or oral) source that provided only the names of Yisra'el's liberator/champion and of Aram's king; it possibly may also have included a mention of the number of years that Kushan oppressed the Yisra'elites. Everything else in the *parashah* has been composed by the author to fit the larger cyclical framework of apostasy-punishment-repentance-salvation that the Josianic historians used to tie originally unrelated stories together and give the narrative of Judges its structure.

11b Aram of the Two Rivers: The two rivers are most likely the rivers we know as the Tigris and Euphrates. If this is correct, Kushan Doublywicked's kingdom would have been located in the region of what today is eastern Syria and northwestern Iraq.

11c a liberator: The Hebrew term used here is מושיע ("rescuer, savior, liberator"). This term likely was present in the source used by the Josianic historians; their own preferred term is "champion" (שפט). The use of the term "liberator" instead of "champion" in several places in Judges is one of the key reasons that scholars have proposed a literary precursor to Judges that they call the "Book of Saviors." On this proposal, see footnote 26 in my introductory note.

11d a kinsman of Kalev who was much younger than him: I believe this phrase is a late addition to the text, likely added as part of the editorial work in the sixth compositional stage. The addition was made to harmonize the reference to Othniy'el with the information about him in P2—in fact, the phrasing of the addition here is identical to the language found in P2.

I believe that the authors of the Josianic History were not aware of a tradition connecting Othniy'el to Kalev. For them, Othniy'el is simply the first champion of Yisra'el. The authors of the Josianic History appear to have had very little information about Othniy'el. For example, they don't provide us with Othniy'el's tribal affiliation—most likely because they did not know it. By contrast, all other champions in the Josianic History's version of Judges are given tribal affiliations; thus we are told that Ehud Gerasson is from Binyamin, Devorah Lapiydothswife from Ephrayim, Gid'on Yo'ashsson from Menashsheh, and Yiphtah the Gil'adite from Gil'ad. (Gil'ad was considered a tribe by the Josianic historians; it is only in the Israelite History that that the tribe of Gil'ad is replaced by the tribe of Gad and the clans of the eastern Menashshehites.)

11e his power was firm against Kushan Doublywicked: That is, he didn't kill Kushan, but he did defeat him and hold him at bay so that the Yisra'elites were no longer subjected to his rule.

12a The Yisra'elites did what Yahweh considered the worst thing: That is, abandoned Yahweh and did service to the gods of other peoples. It is worth noting here that the author no longer feels the need to define what the worst thing is, as he expects the reader to recall this from the previous mentions in P9 and P11. See notes 9b and 11a above.

Notes to P12

This *parashah* tells the story of Ehud the Binyaminite's daring murder of Mo'av's king Eglon. The story contains a number of humorous elements, and the author clearly intended for his readers to find the story entertaining. If we are to imagine the earliest version of Judges as part of the young king's curriculum (on this idea, see footnote 23 in my introductory essay), it is easy to see that the thrilling events in the narrative and the humor in the story of Ehud would certainly have appealed to the teenage student. If there is a leadership lesson in the story, it is simply that a good leader seizes the opportunity when it presents itself and, trusting in Yahweh's support, should have the confidence to act boldly. With respect to the humorous elements in the story, note the following: the king's name (Eglon means "Little Calf" in Hebrew) and the contrast of his name with his obesity; the description of Eglon's death (the feces oozing out from his wound to "complete" his bowel movement); and the actions of Eglon's officials, first waiting for their lord to finish relieving his bowels and then dithering about before finally fetching the key to Eglon's roof-chamber.

12b Palmville: This town is also mentioned in P3; from the reference there, we know that the town was located in the far south of Yehudah's territory, near Arad and close to the Qeynites' settlements.

12c the Yisra'elites were subjects of Mo'av's king Eglon: Note how the author has fit this story into his larger framework of the Yisra'elites abandoning Yahweh and then losing their sovereignty to foreigners (a theme of both the Josianic History and the Israelite History). The source story records that Eglon captured a single town in the far south of Yehudah—hardly sufficient to establish control over all of Kena'an for eighteen years.

12d But then the Yisra'elites cried out...: The Leningrad Codex has a "closed" blank space before this sentence to indicate the beginning of a new *parashah setumah*.

12e about a *gomed* in length: The unit of measure used here, the *gomed* (גמד), does not appear elsewhere in the Tanakh. Traditionally, the term has been understood as close to, if not identical with, the cubit (אמה)—that is, roughly eighteen to twenty inches. That seems a little too long to me, however, for the dagger to remain easily concealed underneath Ehud's clothing, especially when Ehud moves about. For that reason, I suspect the author may have understood the term to indicate a slightly shorter length—perhaps twelve inches or a little less.

12f Once he had returned from the gods' statues at the Circle district: The prose is elliptical, and it is not clear what the author is describing. It is possible that one or more clauses have fallen out of the text. Assuming the text is not corrupt, I read the narrative as follows: Ehud has his men present the Yisra'elites' tribute to Eglon in Eglon's residence; after Eglon has seen (and approved of) the tribute, Ehud sends his men and the tribute back out of the room. Then Ehud and his men go to deposit the tribute at the foot of the statues of the Mo'avite gods in a shrine (or shrines) located nearby in a part of town called "the Circle." But I do not have much confidence in this reading, and there are other reasonable ways to understand the text. (BDB, p. 166, understands הגלגל here as a reference to Gilgal in Yisra'el, which seems completely nonsensical to me.)

12g Now Ehud had come to see him when he was sitting by himself in the breezy roof-chamber that belonged to him: The narrative is disjointed, as the scene suddenly jumps from a formal audience with the king in his throne room to a private meeting in the king's breezy roof-chamber (a place that the king used for relieving his bowels, as we learn later in the *parashah*). I believe that one or more clauses preceding this sentence must have fallen out of the text. It is also possible, but less likely in my opinion, that the two locations represent variant versions of the story that have been partially preserved in the text, with the murder in one version taking place in the throne room and in the other version taking place in the king's breezy roof-chamber.

12h I have a message for you from God: Ehud's statement should be read as a threat—this explains why Eglon rises from his seat in the following sentence.

12i Ehud grabbed the dagger hidden under his clothes with his left hand: This clause provides a good example of the ways in which the translator must depart from a literal rendering of the text to produce natural-sounding English. A literal translation is "Ehud sent his left hand and took the dagger from his right thigh." The author's play on "right" and "left" has a literary quality in Hebrew. But in English this contrast comes across as clumsy and uninteresting, and retaining the imagery with a literal translation fails to do justice to the quality of the Hebrew prose. For this reason I have chosen to describe the dagger's location as under Ehud's clothes, repeating the detail about the dagger given when the author introduces Ehud to the reader.

12j Ehud went out…shutting…behind him: The author's language here cleverly plays on the previous sentence, expressing Ehud's actions in the same terms used to describe the dagger attack. Note the following parallels: Ehud "going out" from the colonnade parallels the feces "oozing out" (the verb in both sentences is the same—יצא—and the Hebrew words for "to the colonnade" (מסדרנה) and "feces" (פרשדנה) rhyme with each other); and Ehud "shutting" the doors "behind him" parallels the fat "closing up behind" the blade (both sentences use the construction סגר בעד). Unfortunately, I was not able to capture this play on words in translation without marring the overall sense of the passage.

12k having a sit: The author here uses a euphemism for evacuating the bowels. Literally, "covering his feet." The euphemism also appears in Samuel P51,18, when Sha'ul relieves himself in a cave where Dawid and his men are hiding.

12l He passed by the gods' statues: See note 12f above. It is unclear why the author has mentioned this detail, and it is possible that a clause has fallen from the text.

12m **: The Leningrad Codex has a *parashah setumah* here.

13a **: The Leningrad Codex has a *parashah setumah* here.   Note to P13

14a Once Ehud was dead…: Note the tension between P13 and P14-P15. In P13,   Notes to P14
Ehud's successor is Shamgar Anathsson; in P14-P15, Ehud's successor is Devorah. P13 lacks the cyclical narrative frame that was important to the authors of the Josianic History and the Israelite History; for that reason, I view P13 as a Persian period addition to Judges. I understand P14-P15, which does contain the cyclical narrative frame, as original to the Josianic History. These two *parashot* (P14-P15) tell the story of a famous battle in which an alliance of Yisra'elite tribes defeats the army of Yaviyn King of Hatzor and his general Siysera. As I discuss below, this battle was the subject of the much celebrated Song of Devorah (P16), and the authors of the Josianic History must have composed P14-P15 so that they could include the song in their history.

It is interesting to note that the story of the battle with Yaviyn's army and the death of Siysera in P15 is inconsistent with the view of the occupation of the land in the earliest version of Joshua, which I associate with the composition of the Israelite History in the sixth century BCE. In P14-P16, the enemy is the Kena'anite king Yaviyn, who is based in Hatzor. But in the earliest version of Joshua and the Israelite History, the Yisra'elites killed all the inhabitants of Kena'an including Yaviyn, and took control of Hatzor (see Jos P22 and P23,1). It seems likely to me that even though the story of Siysera was at odds with the views of the authors of the Israelite History regarding the occupation of Kena'an, they could not remove this story from their version of Judges when they composed Joshua, as the story contained what was perhaps the most famous song known from the northern traditions—the Song of Devorah.

14b Harosheth-of-the-Nations: This town has not been identified, but presumably it is near Hatzor, which is approximately ten miles north of the Sea of Galilee. The Yizre'el Valley (the site of the battle between Siysera's army and the Yisra'elites) lies some thirty miles southwest of Hatzor.

14c **: The Leningrad Codex has a *parashah setumah* here.

NOTES AND COMMENTS   67

Notes to P15

15a to settle their legal disputes: This is the sole instance in Judges in which the "champion" acts in a judicial capacity; apart from the brief mention here, the "champions" in the Josianic History's version of Judges act solely as military leaders and/or tribal leaders.

15b You should know: Devorah's message begins with the interrogative particle, הלא ("Is it not?"). The particle is often used to introduce statements of fact. Here it functions as a polite way of informing Baraq of an oracle involving Baraq that Devorah has received from Yahweh.

It should be noted that Devorah's speech to Baraq here is made in person, not by message. In the previous sentence, she summoned him to come see her, and in the elliptical style typical of ancient Hebrew prose, the author moves directly to Baraq's audience with Devorah, omitting any mention of Baraq's arrival. While the text reads as natural in Hebrew, the transition in scene would come across as awkward and abrupt in English if the reader were not informed of Baraq's arrival. In my translation, I have added the phrase "when he arrived," as this information is required by natural English usage.

15c I will lead the head of Yaviyn's army Siysera to you: Note that this is still the direct speech of Yahweh. Thus it is Yahweh, not Devorah, who will lead Siysera to Baraq.

15d Yahweh is going to sell Siysera into the hands of a woman: The author of P15 has composed this *parashah* on the basis of the narrative in the song that Devorah and Baraq sing in P16; it is likely that the song was the only source that the author had at his disposal for the narrative in P15.

Note the small inconsistency in the narrative here: Devorah earlier relays an oracle from Yahweh to Baraq in which Yahweh states that he will "deliver" Siysera into Baraq's hands. But now she says Baraq won't receive any glory because Yahweh is going to "sell" Siysera into the hands of a woman. This sort of inconsistency is commonly seen in the stories in the Tanakh, as narrative consistency was not especially important to ancient Hebrew authors—they often sought to achieve emotional and dramatic impact in their narratives even when this meant sacrificing consistency. In the particular case here, I believe the inconsistency is simply due to laziness on the part of the author, who has used formulaic language ("deliver into your hands") in Yahweh's oracle without giving much thought to the fact that in the story it is Ya'el who kills Siysera and receives the glory.

15e Devorah then went straight away with Baraq to Qedesh: Devorah now accompanies Baraq back to Qedesh, where he will marshal his men and they will prepare for battle.

15f He then led ten thousand men on foot, and Devorah went with him: The Hebrew is somewhat ambiguous because of the fluidity in ancient Hebrew pronoun usage. It is possible to understand this sentence as "Ten thousand men went on foot, and Devorah went with them," although I think this reading less likely than the way I have translated it.

15g (Now Hever the Qeynite... which is near Qedesh.): The sentence that I have translated within parentheses provides no essential information to the narrative, and I understand it as an addition to the text, likely made as part of Judges' sixth compositional stage. This comment likely was added to offer an explanation for how it happened that a Qeynite (from a tribe to the south of Kena'an) appears in a story set in the far north of Kena'an.

15h Hovav: Mosheh's father-in-law is known under various names in the Tanakh, including Yithro, Yether, and Re'u'el. In Numbers P47,1, Mosheh's father-in-law is also named Hovav. See note 47,1b to my translation of Numbers for a brief discussion.

15i he marshaled…: The Leningrad Codex has a "closed" blank space before this clause to indicate the beginning of a new *parashah setumah*.

15j today's the day that Yahweh delivers Siysera into your hands: Note the inconsistency here. Devorah has already informed Baraq that Yahweh will deliver Sisyera into "the hands of a woman." See note 15c above.

15k she opened a skin of milk and gave him some to drink: The author has clearly borrowed this detail from the song in P16: "He asked for water, she gave him milk."

15l But Ya'el Heverswife instead took a tent stake… His body convulsed and then he was dead: This short paragraph is entirely based on the famous lines of the song in P16 telling of how Ya'el killed Siysera.

15m at the hands of the Yisra'elites: Literally, "in front of the Yisra'elites." The preposition לפני ("in front of") often expresses agency (that is, "by, at the hands of") when used in conjunction with verbs describing military actions in the passive voice. This is most commonly seen with the passive forms of the verb נכה ("strike, attack, kill, defeat"), but the preposition is used this way with other verbs as well. I believe that is how the preposition is being used here. On this usage of לפני, see notes 55b and 68b in my translation of Numbers. For other examples, see notes 14k and 35b in my translation of Joshua.

15n The Yisra'elites' power grew more and more oppressive against Yaviyn: Again, note the tension with the account of the Yisra'elites' battle with Yaviyn in Jos P22-P23,1. It is easiest to explain this tension if P14-P16 were part of a predecessor to the Israelite History (i.e. the Josianic History) or if it were added to Judges after the Israelite History was composed. The authors of the Israelite History would not have added this material, as it is entirely at odds with their presentation of the conquest of Kena'an as a ban devotion of the native peoples. If it were part of an earlier work that they expanded, however, it is easy to see how they would have been reluctant to remove this story.

16a "When in Yisra'el commanders commanded—when men joined up for war (give praise to Yahweh!)": I understand this to be the name of the song that Devorah and Baraq sing. The song is commonly known in English as the Song of Devorah (although since both Devorah and Baraq sing it, perhaps it should be called the Song of Devorah and Baraq). The song is considered by scholars to be among the oldest pieces of ancient Hebrew literature, with most dating it to anywhere from the ninth century to the eleventh century BCE. Songs were often given names based on famous lines that appear in the song, and that is the case here as well—the two lines on which the title is based begin what I have represented as the fifth stanza.

Notes to P16

The phrase in the title that I translate "when commanders commanded" is obscure. The Hebrew root פרע that I understand as "command" in other contexts may also mean "long hair" or "let go, let loose." However, based on the beginning of the fifth stanza, which is a variant of the title given here and which uses a word that clearly means "commanders" (חוקקים), I think it is certain that פרע in the title must be understood as "command." See note 16j below for my comment about the beginning of the fifth stanza.

For the Song of Devorah, the Masoretes used a special form of display that laid out the text in the form of what to the modern eye resembles a checkerboard;

in this form of display, they placed "closed" blank spaces (identical to the blank spaces used to mark a *parashah setumah*) in the text placed between each line of song. The two Masoretes who wrote the Aleppo Codex—Aharon ben Mosheh ben Asher (responsible for the vowel points, accents, and the *Masorah parva* and *Masorah magna*) and Shlomo ben Buya'a (responsible for the consonsantal text)—took great care in their arrangement of the song and the display of the line divisions, and I have tried to respect their effort in my translation by following their line divisions exactly. It is worth noting here that the display of the Song of Devorah in the Leningrad Codex, which was written by Shmu'el ben Ya'aqov, is much less faithful to the natural line divisions of the song. In all my translations, I have consistently noted the places where the Aleppo Codex and the Leningrad Codex differ in their use of "closed" and "open" blank spaces to mark *parashot setumot* and *parashot petuhot*. However, I have opted not to comment in most instances on the different line breaks in the Song of Devorah shown by the two codexes, as the differences are so numerous and the Aleppo Codex's display is so obviously superior that such comments would quickly become tedious to the reader. For a detailed discussion of the Masoretic display of songs and the special format the Masoretes used for the Song of Devorah, see my essay in the appendix to this book.

With respect to the display of the song on the page, I have taken the liberty of dividing the song into stanzas, as is the normal practice for English-language poems and songs, in order to create a "functionally equivalent" reading experience in English. In the Hebrew text, there is no organizing principle for the song's content except for the "closed" blank spaces marking the line divisions. Two other places I have departed from the display of the text on the page are the first sentence of P16, which introduces the song, and the sentence after the conclusion to the song that I have marked as P16,1. In both the Aleppo Codex and the Leningrad Codex, these two sentences are displayed on the page as though they are part of the song. I have chosen instead to separate both sentences from the rest of the song so as not to create a confusing experience for the reader.

16b Listen here, kings and viziers...I shall sing...: Ancient Hebrew narrative songs often began with a stanza addressing the audience and letting them know they are about to hear a song. The language in these introductions is relatively formulaic. For other examples, see Deut P31 (the Song of Mosheh) and Exod P26 (the Song of the Sea). In Exod P26, for example, Mosheh announces to the audience the name of the song that he is about to sing. (I unfortunately did not show the first line of Exod P26 as the title of the song in my translation; however, I did correctly reflect the song title in my translation of Exod P27.)

Here in Jud P16, the audience is "kings and viziers," which prompts one to wonder whether this song might have originally been part of the repertoire that was sung at the royal court of the northern kingdom of Yisra'el. If so, then we should presume that refugees from the north brought this song with them (along with other literary works) to Yehudah after the fall of the northern kingdom.

16c [*When you, Yahweh...at the approach of Yahweh, god of Yisra'el!*]: I believe that this stanza is not original to the song, but is a fragment of some other ancient song that has been added to the song here. The subject matter of this stanza—a theophany of Yahweh—fits poorly with the remainder of the song, which is about the great battle with Siysera. It is most likely, in my opinion, that this stanza was inserted as part of the editorial work on Judges during the late Persian period or Hellenistic period, although there is no way to know precisely when it might have been added. The likely rationale for the addition was to address the lack of Yahweh's involvement in the battle as portrayed in the original song.

16d *Mountains judder and quake at Yahweh's approach*: The verb is ambiguous. I follow many scholars who understand the root as the *niph'al* of the root זלל (z-l-l). However, some scholars prefer to understand the verbal root as נזל (n-z-l). If the latter option is adopted, the appropriate translation would be "mountain torrents rage at Yahweh's approach."

It should be mentioned that language nearly identical to the line here appears twice in Isaiah, in Is 63.19 and 64.2. It is likely that the language in Isaiah is a direct allusion to this line in the Song of Devorah, although it is certainly possible that Persian period or Hellenistic period editors of Judges may have borrowed this language from Isaiah in order to compose this line and insert it into the song.

16e (that is, Siynai): I understand this phrase to be an addition to the text. It is a gloss on the word הרים ("mountains") in the previous line—that is, the editor wishes the reader to understand that it is Mount Siynai that "judders and quakes at Yahweh's approach."

16f Back in the days of Shamgar Anathsson...: This stanza and the one that follows describe this period as a chaotic and lawless time—"highways had vanished" and roads were "tortuous;" the rural population had "disappeared" (i.e. fled to the safety of walled towns) and the Yisra'elites suffered from a lack of weaponry ("neither shields nor lances were to be seen"). One of the leading themes of the book of Judges is the chaos and lawlessness of the period prior to the establishment of the monarchy, and one wonders if the original authors of Judges—the Josianic historians—were influenced by the song in P16 in their decision to adopt this theme for their book.

Regarding Shamgar Anathsson, recall that this champion is mentioned in P13.

16g until Devorah appeared, until a great mother rose in Yisra'el: This is presented as a single line in the Aleppo Codex. It is an unusually long line in Hebrew—fifteen syllables, which is about twice as long as the typical line in this song—and it would be more natural to show a line break after the first clause. This is one of three lines in the Aleppo Codex's version of the song where the line breaks indicated by the "closed" blank spaces do not obviously follow the natural parallelism of the song's language. Although the line breaks in the Leningrad Codex are often out of sync with the song's parallelism, it's worth noting that here the Leningrad Codex has a "closed" blank space at the natural position after the first clause.

16h God chose new things: It is not clear to me what the phrase "new things" refers to. In any case, this stanza, like the previous stanza, sets the stage for the battle: it was a chaotic time when travel was dangerous and people had fled to the safety of towns; commerce was limited to buying and selling food, and metal-workers and smiths were unable to ply their trade (presumably due to lack of raw materials).

It should be noted that in the Aleppo Codex this line is also unusually long; it would be more natural to make the clause "food was bought and sold" serve as its own line. In fact, this is how the Leningrad Codex displays the text.

16i food was bought and sold: The Hebrew is obscure and the meaning is uncertain. I understand שערים to be derived from שער II ("calculate, reckon [a market price]"); see BDB, p. 1045. But my translation here is little more than guesswork.

16j Sing of the plans of Yisra'el's commanders: The line is difficult because the verb governing it—"sing" (שׂיחו)—appears three lines later (in Hebrew, it is the last word in the entire four-line stanza). The word לב, which is typically translated as "heart, mind," sometimes is used with the meaning "idea, plan," and that is how I understand its meaning here. See BDB, p. 523, def. 4 and p. 525, def. 4.

This line and the following line ("of men joining up for war") must have been very famous lines, for they gave the song its name (see note 16a above). I believe that the line here—"of the plans of Yisra'el's commanders" (לבי לחוקקי ישראל) must have been a variant of the line appearing in the title "when in Yisra'el commanders commanded" (בפרע פרעות בישראל).

A literal translation of the entire stanza is: "Of the plans of Yisra'el's commanders, of those among the people joining up [for war] (praise Yahweh!), of men astride tawny jenny-asses, of those sitting atop saddle-blankets, of those traveling down the road, sing!"

16k men astride tawny jenny-asses: The image is of men travelling to where forces are being mustered in order to join up for war, riding their donkeys rather than going on foot.

16l sitting atop saddle-blankets: The Leningrad Codex has a line break (i.e. a "closed" blank space) after this clause, with the following clause "and traveling down the road" serving as a whole line.

16m Arrows whizzed to and fro...: The lines of this stanza describe the beginning of the battle, which commences with fusillades of arrows from both sides in an attempt to disorient the opponents before the initial charge. A literal translation of the first phrase in the stanza is "At the sound of arrows." That is, at the sounds of the arrows, Yahweh's forces begin their attack and swoop down on the enemy gates.

This stanza, like several of the stanzas in the song, appears to be out of order—it would read best immediately after the stanza about the kings of Kena'an entering battle. I think it is clear that the song has suffered significantly in its transmission history, with numerous lines inadvertently moved to new places and other lines being lost entirely.

16n 'Get up, Devorah, get going!: Ancient Hebrew songs often have multiple voices, likely reflecting the fact that many songs were sung by a group of individuals rather than a single person. The song in P16 also appears to have multiple voices, which is consistent with the statement at the beginning of the *parashah* that both Devorah and Baraq sang the song. The voice of the song's narrator has been singing up to this stanza. But the line beginning this stanza, which directly addresses Devorah ("Get up, Devorah, get going!"), appears to introduce a new speaker. The following two stanzas and the fourth stanza following appear to be sung by different voices as well, which I have reflected in the translation with quotation marks. See notes 16o, 16r, and 16v below.

One also wonders if some of the voices were sung in harmony. For example, it is possible to imagine this stanza, which addresses Devorah and Baraq directly, being sung in harmony with the preceding stanza, which is in the voice of the narrator.

16o 'But then a fugitive arrived, one of the nobles...: I have translated this stanza as the direct speech of a person involved in the events the song describes. The fugitive who is a nobleman and valiant warrior is none other than Siysera. The speaker is presumably Ya'el's husband, Hever the Qeynite (see note 16q below).

This stanza about the arrival of Siysera seems to be in the wrong location in the song, and it is conceivable that it was inadvertently moved at some point in the song's transmission history. The stanza would fit much better a few stanzas later, after either the stanza mentioning the attack on Siysera or, most likely, the stanza about the Wadi Qiyshon.

16p [Yahweh's people]: This phrase is a gloss by an editor of the sixth stage. The editor has misunderstood the text; his gloss indicated that the word "nobles" (אדירים)

should be understood as referring to Yahweh's people, but in fact "nobles" here simply denotes military leaders in general.

16q someone from Ephrayim, whose ancestors lived in Amaleq: I understand this line to refer to Hever the Qeynite, who was Ya'el's husband. (The Qeynites and the Amaleqites occupied the desert lands south of Yehudah. It's worth noting that Qayin and Amaleq are loosely associated with each other in the epigrams delivered by Bil'am near the end of Num P72,1.) In P15, Hever is said to live in Qedesh, which is in Naphtaliy, but in the tradition in the song itself, he lives in Ephrayim.

16r 'After you, Binyamin, right there with your troops!': This line represents the third different voice in successive stanzas. The voice here is that of one of the leaders of the other tribes, who in this line reassures Binyamin that his men will be following right behind Binyamin as they march to battle. This, in my opinion, is the best way to understand this line given its placement next to the following stanza, which describes the various tribes taking position and preparing for the battle. It is also possible to understand this line as an alert of a threat to Binyamin ("Behind you, Binyamin! There among your troops!"), but I think this reading is less likely than how I have translated.

16s Makiyr: That is, the tribe of Menashsheh. Makiyr was Menashsheh's only son—thus, all the descendants of Menashsheh are also the descendants of Makiyr. As a result, authors of the Tanakh sometimes use Makiyr as a substitute for the name of the tribe of Menashsheh.

16t as Yissakar...planning their attack: The Aleppo Codex displays this text as two lines in accord with the accent marks. The Leningrad Codex displays it as three lines in contravention of the accent marks. If one follows the line breaks in the Leningrad Codex, the sense is quite different, and I believe that in this instance—despite going against the accent marks—it is an improvement upon the Aleppo Codex. Following the line breaks in the Leningrad Codex, the translation would be:
"As Yissakar, so too Baraq: positioned in the valley—
deployed on foot with Re'uven's brigades—
the leaders having fashioned their plans."

16u deployed into the valley on foot: The valley is the Yizre'el Valley. The stanza describes the leaders and troops from Makiyr (i.e. Menashsheh), Zevulun, Yissakar, and Naphtaliy (represented by Baraq) marching from Mount Tavor down into the Yizre'el Valley to engage Siysera's forces.

16v 'Why do you sit amongst desolate encampments...: This is the fourth new voice introduced in the song after the narrator. It is not certain who this voice is addressing. The Yisra'elite forces are a coalition of the northern tribes and the tribes east of the Yarden, so the voice must be addressing one of the tribes that has not joined the coalition. The tribes not mentioned as part of the coalition in the material that I understand to be original to the song are Asher, Dan, and Gil'ad. (Recall that Gad was not considered a tribe in the early literature; see note 11d above.) The tribes of Naphtaliy and Ephrayim are not mentioned by name in the song, but the leaders of those two tribes—Baraq and Devorah—are the song's protagonists and "co-singers"; moreover, in the previous stanza, both Devorah's forces [i.e. Ephrayim] and Baraq's forces [i.e. Naphtaliy] have taken their battle positions.

Given that the following line in the stanza is about Re'uven, and given that the territories of both Re'uven and Gil'ad were east of the Yarden, I think it most likely that the tribe being addressed here by the singer is Gil'ad. The comment added at the end of this stanza by the editors of the sixth compositional stage also suggests that the tribe being addressed here is Gil'ad; see note 16w below.

It's worth noting that the word I translate as "desolate encampments" (מִשְׁפְּתַיִם) also appears in Gen P43, which is the part of the Blessing of Ya'aqov devoted to the tribe of Yissakar. This is one of a number of touchpoints between the Song of Devorah and the Blessing of Ya'aqov.

16w [*Across the Yarden, Gil'ad stays put.*]: I understand this sentence to be a comment added by the editors of the sixth compositional stage; in this comment, they tell the reader that the tribe sitting in "desolate encampments listening to the bleatings of goats" is the tribe of Gil'ad.

16x [*As for Dan...the heights of the countryside.*]: I believe this entire stanza is a Persian period or Hellenistic period addition to the text, made in order to address the absence of the tribes of Asher and Dan. The addition about Asher and Dan uses language similar to that found in Gen P42, which is the part of the Blessing of Ya'aqov (Gen P39 - P44) that is devoted to the tribe of Zevulun.

It is unclear to me why this addition to the Song of Devorah also mentions Zevulun and Naphtaliy, as the original song has them as participants in the battle. Possibly the author of the addition had access to fragments of some song he believed to be ancient, and he may have decided to include them here in order to contrast the cowardice of Dan and Asher with the bravery of Zevulun and Naphtaliy.

16y [*As for Dan, why does he tarry... Or Asher, why does he stay...*: The author of the lines about Dan and Asher has modeled them on the statement about Zevulun in Gen P42, which is part of the Blessing of Ya'aqov in Genesis.

16z Kings arrived...: Beginning here and for the rest of the song, the line breaks in the Leningrad Codex are completely out of sync with the Masoretic accent marks. The line breaks in the Leningrad Codex clearly do not reflect the way the song was sung and hinder the reader's ability to understand the song. For this reason, I do not comment on the Leningrad Codex's line divisions for the remainder of the song.

16aa at Ta'nak, alongside Megiddo's watercourses: There is some tension between the song and the preceding narrative regarding the location of the battle. In the narrative in P15, Baraq's forces are camped on Mount Tavor, which is at the northeastern end of the Yizre'el Valley, and they swoop down into the valley to meet Siysera's forces. Siysera's forces are camped on the Wadi Qiyshon, which flows through the western end of the Yizre'el Valley, and is approximately twenty-five miles southwest of Mount Tavor. Presumably, then, the author of the narrative in P15 envisioned the battle taking place at a midpoint in the valley. In the song, however, the battle takes place at Ta'nak, near the Wadi Qiyshon—that is, where Siysera's forces are camped.

Regarding the phrase "Megiddo's watercourses," I believe this is simply a literary term for the Wadi Qiyshon—similar to how an American might refer to the Potomac River poetically as "Washington's watercourse."

16ab while plunder of silver they forswore: That is, they devote all their efforts to fighting.

16ac from their tracks the stars at Siysera struck: In the cosmology of the song's author, Yahweh is the sky god, and the stars are his warriors. The word צבא means both "star" and "army." This is the background for the name "Yahweh Tzeva'oth," which means "Yahweh of Armies."

16ad The Wadi Qiyshon swept them away: The Wadi Qiyshon is a river that runs by Megiddo. This is "Megiddo's watercourses" referenced in an earlier stanza. The image is of the river carrying the bodies of the slain soldiers of Siysera's army downstream until they are submerged entirely ("stamping them under").

16ae Then the horses' hooves hammered down...: This stanza seems out of place. It would fit better five lines above, immediately before the stanza beginning "Swooping down from the sky."

16af ['*Damn Meroz...to Yahweh's support!*]: I understand these three lines as a late addition to the song, likely made as part of the editorial work on the sixth compositional stage. There are two reasons to think these lines are an addition. First, the initial line of the addition has no notable lyric qualities, and—with eighteen syllables in Hebrew—is too long to function as the line of a song. And second, Yahweh's envoy plays no role elsewhere in the song, and the mention of the envoy here is jarring and out of place.

The addition fits better with the earlier additions regarding Dan and Asher, and one wonders if the addition here was displaced from its original position during the song's transmission history. The authors of this addition must have known of an ancient tradition about the cowardice of the town of Meroz, and decided to insert it into the Song of Devorah because of its relevant subject matter.

16ag went not with the valiant: The Hebrew is ambiguous, and the term בגברים may refer either to the foe or to the allies. I prefer the latter interpretation, as the term used—גבורים ("valiant ones, warriors")—typically has a positive connotation. In the former interpretation, which is certainly plausible, the translation of the line would be "went not to support Yahweh against the valiant foe."

16ah Most bless'd of women...: The narrative flow at this point of the song is very disjointed. Originally, this stanza was likely preceded by the stanza about the fugitive's (i.e. Siysera's) arrival, which I suggested above is out of place (see note 16o). In addition, I think it is likely that there was originally a stanza about Siysera dismounting his chariot and fleeing the battle that has fallen out of the text. The fact that these actions are described in P15 offers some support for the proposal that a stanza describing Siysera's flight from battle was also present in the song, for I think it is clear that the authors of the Josianic History used the Song of Devorah as their source when composing P15 (see note 15d above).

16ai She reaches with her hand: Literally, "Her hand reached." The verb "reached" is conjugated as the third person feminine plural, but the subject "hand" is the feminine singular. Hebrew often has grammatical oddities such as this, as there was a much looser attitude toward grammatical consistency than we modern-day English speakers have. It would be wrong, in my opinion, to suppose that the text is corrupt here, or to attempt to "fix" the grammar with an emendation, as is sometimes done by scholars.

16aj Siysera's mother gazed out the window, squealed thru the lattice: This is a single line in the Aleppo Codex. At twenty-one syllables, the line is by far the longest in the song, and it is one of three lines in the Aleppo Codex's display of the song where the line breaks indicated by the "closed" blank spaces do not follow the natural parallelism of the song's language. It would be most natural to show a line break after the first verb in the Hebrew; however, Shlomo ben Buya'a, the author of the consonantal text, likely elected not to do that because he needed to end the poem at the end of the text column, and if he displayed this sentence about Siysera's mother as two lines, it would have added another line to the checkerboard pattern he was following, and the poem would have ended in the middle of the text column.

16ak Surely they found…borne on captives' backs: The song ends with Siysera's mother and her attendants speculating that Siysera's delay is due to all the spoils he and his men are collecting—a powerful note of irony that achieves a wonderful literary effect, and an astonishing ending to this most famous song. The element of irony is heightened when one recalls that in a stanza earlier in the song, the narrator informs us that when "the kings of Kena'an waged war" (i.e. Yaviyn's army and his allied forces, all led by Siysera), they did not take any plunder ("plunder of silver they forswore").

16al Thus may all your enemies, O Yahweh, perish!: I treat this line as the original conclusion to the song; it is possible, however, that the song may originally have ended with the previous line.

16am [*And may all those who love him stay strong as the rising sun!*]: This sentence is clearly a very late addition; note, in particular, the shift from addressing Yahweh in the second person in the previous line to the third person address here.

16an —: The Leningrad Codex does not have a "closed" blank space here. Although it is possible to view the closed blank space here in the Aleppo Codex as part of the song, I instead treat it as the beginning of a new *parashah setumah*.

Notes to P17

17a But then the Yisra'elites did what Yahweh considered the worst thing…: This *parashah*, which I believe was composed by the authors of the Josianic History, serves as the introduction to the stories about the hero Gid'on Yo'ashsson, which appear in P19-P26. These stories form the core of the book of Judges—both in its current form, and in the form it had as part of the Josianic History. In the stories following P17, Gid'on is presented as the greatest of the "champions" of Yisra'el, and he demonstrates all the characteristics of a model leader (see the list of his personal characteristics in note 24k below). If we accept the idea that the Josianic History was composed to serve the educational curriculum of the young king, then Gid'on can be understood as an ideal role model for the king, who is being forced to grow up quickly and "learn on the job." With respect to the proposal that the Josianic History was composed primarily for the young king, it is perhaps worth noting here that P17 reads as something that would appeal strongly to a young teenage boy.

17b nor any sheep, nor cattle, nor asses: The author's inclusion of asses here is surprising, as asses are not treated elsewhere in the Tanakh as a source of food. It is possible that the author intended for the reader to understand the mention of sheep, cattle, and asses not as an elaboration of the term "form of sustenance" (מחיה), but simply as examples of the animals that the Midyanites killed when they destroyed the Yisra'elites' sources of sustenance.

With respect to "forms of sustenance," dietary practices varied quite a bit locally. The dietary rules preserved in Lev P24 and in Deut P13,4 - P13,6 represent cult rules associated with individual shrines and wouldn't necessarily have been observed by families who made offerings at other cult sites. That said, it's worth noting that the dietary rules in Leviticus explicitly prohibit the consumption of "animals that have hooves but that don't divide them and that don't bring up their cud"—that is, animals belonging to the genus *Equus*, which includes horses, asses, and zebras.

17c It was impossible to count: Ancient Hebrew writers often used the particle אין ("there is not") in places where a native English speaker would say something was "impossible." That is how the particle is used here, and I have translated accordingly.

I have commented frequently in my other translations on this usage of אִין; see, for example, note 37w in my translation of Genesis and note 1v in my translation of Deuteronomy.

18a Now when the Yisra'elites...: The entire *parashah* reads as a late addition to the text. The sending of a prophet rather than a champion suggests that the *parashah* is not from the hand of the Josianic historians. Although the allusions to the exodus from Egypt and the narratives of Numbers and Joshua can certainly be understood as an addition by the exilic authors of the Israelite History, the phrasing used at the end of the *parashah* specifically recalls Yehoshua's farewell speech in Jos P54 - P56, which is a Persian period addition to that book.

Notes to P18

With respect to the date of this *parashah*, it is interesting to note that in the fragments of Judges found in cave 4 at Qumran (4Q Judg^a), the text goes directly from the end of P17 to the beginning of P19—that is, the entirety of P18 is absent. This offers strong support for understanding P18 as a very late addition to the text, almost certainly dating to the Hellenistic period.

18b I rescued you from Egypt: An allusion to the destruction of Phar'oh and his army at the Reed Sea in Exod P25.

18c all those oppressing you, driving them out of your path and giving you their land: An allusion to Num P72, which relates the story of how the Yisra'elites took possession of land east of the Yarden after they defeated Siyhon King of Heshbon and Og King of Bashan, both of whom engaged the Yisra'elites in battle rather than allow them to cross through their land.

18d 'I am your god Yahweh,' I said to you. 'Don't give reverence to the gods of the Amorites, in whose land you're living: An allusion to Yehoshua's farewell speech to the Yisra'elites at Shekem in Jos P54 - P56. The author here borrows language directly from Jos P54, which uses the identical phrase "the gods of the Amorites in whose land you're living." It's worth noting that the speech in Jos P54 - P56 is itself a Persian period addition to Joshua. On the Persian period date of this speech, see my comments on those *parashot* in my translation of Joshua.

19a An envoy from Yahweh arrived and sat under the terebrinth tree...: This *parashah* and the one that follows (P20) tell the story of Gid'on's "call" to rescue Yisra'el from Midyan. The interaction of Gid'on with Yahweh, who has taken on the form of a human, is somewhat reminiscent of Yahweh's visit to Avraham and Sarah at the Terebrinths of Mamre in Gen P19, where Yahweh takes on the form of three men and they also sit under a terebrinth.

Notes to P19

One oddity of the story here in Jud P19 - P20 is that the author is inconsistent in describing Gid'on's visitor: sometimes the visitor is described as an envoy (מלאך) of Yahweh, and other times simply as Yahweh. I think it likely that in the earliest written versions of the story (that is, those in the first and possibly second compositional stages), there may have been no mention of an envoy and the visitor was indeed Yahweh. But if this is so, there is no way of knowing when the text was revised so that the visitor was Yahweh's envoy rather than Yahweh himself.

19b Ophrah (the town settled by the Ezrites' ancestor Yo'ash): The author provides little background information at the beginning of the story of Gid'on, likely because he assumed his audience was aware of this information. For the modern-day reader, the critical pieces of background information are that Ophrah is a town or village in the Gil'ad region, that this part of the Gil'ad region belonged to the tribe of Menashsheh, and that the Aviy'ezrites (=the Ezrites) were one of the seven clans comprising the tribe of Menashsheh. On the Aviy'ezrites as a clan, see note 19f below.

The phrase אשר ליואש אבי העזרי ("which belonged to the Ezrites' ancestor Yo'ash") can be understood to qualify either the terebrinth tree or the town of Ophrah. Based on the use of a similar phrase to qualify Ophrah at the end of P20, I think it is certain that the phrase here must refer to the town and not the tree (see note 20e below). There must have been numerous places named Ophrah (which means "Dusty")—the author wants us to know that this is the Ophrah settled by the Ezrites.

19c in order to hide it from Midyan: This clause clearly assumes the events of P17. I view P17 as from the hand of the Josianic historians, who have composed it in order to set the Gid'on stories within the narrative frame of their version of Judges. As I discuss in the essay on the composition history of Judges, I believe the Josianic historians utilized a written collection of stories about Gid'on (the core of P19 - P26), but it is not always possible in my view to identify what in these *parashot* was part of the pre-existing written document and what was added by the Josianic historians.

19d Where are all those amazing things he did...: Although Gid'on's tone is initially respectful ("If I may, my lord"), he follows this up with a comment that has sarcastic undertones ("where are all those amazing things he did"). The "amazing things" Yahweh did is a reference to the exodus tradition and the miracles associated with it. It is unclear how developed the exodus tradition was that was known by the Josianic historian who was largely responsible for the current form of this *parashah*. It is certainly possible that the tradition was still only partially developed as late as the 630s and 620s BCE, when I believe the Josianic historians were active. I argued in my translation of Exodus that the earliest version of the book (which reflects a fully developed exodus tradition) was composed in first half of the sixth century, some five or six decades after the Josianic history.

19e Be assured, I have sent you: The logic of the narrative is somewhat confused. At the beginning of the *parashah* and at various other points in the story, Yahweh (or his envoy) is in disguise and Gid'on doesn't know that he is speaking with Yahweh. However, in Yahweh's speech here and in the following exchange between Yahweh and Gid'on, the author writes as though Yahweh's identity is known to Gid'on. One possible explanation of this inconsistency is that the material where Yahweh's identity is known to Gid'on was not part of the earliest written version (the pre-Josianic source material), but reflects edits made by the Josianic historians. However, it is also possible that this material was original to the story, for ancient Hebrew authors had a much more flexible attitude toward narrative logic than modern-day authors, and they often sacrificed narrative logic to achieve other goals, such as enhancing the emotional impact on the reader or introducing important themes. I have frequently commented on this tendency of the ancient biblical authors in my other translations; see, for example, note 21b in my translation of Genesis and note 29i in my translation of Joshua. See also note 9n above.

19f My clan is the weakest in Menashsheh: Gid'on's clan is Aviy'ezer, which is one of the seven clans of Menashsheh. The references here to Gid'on's clan are confusing because his clan is never specifically named. However, at the beginning of this *parashah*, the author tells us that Gid'on is the son of Yo'ash, and that Yo'ash is the ancestor of the Ezrites—אבי העזרי (Aviy Ha'ezriy), which then gets shortened into the name אביעזר (Aviy'ezer). For the full list of clans of Menashsheh, see Jos P34 and Num P76,6. Note that in Num P76,6, this clan name is further abbreviated as Iy'ezer (איעזר) rather than אביעזר (Aviy'ezer). Note also that the clan of Hepher (the seventh clan of Menashsheh) was subdivided into five clans founded by Tzelophhad's daughters.

Aviy'ezer the clan is mentioned also in Jud P20,2 and P24. Both those references are confusing if the reader is unaware that Aviy'ezer is the Menashshehite clan to which Gid'on belongs.

19g a gift: The word מנחה is a general term for "gift," but within the cult it typically refers specifically to an offering of grain or produce. Because Gid'on is interacting with Yahweh, it is tempting to interpret the word here as meaning an offering; however, the lack of an altar (which is only built at the conclusion of P20) makes clear that it is simply a gift.

19h present it to you: Literally, "place it down in front of you." In English, it is most natural to say that one "presents" a gift to another. The author's choice of verb here (the *hiph'il* of נוח) is a little unusual, but he may have been influenced by the alliteration with the word מנחה.

19i an *eyphah* of flour: The *eyphah* was a dry measure equivalent to twenty-two liters in today's metric system. Presumably the author meant not that Gid'on used a full *eyphah* of flour in making the flat bread, which would have made perhaps two or three dozen loaves, but rather that he used some of an *eyphah* of flour stored at home to make the loaves. For a good overview of weights and measures used in the Tanakh, see "Weights & Measures" at the Jewish Virtual Library website.

19j placed it in front of him: Literally, "and brought [it] near." The *hiph'il* of the verb נגש is associated with bringing out food and putting it in front of a person; see, for example, the identical usage at the conclusion of Sam P60,2.

19k **: The Leningrad Codex has a *parashah setumah* here.

Notes to P20

20a Take the meat and the bread…: The effect of the instructions of God's envoy is to turn what was a meal into an offering to a god. The meat and bread are placed on a rock (which equates to the altar), and then the broth (which equates to the blood) is poured out. Then, in parallel with a whole offering (עֹלָה), the meat and bread are consumed in fire.

20b the being was an envoy from Yahweh: The Leningrad Codex has a "closed" blank space after this clause to indicate the beginning of a new *parashah setumah*.

20c It's okay: The author uses idiomatic language. A more literal translation is, "You'll be fine" (שלום לך). I have translated with a slightly different English phrase that is more appropriate for the altar's name in the following sentence. Note also the logical inconsistency in the narrative: Yahweh (or his envoy) has disappeared from sight when the fire consumed the meat and bread, but now Yahweh addresses Gid'on as though he is still present.

20d Yahweh-It's-Okay: There is an element of humor in the etiology of the altar here in P20. In Hebrew, the altar has a serious sounding name, "Yahweh Shalom." The humor arises from the incongruity of the serious name and the somewhat silly etiology that the author gives for the name—the author ties the altar's name to an idiomatic and casual use of the phrase שלום לך. The phrase usually means "I wish you well," but one of its idiomatic uses in everyday speech is the equivalent of the English phrase "it's okay" (or "it'll be okay") when used to reassure someone that there is nothing to be concerned about. In order to capture the element of humor in this *parashah*, I have had to translate the name of the altar as a humorous one rather than a serious one. As an aside, in thinking about the idea that the Josianic History may have been composed as part of the king's education, it is worth mentioning here that this sort of story with a silly etiology would appeal to a young teenage boy who otherwise might be feeling somewhat bored in his lessons.

20e the Ophrah founded by the Ezrites' ancestor: As mentioned above in note 19b, Ophrah ("Dusty") must have been a relatively common name for a village; thus the author felt the need to specify that he is speaking of the Ophrah founded by the Ezrites' ancestor. Recall from the beginning of P19 that the Ezrites' ancestor is Gid'on's father Yo'ash.

20e —: The Leningrad Codex has a *parashah petuhah* here.

Notes to P20,1

20,1a a second bull seven years: The Hebrew does not read naturally and the text may be corrupt. The word בן ("son") appears to have fallen from the text. Inserting that word into the text yields a very natural Hebrew phrase that I would translate as "a second bull that's seven years old." But the significance of the age of the bull is unclear and the age plays no further role in the story, suggesting that the corruption of the text may extend beyond the loss of בן.

20,1b in the proper arrangement: The author's use of the word מערכה is difficult to understand. Elsewhere, the word is a military term with the meaning of "row, rank, battle-line," but that is clearly not the meaning here. However, I do not believe that the text here is necessarily corrupt. The root of the word is ערך, which means "to arrange neatly, arrange in rows." Of relevance for this passage in Judges is that the verb ערך is associated with the building of the seven altars in the story of Bil'am and Balaq (Num P72,1), where it is used in parallel with בנה ("build") and where context suggests it must mean something like "build in the proper arrangement" or "build in a neat and orderly fashion." Based on that usage in Num P72,1, I understand the noun מערכה here in Judges to mean "orderly, neat, or proper arrangement," and I have translated accordingly.

20,1c at the summit of that refuge: The reference to a "refuge" (מעוז) is nonsensical. I think it is very likely that the text here is corrupt.

20,1c Take the second bull: Note that the first bull is nowhere to be seen. It is likely, in my opinion, that a sentence or two has fallen from the text that describes what Gid'on is supposed to do with the first bull. The gap in the text here may be related to the corruption in the text in the preceding sentence, as discussed in the notes directly above.

20,1e with the wood of the Asherah pole: It is difficult to imagine that this whole offering would meet with the approval of the authors of Leviticus. Rather, those authors would have viewed the wood of the Asherah pole as impure and causing pollution, and it seems inconceivable that they would have approved of allowing any such wood in the vicinity of an altar to Yahweh, much less using that wood for a whole offering.

20,1f "Are you prosecuting this case on behalf of the Ba'al...: The *parashah* concludes with an etiology of the name Yerubba'al, the name that Gid'on was commonly known by. It is possible to read this etiology as a humorous one. The name means "Ba'al contends," but the author humorously turns the name on its head by reading the name as "he contends with the Ba'al"—thus, he makes it not about the Ba'al contending on behalf of one of his devotees, but rather about a man challenging a (weak) god.

The Gid'on stories have numerous elements of humor in them, as does the story of Ehud. While this obviously is entirely speculative, it is tempting to see the many humorous elements in the Josianic History's version of Judges as being intended to make the young king's educational curriculum more appealing to him. See notes 12a and 20d above.

20,1g they called him Yerubba'al: The wording of the Hebrew has left the antecedent of the pronoun "him" somewhat ambiguous. However, as we learn in P21, Yerubba'al is the alternate name not of Yo'ash, but of his son Gid'on.

20,1h —: The Leningrad Codex has a *parashah petuhah* here.

20,2a Now all Midyan, Amaleq, and the Qedemites… in the Yizre'el Valley: Midyan, Amaleq, and the Qedemites occupy the desert lands south of Yehudah. They must travel quite a distance—some one hundred and fifty miles—to the north to reach the Yizre'el Valley.

20,2b Aviy'ezer: Aviy'ezer is one of the seven clans of Menashsheh, and it is the clan to which Gid'on belongs. See notes 19b and 19f above.

20,2c Are you really going to rescue Yisra'el through me like you said?: A reference back to Gid'on's initial encounter with Yahweh in P19, when Yahweh (or his envoy) tells Gid'on that he will rescue Yisra'el. The phrasing of the speech here in P20,2 presumes that Gid'on interacted directly with Yahweh in the encounter in P19, and thus supports the view that the envoy (מלאך) language in that *parashah* is a later addition to the text.

Notes to P20,2

21a Quaking Spring… Teacher's Hill: These must be sites in the Yizre'el Valley. At the beginning of P20,2 the author states that Midyan, Amaleq, and the Qedemites established a position in the Yizre'el Valley.

Notes to P21

21b —: The Leningrad Codex does not have a *parashah* break here.

21,1a Whoever is afraid or scared ought to go back: Compare the statement here that Gid'on must offer his forces with the precepts of war in Deut P19,3. Note in particular the precept requiring officers to give soldiers who are weak-hearted the opportunity to return home: "When addressing the soldiers in this fashion, the military officers shall add the following: 'Any man who is afraid or weak-hearted, let him leave here now and return home—his compatriots mustn't lose their courage as he has done.'"

Notes to P21,1

21,1b and chirp away from Mount Gil'ad: The Hebrew is obscure. The Masoretic text reads "let him *ṣ-p-r* from Mount Gil'ad" (ויצפר מהר גלעד). The verb of the root *ṣ-p-r* (צפר) is unattested elsewhere in ancient Hebrew, but the noun form of the root means "bird." In other Semitic languages, the verb form of this root means "chirp, peep, twitter"—that is, to make sounds like those of a bird. If we adopt this meaning for the verbal form of this root in Hebrew, we can understand the phrase as a derisive comment about the men who are too scared to fight—"let them go back and chatter away like birds from the safety of their own homes." I have taken this approach in my translation. That said, there is some doubt in my mind as to whether the text might not be corrupt, as the phrase "Mount Gil'ad" is otherwise unattested.

One alternative would be to understand the verb צפר to denote a different action of a bird—flying. In this alternative, rather than reading "from Mount Gil'ad," one would emend the Masoretic vocalization by transposing the vowels of מֵהַר ("from the mountain") to מַהֵר ("quickly"). In this alternative, the phrase ויצפר מהר גלעד would thus be translated as "winging his way quickly to Gil'ad," which fits the context equally well, if not better, than the translation "and chirp away from Mount Gil'ad."

As an aside, the mention of Gil'ad here proves that the clan of Aviy'ezer (and Gid'on's home town of Ophrah) is located in the Gil'ad region and not in the territory of Menashsheh west of the Yarden. See note 19b above.

21,2a Have them go down to the water: The "water" is a reference to the spring where Gid'on and his forces are camped. Recall from P21 that Gid'on and his forces

Notes to P21,2

established their camp at Quaking Spring. (Recall also from P20,2 that Midyan, Amaleq, and the Qedemites are positioned in the Yizre'el Valley.)

21,2b So Gid'on had his forces go down to the water: The Leningrad Codex has a "closed" blank space after this clause to indicate the beginning of a new *parashah setumah*.

21,2c And anyone who crouches down on his knees to drink: The Hebrew is written in a sort of short-hand colloquial style that is characteristic of spoken language—the verb clause "set him to the other side" is omitted and is understood from context.

21,2d all the rest of the men crouched down on their knees to drink water: It is not clear exactly how this group, which numbered 9,700 men, drinks water; I believe it likely that the author intended the reader to imagine these individuals crouching or kneeling, filling a bowl with water, and then sipping from the bowl.

Notes to P22

22a battalions: These are fifty-man units. The term used here is an irregular plural. See my comments on this term in note 3d of my translation of Joshua.

22b (Now Midyan, Amaleq, and all the Qedemites…like swarms of locusts…as numerous as the sand on the seashore.): The sentence that I have translated within parentheses may be an addition by the editors of the sixth compositional stage. The phrasing here—"swarms of locusts" and "countless numbers of camels"—is borrowed directly from P17, which describes the raids on Yisra'el carried out by Midyan, Amaleq, and the Qedemites.

Notes to P23

23a he prostrated himself on the ground: Gid'on's action is his way of giving thanks to Yahweh, both for advising him to go to Midyan's camp and eavesdrop on them, and for granting him the future victory over Midyan.

23b and then in the way that I do: The Aleppo Codex appears to read באשר ("in [the way] that") here, whereas the Leningrad Codex and the other Masoretic manuscripts read כאשר ("exactly as"). Shlomo ben Buya'a, who wrote the consonantal text of the Aleppo Codex, wrote the letters *beth* (ב) and *kaph* (כ) very similarly, and it is often difficult to distinguish the two letters from one another in his writing; in this instance, however, the letter form is closer to how he usually wrote *beth*. The Leningrad Codex, which has the *kaph*, has the more natural reading and is almost certainly correct. While the reading of the Aleppo Codex is not obviously wrong, I think it most likely that ben Buya'a here has inadvertently written a *beth* in place of a *kaph*. The error may not have been caught in his proofreading the text because his *kaph* and his *beth* were so similar.

23c everyone with me: Of the three groups of one hundred men, this is the one that is with Gid'on.

Notes to P24

24a the night's middle watch: References in the Tanakh suggest that there may have been three watches. From the passage here, we know there was a middle watch, and Sam P22,1 and Exod P24 mention the "morning watch." The first watch is never named, but we may guess that it was called the "evening watch" (אשמרת הערב).

24b Each man remained standing in place…while the entire camp ran and shouted and took flight: I believe the authors of the *parashah* meant for this picture to be humorous. As presented in the Josianic History, the Gid'on stories contain elements of both humor and thrilling action that, in part, are meant to entertain the reader. As mentioned above, such elements make the stories especially appealing to a young teenage boy and are entirely understandable if one of the primary purposes of the

Josianic History was to educate the young king Yoshiyyahu (=Josiah) about the responsibilities of leadership and about the great leaders of his people in the past.

24c Acacia Town: Acacia Town (בית השטה) is likely the same place as The Acacias (השטים or "Shittiym"), which is mentioned in Num 73 and Jos P4 and which was the place in Mo'av where the Yisra'elites camped at the end of their wilderness journeys before crossing over the Yarden River into Kena'an.

24d Yisra'elites were marshaled from Naphtaliy, from Asher, and from all of Menashsheh: Recall that Gid'on sent home 22,000 men in P21,1 and an additional 9,700 men in P21,3. Now—just a day or two after sending the men home and while many of them are presumably still on the road—he summons thousands of men back to the fight. The act of sending away nearly the entire army and then almost immediately calling up a new army to help in the fight strikes the modern reader as absurd and illogical. This sequence of events, however, is a good example of one of the principal techniques of ancient Hebrew narrative art, in which writers sought to create a heightened emotional impact on the reader, even at the cost of sacrificing narrative logic. The story is more exciting and dramatic because the Yisra'elites are vastly outnumbered, and then the resulting chase is also more exciting and dramatic because fighters are summoned at a moment's notice from multiple tribes in the surrounding area. If Gid'on had simply kept the 31,700 men instead of sending them away, much of the drama and excitement of the battle narrative would have been lost.

24e back on the other side of the Yarden: That is, back in Kena'an where Gid'on still is (recall that the Midyanites were camped in the Yizre'el Valley.) The phrasing of the Hebrew here is somewhat confusing. The author uses the phrase מעבר לירדן ("on the other side of the Yarden"). Usually this phrase refers to the region to the east of the Yarden (that is, the side of the Yarden that the speaker is not on). In this instance, however, the phrase is used relative to the location of the Ephrayimites, who have crossed east of the Yarden in pursuit of Midyan.

24f What in the hell is this thing you did: In ancient Hebrew, the demonstrative particle זה ("this") is often used in direct speech to express displeasure or contempt. My translation here reflects this use of the particle. I have frequently commented on this use of the particle in my other translations. See note 9q above.

24g Not summoning us when you went to fight Midyan: Recall that in P20,2, Gid'on summons forces from his own clan Aviy'ezer, from other clans in Menashsheh, and from Asher, Zevulun, and Naphtaliy, but he does not summon Ephrayim, whose territory is adjacent to those tribes.

24h How does what I did justify what you're doing now?: The tone of the Hebrew is highly colloquial, as is appropriate for emotional speech. Somewhat more literally, "[How] is what I did now like [what] you['re doing]?" That is, how does my not summoning you to fight justify your attacks on me now? Note: the position of the particle עתה ("now") appears out of place—it would be more natural for it to follow ככם ("like you") than to precede it. I presume the positioning is meant to reflect the emotional speech, which doesn't always observe customary grammatical practices.

24i Aviy'ezer: Recall that Aviy'ezer is the clan in Menashsheh to which Gid'on belongs. See notes 19b and 19f above.

24j I couldn't have captured them if I'd wanted to: The Hebrew is highly colloquial, and I have translated with an English colloquialism that captures the tone and meaning of the Hebrew. Literally, "How was I able to do like you [did]?"

24k Their anger abated at him when he spoke these words: Gid'on assuages the Ephrayimites' anger through a combination of humor (his comment about the leftover grapes) and humility (his admission that he would have been unable to capture Orev and Ze'ev on his own). It is interesting to note the subtlety and richness of the characterization of Gid'on in the stories about him. He is by far the most complex "champion" in the book of Judges. He is skeptical by nature and won't take things on faith but demands empirical proof (P19 - P20, P20,2, and P22); he is appropriately cautious when the situation demands it (P20,1 and P22); he is creative and clever in formulating battle plans (P23) and decisive in seizing opportunities (P24); he is diplomatic and skilled in managing conflict (P24), but vengeful to traitors (P25); and he is unmotivated by power (P26). His one flaw is that he gives in to the temptation for material wealth (P26). As mentioned above in note 17a, the character of Gid'on would serve as an excellent role model for a leader in training, such as the young king for whom the Josianic History might have been composed as part of his educational curriculum.

24l proceeded to the Yarden, crossing over: Recall that earlier in the *parashah*, the Ephrayimites take the heads of Orev and Ze'ev to Gid'on, who was still in Kena'an (see note 24e above). Now Gid'on and his men cross the Yarden, and the action takes place at sites east of the Yarden—Sukkoth and Penu'el here in P24, and Qarqor, Novah and Yogbehah, and Heres Pass in P25.

24m the leaders of Sukkoth: The Hebrew reads אנשי סכות ("men of Sukkoth"). In ancient Hebrew, the phrase "men of TOWN NAME" has different shades of meaning, depending on context. It can mean the adult males of the town, the residents of the town (including women), or the leaders (or "leading men") of the town. We can infer that the latter meaning is intended here, as in the following sentence it is the town chiefs (שׂרים) who respond to Gid'on's request.

24n we're chasing after Midyan's kings: Literally, "I'm chasing after Midyan's kings." This clause is a good example of the subtle departures one must make from a literal rendering of the text to produce a functionally equivalent translation. The clause serves as Gid'on's rationale for why Sukkoth's leaders should give food to his men. It would be unnatural in English to exclude the men who will receive the food from the statement providing the rationale for why the food should be given to them; thus the translation required by natural English usage is "we're chasing" rather than "I'm chasing."

Notes to P25

25a Gid'on proceeded north...and attacked the army: At the end of P24, Gid'on is still leading only three hundred men (despite having just marshaled thousands of troops from Naphtaliy, Asher, Menashsheh, and Ephrayim); moreover, all three hundred of the men under his command are exhausted and hungry. Yet now these three hundred men attack and "rout" the Qedemite armies still with Midyan's kings Zevah and Tzalmuna, which numbered fifteen thousand men. The lack of logic in the narrative here is likely due to the fact that the authors have joined up two originally independent stories—a story about seeking provisions from Sukkoth and Penu'el (the conclusion to P24) and a story about Gid'on's defeat of the Qedemites' army and the capture of Zevah and Tzalmunah (the beginning of P25). By linking the stories together, the authors imply that Gid'on's forces who defeated the Qedemites' army numbered only three hundred men. But when the story of the Qedemites' defeat and the capture of Zevah and Tzalmuna in P25 is viewed on its own, there is no reason to believe that Gid'on's forces were anything less than a full-size army.

25b along the Occupied-Tents Highway, to the east of Novah and Yogbehah: The name of the highway is unusual, and it is possible that the text is corrupt. The highway must be a north-south road, for it is to the east of Novah and Yogbehah. We know from Num P87 that Yogbehah is in the territory belonging to Gad and that Novah is to its north, in the territory belonging to the eastern Menashshehites. Gid'on is coming from the area around Sukkoth and Penu'el, both of which are in Gad. We know from Jos P27 that Sukkoth is in Gad's territory, and we know from Gen P28 that Penu'el is located on the Wadi Yabboq (in Joshua, the territory to the south of the Yabboq belongs to Gad and the territory to the north belongs to Menashsheh).

25c Where are the men you killed in Tavor: There is no previous mention of this incident in the narrative. It is possible that a sentence or two relating this incident has fallen out of the text. BDB, p. 33, proposes that איפה ("where") in this instance means "of what kind;" however, this meaning of the word is otherwise unattested, and the sentence reads naturally if one understands איפה to mean "where." That is to say, Gid'on is simply asking what they did with the bodies of the men whom they killed.

25d 'At once,' you coward: Zevah and Tzalmuna repeat back Gid'on's command to his oldest son (קום, used idiomatically with the meaning "at once"). They belittle and insult the boy in a final act of defiance before Gid'on kills them.

25e like a real man: The Hebrew is idiomatic and colloquial, and I have translated with the appropriate English idiom. Literally, "for like the man is his strength"—that is, a man's strength (or courage) is the true measure of his character. In his inability to summon the courage to kill Zeva and Tzalmuna, Yether demonstrates that he is fundamentally a weak young man who is undeserving of respect. If we accept the idea that the Josianic History was composed to educate the young king about his role, it is possible to see in the story a lesson for the boy about the courage that a true man must exhibit.

25f **: The Leningrad Codex does not have a *parashah* break here.

26a I certainly will not rule over you... Rather, Yahweh is the one who rules over you: The author here uses the verb משל, which means "rule, have dominion over." It is a term to describe the power in general that one person has over a group of people, and it is not necessarily associated with kingship. When it is used in reference to a king, it is almost always used to describe a king's power over vassal states; it is only rarely used to describe a king's relationship to the people of his own country. Given that the verb here in P26 is משל and not מלך (which is a term specifically applied to a king's power over his own people), I do not believe the authors of the Josianic History in this *parashah* are necessarily making any specific point about kingship. That said, however, the general idea—that Yahweh is the proper ruler of Yisra'el—is consistent with the ambivalence towards the institution of kingship expressed in Sam P21, which I believe belongs to the Josianic History's version of Samuel.

Notes to P26

26b (Now, the earrings they had were gold because they were taken from the Yishma'elites.): The Hebrew is awkwardly expressed, and I have tried to reflect that in my translation. Literally, "Now, they had gold earrings because they were Yishma'elites." The author is reminding the reader that the Yisra'elites' opponents—Midyan, Amaleq, and the Qedemites—are all from the south, and as such are of Yishma'elite descent. The author seems to allude to a belief common in his day that the Yishma'elites were especially fond of gold. (On the association of the Yishma'elites with the Paran Wilderness in the south, see the conclusion of Gen P19,2.)

26c seventeen hundred sheqels of gold: The author omits the unit of weight (sheqels), as is common in ancient Hebrew prose. A sheqel was equivalent to 11.3 grams. Thus, seventeen hundred sheqels is equal to 19 kilograms, or 42 pounds—an enormous amount of gold. For a convenient discussion of weights and measures in the Tanakh, see the article "Weights and Measures" in the Virtual Jewish Library.

This is far too much gold for just three hundred earrings (one from each of Gid'on's men), suggesting either that Gid'on's men numbered in the thousands in this story, or that the author simply hasn't given much thought to what three hundred earrings would actually weigh.

26d (But all Yisra'el... Gid'on and his family.): This sentence reads as a comment made as part of the second compositional stage. Apart from a few comments such as the one here and the addition of a narrative frame in several places, the Josianic editors seem to have left the pre-existing stories about Gid'on largely untouched—there are very few elements elsewhere in the story that clearly show the influence of the Josianic historians apart from the statements at places in the narrative that treat Yisra'el (or the Yisra'elites) as a unified collection of tribes.

Notes to P27

27a Yerubba'al Yo'ashsson...: This *parashah* introduces the character of Aviymelek, who does not fit the profile of the champions found in the Josianic History (Othni'el, Ehud, Devorah, Gid'on, and Jephthah). I understand all the material about Aviymelek, which consists of P27-P33, to be a Persian period addition composed by an author from Yehud. I believe that these *parashot* were written primarily to depict the dangers of leaders who were neither chosen nor approved by Yahweh, the authors' message being that such leaders must resort to murder to come to power and that ultimately Yahweh will bring retribution on them to satisfy their bloodguilt. Perhaps most interesting, however, is that within the larger story of Aviymelek, there is a polemic against the traditions of syncretistic Yahwism found in the Samarian book of Genesis and which in that book are associated with Shekem and the town of Beyth-El. See note 28a below, where I discuss this idea in more detail.

There are numerous indications that P27-P33 are not part of the editions of Judges belonging to either the Josianic History or the Israelite History. Most significantly, unlike the other material in Judges belonging to these two histories, there is no foreign oppressor, nor is there a champion who rescues Yisra'el and facilitates the Yisra'elites' return to Yahweh. The narrative of the Aviymelek story is completely at odds with the narrative structure and themes of Judges as it existed in its earliest versions: the story's focus is on a villain, not a hero, and it is concerned exclusively with the citizens of a single town rather than the people as a whole. Moreover, this is the only story in Judges where the apostasy of the Yisra'elites is connected to a specific god who is named. It is these latter two points—the focus on a single town and the focus on a single named god—that provide important clues to understanding the polemic within the Aviymelek material against syncretistic Yahwism.

27b [*the one founded by the Ezrites' ancestor*]: I understand this comment to be a late addition to the text. The comment is a gloss on Ophrah, reminding the reader that this is the Ophrah settled by the clan of Aviy'ezer. This gloss repeats the characterization of Ophrah in P20 above; see my comment in note 20d.

Notes to P28

28a they adopted Ba'al Beriyth as their god: I understand Ba'al Beriyth to be equivalent to the god El Beriyth and/or the god Beyth-El Beriyth. In abbreviated form, these gods' names are El and Bethel. The term *ba'al* simply means "lord, owner, master," and it was often used in place of a god's name as a way to show respect for the god.

There is a great deal of evidence for the gods El and Bethel in both the Tanakh and in ancient Near Eastern literature, whereas a god by the name of Ba'al Beriyth is otherwise unattested.

Specifically, it is my view that the god in the Aviymelek story in Judges, who is called Ba'al Beriyth in P28 and (Beyth) El Beriyth in P32, is identical to the gods Bethel and El Shaddai known from the Ya'aqov stories in Genesis. These two gods are mentioned in five places in the Ya'aqov stories: (1) in Gen P27,3, Ya'aqov has dream in which Yahweh appears to him and he names the place of his dream Beyth-El, which is associated with the town of Luz; (2) later in P27,3, Ya'aqov recounts a dream to his wives in which the god Beyth-El appears to him (and tells him that he is the same god who appeared to him earlier); (3) in Gen P28,1, after his return from Paddan Aram, Ya'aqov arrives at Shekem where he builds an altar named "El, god of Yisra'el;" (4) in Gen P29, Ya'aqov and his family travel to Beyth-El (=Luz), where he builds an altar and names the place "El Beyth-El" (or "[the] god Beyth-El"), which in the story is also equated to the god from P27,3; and (5) in Gen P30, El Shaddai shows himself to Ya'aqov, following which Ya'aqov erects a sacred pillar, makes an offering on it, and names the place Beyth-El. Most importantly, this last reference indicates El Shaddai and Bethel were viewed as the same god by the Genesis authors; it is also important to note that the two gods are equated in Gen P38, where Ya'aqov says El Shaddai appeared to him in Luz.

As stated above in note 27a, I believe that the material in P27-P33 contains a polemic against the syncretistic Yahwism depicted in the Samarian book of Genesis and which in that book was associated with the sites of Shekem and Beyth-El. Over the course of my translation work on the books of the Torah, I have argued that the composition of the Torah was primarily a joint effort of the priesthoods of the two principal cults of Yahweh during the Persian period—the Samarian cult on Mount Gerizim at Shekem and the Yehudean cult on Mount Zion at Yerushalem (see the introduction to my translation of Joshua for a summary of my views on this topic). The principal contributions of the Samarians were the books of Genesis and Leviticus, and the principal contributions of the Yehudeans were Deuteronomy, Exodus, and Numbers. As I have pointed out in my translations of Leviticus and Joshua, this collaborative effort required the leaders of each cult to make compromises and to allow their counterparts to include material which they did not fully accept or which they disagreed with outright. For that reason, this must have oftentimes been an uneasy partnership.

This I believe is the background for understanding the polemic against the local Shekemite god in the Aviymelek material in Judges. Relatively early on in the partnership between the cults at Mount Gerizim and Mount Zion, the leaders of the two cults agreed to share some of the books in their cult libraries, and this prompted the effort to connect the Samarian book of Genesis (likely a composition of the late eighth and early seventh centuries BCE) with the Yehudean book of Exodus-Numbers through the composition of the Yoseph narrative that today concludes Genesis. But there likely would have been some discomfort among the leadership at Mount Zion concerning the material in Genesis that reflected a merging of Yahweh with some of the local gods of Kena'an and Aram—in particular the merging of Yahweh with the Kena'anite god El (Shaddai) and with the Aramean god Bethel as known from the stories about Yisra'el's ancestor, Ya'aqov. (Perhaps our most vivid picture of the syncretism of northern Yahwism of the eighth century is provided by the Yahwistic psalms and other material known from Papyrus Amherst 63; these psalms, which K. van der Toorn has proposed reflect songs used in the eighth-century Samarian cult to Yahweh, explicitly equate Yahweh and the god Bethel. See K. van der Toorn, "The Background of the Elephantine Jews in Light of Papyrus Amherst 63" in R. Kratz and

B. Schipper (eds.), *Elephantine in Context: Studies in the History, Religion and Literature of the Judeans in Persian Period Egypt* (Tübingen: Mohr Siebeck 2022), pp 353-365.)

While this is of course wholly speculative, it is reasonable to think that during the fifth century or fourth century BCE, the leaders of the cult in Mount Zion agreed to the composition of the Aviymelek narrative and its insertion into Judges (a book not shared with their counterparts at Mount Gerizim) to assuage the concerns of individuals—perhaps including the leaders themselves—who were uncomfortable with Genesis' explicit connection of Yahweh with the gods Bethel and El (Shaddai). In previous centuries, both gods' cults were popular in many parts of Samaria, and it is possible that a cult that equated both gods may have still been active around Shekem in the Persian period. We know, for example, that during this time the Yahwistic community in Elephantine equated Yhw (their name for Yahweh) with the god Bethel, and they acknowledged the god in their cult under both names. (For a good recent discussion of the evidence for the merger of Yahweh/Yaho and Bethel, see T. Holm, "Bethel and Yahō: A Tale of Two Gods," *Journal of Ancient Near Eastern Religions* 23 (2023), pp. 25-55.)

With respect to the potential association of the god Bethel with Shekem, it is very interesting to note that Samaritan tradition identifies the site of Beyth-El (=Luz) with Mount Gerizim (which abuts Shekem)—that is, in later centuries the Samaritans themselves associated Shekem and Mount Gerizim with the Beyth-El of the Ya'aqov stories.

28b the Yisra'elites no longer honored their god Yahweh: Literally, "the Yisra'elites didn't remember their god Yahweh." The verb זכר ("remember") is sometimes used with the nuance of "honor, give reverence to," and that is how I understand the usage here. The opposite of זכר is שכח ("forget"), and to "forget one's god" is to cease to honor or revere the god. A good example of this usage of שכח is at the beginning of P11, where the author tells us the Yisra'elites "forgot their god Yahweh and did service to the Ba'als and Asherahs."

Notes to P29

29a they were persuaded to follow Aviymelek: Literally, "he turned their heart after Aviymelek." It was common in ancient Hebrew to use an active verb with an indefinite subject in place of the passive, and I believe that is the best way to understand the sentence here. I have commented frequently on this practice in my other translations; see notes 3e and 8d above.

29b seventy sheqels of silver: This is a significant sum of money. In the case law decisions preserved in Exod P37, for example, thirty sheqels is the appropriate compensation for the loss of a manservant or maidservant due to death or disability. In modern terms, a sheqel was equivalent to a little more than eleven grams; so seventy sheqels is equivalent to just under 800 grams, or 1.7 pounds. For a good discussion of weights and measures in the Tanakh, see the article "Weights & Measures" at the Jewish Virtual Library.

29c Ba'al Beriyth: I believe this is an honorific term for the god El (Beriyth), who was equated with the god Bethel (Beriyth); see note 28a above.

29d killing each of them with a single stone: Literally, "upon a single stone." The phrase appears to be a Hebrew idiom. Because the idiom is otherwise unattested, its meaning is not entirely clear.

Notes to P29,1

29,1a terebrinth post: The Hebrew is difficult, and the text may be corrupt. Literally, "the terebrinth tree [that had been] stood up." The author almost certainly intended the reader to think that this terebrinth post is the same terebrinth mentioned in Gen P16 (the "Teacher's Terebrinth" at Shekem), in Gen P29, and possibly also in Jos P55 (the text in Jos P55 reads אלה, which is vocalized as "oak," but which can also be vocalized as "terebrinth"). In Jos P55, which is by a Samarian author, this tree is associated with Yahweh's cult, as it is located "in Yahweh's sanctuary." By contrast, the author of the Aviymelek material in Judges (who seeks to disassociate Yahweh from the god Bethel/El Shaddai) has associated this tree not with the cult of Yahweh, but with the cult of Ba'al Beriyth (that is, the cult of Bethel/El Shaddai).

29,1b Mount Gerizim: Yotham stands on the Samarian cult's sacred mountain—the most holy spot in Samarian Yahwism during the Persian period, the place "that Yahweh chose" for his name—to deliver what is effectively a curse upon the citizens of Shekem and the nearby town of Beyth Millo. Our author views Mount Gerizim in a positive light, unlike the terebrinth in Shekem. Mount Gerizim is the place where Yotham delivers a curse heard by "God." The terebrinth is the place where the Shekemites make Aviymelek their king.

The mention of Mount Gerizim here makes most sense if we understand the Aviymelek material to be a Persian period composition. It is more difficult to understand the mention of Mount Gerizim in this passage if we take the Aviymelek material to be part of the Josianic History or the Israelite History, because there is no evidence for Mount Gerizim's special role prior to the Persian period. (In my translation of Deuteronomy, I viewed the mention of Mount Gerizim in Deut P24,2 as one of the early sixth-century BCE expansions to the book; however, I now think it more likely that this material dates to the Persian period, when there was close collaboration between the priesthoods at Mount Gerizim and Mount Zion on the books of the Torah.)

29,1c so that God may hear about you: Yotham here alludes to the fact that the Shekemites believed Yahweh was present on Mount Gerizim. Yotham is letting the Shekemites know that because he is denouncing them from atop Mount Gerizim, God (that is, Yahweh) will hear his denunciation. The construction שמע אל typically means "listen to," but it sometimes—as here—has the meaning "hear about." See BDB, p. 1033, def. 1c and 1d.

29,1d take shelter in my shade: The author intends the reader to find the conclusion to his parable humorous. No reasonable person would seek out a thornbush for shade or shelter.

29,1e A fire sparked from a thornbush consumes mighty cedars: The thornbush threatens his future subjects by quoting what was almost certainly a well-known proverb. I have recast the proverb's wording so that it reads naturally in English. A literal translation of the proverb is "A fire goes forth from a thornbush, and it consumes Levanon's cedars." The point of the proverb is that the most insignificant thing—such as sparks from a fire in a thornbush—can destroy the mightiest things.

29,1f So now, have you acted... Have you treated... or have you dealt: The particle אם is sometimes used to begin a question where the expected answer is "no." In certain instances, as here, the particle is repeated to express two or more closely related questions (all expecting a "no" answer). For other examples of the repeated use of אם in this fashion, see BDB, p. 50, def. 2a (*a*).

29,1g 'a fire will spark': Yotham quotes the first words of the proverb spoken by the thornbush to drive home the point of his parable that neither Shekem nor Beyth Millo will be happy with Aviymelek as their king, nor he with them as his subjects, and the result will be the destruction of them all.

Notes to P30

30a Aviymelek ruled over Yisra'el: It is noteworthy that the author avoids specifically calling Aviymelek king; he uses the verb שרר ("rule, be a chief, be a prince") rather than מלך ("reign, serve as king"). Also worth noting is that the verb מלך is used throughout Yotham's parable in P29,1.

30b atop the mountains: The author likely means the mountainous area directly to the east of Shekem; the reference almost certainly does not include either Mount Eval or Mount Gerizim, which abut the town respectively to the north and south.

Notes to P31

31a showed up: The author's use of the verb בוא ("come, go, arrive, enter") in this sentence is a little unusual. Typically the verb בוא is followed by a mention of where the subject of the verb is arriving or entering, unless the location is obvious from context. Here, however, the location is not obvious, yet there is no mention of the place arrived at.

31b their god's temple, where they ate and drank: That is, the temple of Ba'al Beriyth (=the temple of the god Bethel/El Shaddai). Recall from P28 that the Yisra'elites at this time have abandoned Yahweh and adopted Ba'al Beriyth as their god. Furthermore, recall from P29 that Ba'al Beriyth's temple appears to be located near Shekem. In P32, we learn that the *tzeriah* of the god Beyth El Beriyth (or, if we choose a different translation strategy, the *tzeriah* of the temple of the god El Beriyth) is atop Mount Tzalmon. This structure (whatever the word *tzeriah* means) is almost certainly part of the compound where the temple referred to in P29 and here in P31 is also located.

It is worth noting that this celebration in the god's temple is the festival of the annual harvest—a festival that was sometimes conjoined with the new year's festival. As celebrating the vintage was part of the annual harvest festival, we should imagine that it was common for the celebrants to get quite inebriated. There is, in fact, a fascinating picture of the drunken celebration of the harvest festival within Yahweh's cult in one of the Yahwistic "psalms" in Papyrus Amherst 63. This document dates to the fourth century BCE and represents a compilation of different hymns and stories from foreign communities in Egypt, including a community that acknowledged Yhw (=Yahweh) as their principal god. The three Yahwistic psalms in the papyrus, which may reflect traditions stretching back several centuries, show notable Samarian influences (including the identification of Yhw with the god Bethel). The harvest festival/new year's festival psalm is worth quoting in full (the following translation is adapted from R. Steier and C. Nims, *The Aramaic Text in Demotic Script: Text, Translation, and Notes*, 2017):

> "Listen to me, my god and my king: fine young sheep—
>   we offer up to you alone among the gods!
> Out of all the people's divinities, our banquet honors only you—
>   yes lord, you alone, out of all the people's divinities!
> The people bless you, my lord—your yearly offering we take in hand.
> Get drunk, my god, from this pitcher—I fill it with new wine, towering father!
> The merciful one, Yaho, my benefactor—a vat of wine they pour into cups.
> So from silver cups drink, Yaho! Yes, from a thousand bountiful basins!
>   Get drunk, my lord, from the bounty of men!
> Musicians stand in attendance upon the lord with songs of the harp!
>   Songs of the lyre and songs of the harp you let me hear—
>   things sweet to the ears, at the banquets of mortal men!

31c Who is Aviymelek and who the Shekemites...: The author's statement in the previous sentence that the celebration at the temple involved drinking and insults against Aviymelek makes it clear that we should understand Ga'al's speech here to be drunken braggadocio.

31d Isn't he Yerubba'al's son and Zevul just his henchman?: Ga'al belittles both Aviymelek and Zevul—Aviymelek isn't a proper ruler, he is just one of Yerubba'al's many sons, and Zevul is a mere henchman of Aviymelek, not a proper town leader.

The literal meaning of the word פקיד is "appointee," but as the context (Ga'al's drunken speech) calls for a term of derision, I have translated as "henchman."

31e Shekem's founder Hemor: For Hemor, see Gen P28,2. The author of this *parashah* appears to know of a different tradition about Hemor than that preserved in Genesis. The author here assumes that Hemor is still revered in Shekem and has many descendants living in town. But in Genesis, Shim'on and Lewiy kill Hemor, his son Shekem, and every male in the entire town, in revenge for Shekem's rape of their sister Diynah. The inconsistency between the two traditions about Hemor is striking, and it is likely due to the Genesis author departing from the tradition in his story in order to make a larger theological point about the issue of intermarriage.

31f Make your army even larger, and then go and shit yourself: There is a pun in the Hebrew that is difficult to capture in English. Literally, "Enlarge your army, and then come out [to fight]!" But the masculine singular imperative for the verb יצא ("go out") is identical to the word for feces (צֵאָה). In imagining this scene, the reader should keep in mind that Ga'al has been feasting and drinking copious amounts of wine in celebration of the vintage. The author almost certainly intended the reader to understand that Ga'al is drunk.

31g surreptitiously: Translation of תרמה (which occurs only here in the Tanakh) from context. The root of the word indicates some such meaning as "deceitfully, craftily, with false intent," which is not far from my translation "surreptitiously." But the text may be corrupt; see BDB, p. 941. The change of a single letter would make the clause read, "So he sent messengers to Aviymelek in Arumah." We know from the end of P31 that Aviymelek is staying in the village of Arumah.

Recall that Zevul is a close ally of Aviymelek. He would have needed to act surreptitiously because Ga'al Evedsson has won over the Shekemites, and they might harm him if they learned he was informing on Ga'al to Aviymelek.

31h securing the town against you: Literally, "binding the town against you." The root is צור (besiege, bind), but possibly the author had the root צרר (tie up) in mind. But neither verb is otherwise used in this fashion in the Tanakh, and the text may be corrupt.

31i bring the full brunt of your power against him: The author's prose here is highly idiomatic. More literally, "you should do to him in accord with what your hand finds." The phrase "what your hand finds" is a common Hebrew idiom meaning "as much as you are able, to the full extent of your abilities."

31j Aviymelek and all his men...: The Leningrad Codex has a "closed" blank space before this sentence to indicate the beginning of a new *parashah setumah*.

31k "Look!" repeated Ga'al: The Leningrad Codex has a "closed" blank space before this sentence to indicate the beginning of a new *parashah setumah*.

31l the Soothsayers' Terebrinth: It is unclear whether this is identical with the terebrinth in P29, or whether it is a different terebrinth.

31m Aren't those the troops that you mocked?: Zevul reminds Ga'al of his drunken insult of Aviymelek and his army at the celebration at the temple, when he proclaimed that Aviymelek should "make his army even larger, and then go and shit himself."

The word that I translate as "mock" is מאס, the core meaning of which is "reject, detest, despise." But in contexts where the verb is used in relation to spoken words, the meaning shades into something close to "deride, disdain, mock." See, for example, Job 19.18, where מאס is used in parallel with דבר ב ("speak against, verbally attack, criticize"). See BDB, p. 181, def. 4d.

31n And so Ga'al marched out...: The Leningrad Codex has a "closed" blank space before this sentence to indicate the beginning of a new *parashah setumah*.

31o Arumah: Possibly this is the name of a village near Aviymelek's home town of Shekem. See note 31g above.

31p Zevul having driven Ga'al and his kinsmen out...: The narrative is confused, but the text does not appear to be corrupt. It was Aviymelek, not Zevul, who drove away Ga'al and his kinsmen. Possibly the entire clause is a late addition to the text, but if so, the rationale for the addition is unclear.

31q —: The Leningrad Codex does not have a *parashah* break here.

Notes to P31,1

31,1a as was their normal practice: This phrase is not in the Hebrew. I have added it to provide the necessary context for the reader—context that would not have been needed by ancient readers. The people are leaving the town to work in the pastures and farmland surrounding the town, as they do every day.

31,1b they stood outside the entrance to the town gate while two of the gangs carried out raids: Aviymelek has divided his men into three gangs. One gang guards the town gate to prevent anyone from entering or leaving, while the other two gangs attack and kill all the townspeople who are working in the surrounding fields.

Notes to P32

32a Shekem Tower: I understand Shekem Tower to be another name for Beyth Millo (mentioned in P29,1). The term *millo'* (מלוא) means "citadel, fortification," and the term usually translated as "tower" (מגדל) is often used in reference to a citadel or imposing fort.

32b the *tzeriah* of Beyth El Beriyth: The word *tzeriah* (צריח) is obscure, and the meaning is uncertain. The word appears only here and in Sam P25 (where I translated as "hollows"). BDB, p. 863, proposes "underground chamber" based on the usage in Samuel. However, given the large size of the *tzeriah* here in P32 (the author tells us one thousand people were inside it), I think it more likely that the author of the Aviymelek story used it to refer to an above-ground structure—perhaps some sort of fort or treasure house where the god's possessions were stored.

I understand the phrase *beyth el beriyth* (בית אל ברית) to be the name of a god. Specifically, this god is identical with Ba'al Beriyth mentioned in P29, and—most importantly—this god is also identical with the god Bethel known from the Ya'aqov traditions in Genesis and mentioned in Jer 48.13. (As discussed above in note 28a, the Genesis authors equate this god with El Shaddai.) It is also possible to read the phrase as בית אל ברית as "the temple of El Beriyth," in which case it would refer specifically to El Shaddai. But regardless of how one understands the phrase, I believe the god being referenced is the god of Ya'aqov mentioned in Genesis: Bethel, who is also known as El Shaddai.

It's worth noting here that in both the Aleppo Codex and the Leningrad Codex, the phrase בית אל ברית is spread across two lines. In both manuscripts, בית is the final word of one line, and אל begins a new line. The fact that בית and אל were not kept together on the same line suggests that the Masoretes understood the phrase בית אל ברית as "the temple of El Beriyth."

32c Mount Tzalmon: The shrine of Beyth El Beriyth (or El Beriyth) must have been located atop Mount Tzalmon. Mount Tzalmon has not been identified, but it must have been one of the mountains just to the east of Shekem (Mount Eval lies immediately to the north of Shekem, and Mount Gerizim lies immediately to the south). The village of Shekem Tower likely lay at the foot of Mount Tzalmon.

32d Taking axes in hand: The plural "axes" is nonsensical, and there may be an error in the text. BDB, p. 899, proposes removing the final letter of the word, which would produce the reading "his ax."

32e also died: By writing "also," the author reminds the reader that the inhabitants of both Shekem and Shekem Tower are dead. With the immolation of the residents of Shekem Tower, the curse of Yotham at the end of P29,1 has come to pass: "'A fire will spark' from Aviymelek and consume the citizens of Shekem and Beyth Millo."

33a Aviymelek next went to Tevetz...: This *parashah* is the account of Aviymelek's death and the conclusion to the Aviymelek material. The mention of the town of Tevets comes out of the blue, and the author may have felt he had to include Tevetz in his account because the story of Aviymelek's death was so well known. (It is clear that the story of his death must have been famous, for it is referenced in Sam P84,2.) There is no reason to suppose that Tevetz is necessarily near Shekem. The entire story of Aviymelek in P27 - P33 reads as a literary composition, and the Shekem setting is essential for one of the author's larger purposes, which was to attack the syncretistic practices that equated Yahweh and the god Bethel/El Shaddai (and for which Genesis provided some support). But there is not necessarily any connection between Shekem and Tevetz.

33b a woman on the roof threw a mill-stone...it shattered his skull: I have added the phrase "on the roof" as normal English usage requires some information about the woman's location; this is not required in Hebrew. It is interesting to note the parallel with Ya'el's murder of Siysera, whose skull was "smashed" and "obliterated." It is likely that the parallel was intentional on the part of the author.

33c Take out your sword and finish me off...: Compare the account of Aviymelek's death with the two accounts of Sha'ul's death in Sam P64 and Sam P66.

33d When the Yisra'elites saw...they all returned home: The author has included this sentence as part of his conclusion in order to integrate the story of Aviymelek into the larger structure narrative of Judges. The effect, however, is very awkward, as prior to this point the entire story has focused wholly on Shekem and Beyth Millo and their citizens.

33e God brought punishment upon Shekem's citizens for their wickedness: Their wickedness consists of both supporting Aviymelek's murder of his brothers and making Ba'al Beriyth (=Beyth-El Beriyth/El Beriyth=Bethel/El Shaddai) their god.

33f Yotham Yerubba'alsson's curse about them came to pass: I have recast the Hebrew into natural-sounding English. More literally, "Yotham Yerubba'al's curse happened to them." Recall from the end of P29,1 that Yotham declared "a fire will spark" from Aviymelek and consume the citizens of Shekem and Beyth Millo. (For the equivalence of Shekem Tower and Beyth Millo, see note 32a above.)

Notes to P33

Note to P34	**34a Tola Pu'ahsson Dodosson...:** This short *parashah* was most likely added in Judges' fourth compositional stage as part of the numerous early expansions made to the text during the fifth century BCE. I believe that as part of the work in this stage of Judges, the authors and editors wished to create a comprehensive record of the period before the establishment of the monarchy, and this involved the addition of material about several champions about whom little was otherwise known: Shamgar Anathsson (P13), Tola Pu'ahsson Dodosson here in P34, Ya'iyr the Gil'adite (P35), Ivtzan from Beyth Lehem (P46), Eylon the Zevulunite (P47), and Avdon Hillelsson the Pir'athonite (P48).
Notes to P35	**35a Succeeding him was Ya'iyr the Gil'adite...:** Ya'iyr is also mentioned at the end of Num P87 (which I understand as a Hellenistic period addition to Numbers).
	35b [*That is, they owned thirty jackasses.*]: I understand the sentence I have placed in brackets to be a late comment added to the text; the purpose of the addition possibly was to correct the text, to inform the reader that Ya'iyr's sons owned the jackasses, but didn't necessarily ride them. Alternatively, the phrase may be an unusual example of dittography. If we take this to be the case, one would translate, "He had thirty sons who rode thirty jackasses. thirty jackasses. They They were called 'Ya'iyr's Hamlets,' as they still are today, which are in the Gil'ad region."
	35c They were called 'Ya'iyr's Hamlets,' as they still are today, which are in the Gil'ad region: This sentence fits very awkwardly into the *parashah*. I believe it is a very late addition to the text from Judges' sixth compositional stage, made under the influence of references to Ya'iyr Hamlets in Num P87, Deut P1,4, and Jos P27,1. All the mentions of Ya'iyr's Hamlets, with the exception of Jos P27,1, appear to me to be very late additions.
Notes to P36	**36a The Yisra'elites once again did what Yahweh considered the worst thing...:** This *parashah* (P36) and P37 introduce the story of the Yiphtah, whose story concluded the Josianic History's version of Judges. In setting up the final story of their book, the Josianic historians have written a lengthy introduction that serves as a book-end to the lengthy set-piece that they wrote at the beginning of their book in P9.
	36b subjects of the Philishtines and the Ammonites. They crushed: The Philishtines do not appear anywhere in the story of Yiphtah, and I believe the mention of them here as the oppressors of the Yisra'elites is a late addition to the text. The addition may have been prompted by the mention of the Philishtines' gods earlier in the *parashah* or by the mention of the Philistines in the (corrupt) first part of P37.
	The Masoretes always added a marginal note in their texts marking the midpoint of each book. In Judges, they added that note (חצי הספר) here in reference to the sentence beginning "They crushed" (וירעצו).
	36c the Ammonites crossed the Yarden to go to war with Yehudah, Binyamin, and the people of Ephrayim, putting Yisra'el in great distress: The stories associated with Yiphtah in P39 - 45 are concerned only with the war between the Ammonites and Gil'ad. I think it is likely that the Josianic historians here in P36 have included the mention of tribes living west of the Yarden to make the stories of Yiphtah fit their broader theme about the collective identity of the tribes under the name "Yisra'el." Without the addition of other tribes, it would not be possible for them to present Yiphtah as a champion of Yisra'el.
Notes to P37	**37a Didn't from Egypt and from the Amorites...:** Unfortunately, the beginning of this *parashah* is confusing to the reader because language appears to have fallen from the text in two places: after "from Egypt," and also after "the Philishtines." The

original text may have read something like, "Didn't I take you out of Egypt and didn't I save you from the Amorites?" [הלא ממצרים העליתיכם ומן־האמרי הושעתיכם] The mention of Egypt of course is a reference to the exodus traditions. The mention of the Amorite threat is a reference to the wilderness wandering traditions, in which the Yisra'elites fought and defeated the Amorite kings Siyhon and Og. (On the mentions of the Ammonites and the Philishtines in this sentence, see note 37b directly below.)

This *parashah*, P37, is best understood when read in conjunction P9. Just as the Josianic historians laid out their theme near the beginning of their book in P9, so here in P37 in the preface to the stories about their book's final champion, they make their concluding statement about the period prior to the monarchy: Yahweh has at last lost patience with his people, who have repeatedly abandoned him for other gods despite his saving them time and again from their oppressors. Yahweh's statement that "I won't rescue you again" should be understood as the Josianic historians' attempt to show Yahweh acknowledging the inadequacy of the model in which individual "champions" serve as the chief means of protecting his people, thus paving the way for the adoption of a new institution to serve this purpose—that of the monarchy. It is fitting that the Josianic historians have placed Yiphtah's story last, as he is the most problematic and flawed of the five champions in their version of the book (Othni'el, Ehud, Devorah, Gid'on, and Yiphtah). He is a son of a prostitute who is rejected by his family (P39), his associates are "good-for-nothing men" (P39), he relishes and encourages conflict (P45), and he initiates a civil war among the tribes (P45). Moreover, it is noteworthy that Yiphtah is the only one of the five champions about whom the Josianic historians omit the statement that "there was tranquility in the land" during his time.

37b [*and from the Ammonites and the Philishtines*]: I understand the references to the Ammonites and Philishtines here to be late additions to the text; because of the corruption of first half of this *parashah*, the purpose of the addition and what the author wanted to say in it is unclear. It should be noted that at this point in the narrative, the Yisra'elites have yet to be saved from either people: they are not saved from the Ammonites until P43, and the conflict with the Philishtines doesn't occur until the story of Shimshon, which begins in P52.

37c when the Tziydonians and Amaleq and Ma'on oppressed you, you cried out to me: The mention of the Tziydonians is likely an addition from the fifth compositional stage, made to harmonize this *parashah* (P37) with the mention of the Tziydonians in P10. The Tziydonians are mentioned in the story of the Danites' relocation to Layish in P61 - P63, but there is no mention of the Tziydonians oppressing the Yisra'elites. Rather, the Danites launch an unprovoked attack on Layish (which is portrayed as an isolated Tziydonian outpost located far from its mother city).

The mention of Ma'on is nonsensical, and many scholars—including myself—believe that it is likely an error for Midyan. Recall that Midyan and Amaleq were the Yisra'elites' oppressors in the story of Gid'on beginning in P17. The mention here in P37 that the Yisra'elites cried out to Yahweh is an allusion to the concluding sentence of P17.

37d "We've done wrong!" the Yisra'elites said...: I believe the text from here to the end of the *parashah* was not part of the Josianic History, but was added during the fifth compositional stage. In the earliest version of Judges, the Josianic historians needed to show the inadequacy of the "champion" model in order to lay the groundwork for the establishment of the monarchy in the book of Samuel. Thus, in the Josianic History's version of P37, the *parashah* likely ended with Yahweh's statement that he "won't rescue" the Yisra'elites again and that the Yisra'elites should rely on the gods they've chosen to save them. In the following *parashot*, Yiphtah does rescue the Yisra'elites from the Ammonites, but it is noteworthy that in the material about Yiphtah that I attribute to the Josianic History, Yahweh does not choose or "raise up" Yiphtah as a champion, nor does Yahweh speak to him. This must have been a conscious choice of the Josianic historians, as for all other champions in their book, Yahweh either chooses the champion (Othni'el and Ehud), speaks to the champion indirectly (Devorah the prophetess) or speaks to the champion directly (Gid'on).

The five places in the Yiphtah stories where Yahweh is somehow involved in Yiphtah's actions are all from other compositional stages. The scene in P40 in which Yiphtah invokes Yahweh's name in agreeing to lead Gil'ad against the Ammonites and the statements in P43 and P45 that Yahweh "delivered" the Ammonites into Yiphtah's hands are all clearly from the Josianic historians' source material, and they must have felt it would be wrong to delete or alter that material. In P42, Yahweh's power is said to "fill" Yiphtah, but that entire parashah is a late addition from the fifth compositional stage. And P41, in which Yiphtah recounts Yahweh's great deeds to the Ammonites' king, is an expansion from the fourth compositional stage that was influenced by the versions of the books of the Torah (specifically Numbers and Deuteronomy) that existed in the authors' day.

37e from their communities: The Hebrew phrase is מקרבם ("from their midst"). The preposition קרב is frequently used in the book of Deuteronomy with the meaning "community," and that is exactly how the preposition is used here. This usage of the preposition is not seen elsewhere in material associated with the Josianic historians, and thus the usage here offers additional support for the view that this portion of the *parashah* is a later addition to the text. On the distinctive use of the preposition in Deuteronomy, see note 21,5b in my translation of Deuteronomy and note 56j in my translation of Exodus.

Note to P38

38a Let him be the leader: The imperfect verbal form in ancient Hebrew is sometimes used with the force of the jussive, as here. On the use of the imperfect in place of the jussive, see GKC § 107 *n*.

Notes to P39

39a our father's wealth: The noun בית ("house") is often used with the meaning of "personal property, possessions," and that is how I understand the word's use here. See BDB, p. 110, def. 6.

39b your mother's a foreigner: Literally, "you are the son of a foreign woman." The adjective אחרת ("another") is often used with the meaning "strange, alien, foreign," which is how the author uses it here.

39c some good-for-nothing men: This detail is unusual insofar as these men do not appear later in the story of Yiphtah. It is possible there were one or more stories about Yiphtah that involved these men, but if so, the Josianic historians and their successors did not see fit to use those stories for their book of Judges.

39d went out on missions: The verb יצא ("go out") is often used as military terminology to mean "go on a campaign" or "go on a mission," and that is how I understand the use of the verb here. See note 9g above.

Notes to P40

40a summon: For this use of לקח, see BDB, p. 543, def. 6.

40b Didn't you in fact oppose my lawsuit: Literally, "Didn't you hate me?" In ancient Hebrew legal terminology, the verb שנא ("hate") denoted the act of opposing a person in a legal action, and the participle form of the verb ("hater") was the term for one's legal adversary. I believe that this is the use of the verb here. Yiphtah is referring to his being disinherited from his family, which must have involved a lawsuit to adjudicate the dispute. His response suggests that Gil'ad's elders supported his family members in the legal dispute resulting in his disinheritance.

40c Let Yahweh be the judge: The author uses the construction שמע בין ("hear between"), which is a legal idiom meaning "to hear [i.e. judge] a legal dispute." A literal translation of the Hebrew is "Yahweh will be the one who hears between us"—that is, Yahweh will hear the legal case that Yiphtah would bring against the elders for not keeping their part of the agreement. The elders make this statement to Yiphtah to reassure him that he can trust their intentions toward him.

On the use of the imperfect in place of the jussive, see note 38a above and GKC § 107 *n*.

40d whereupon Yiphtah repeated all his demands in front of Yahweh there in Mitzpah: The author here portrays Yiphtah as distrusting Gil'ad's elders (recall that they supported his family in the lawsuit over his disinheritance). In order to hold the elders accountable to their agreement that he will be their leader if he returns and fights the Ammonites, he goes to Yahweh's shrine in Mitzpah where he formally recites the terms of his agreement with the elders in Yahweh's presence. This will ensure that Yahweh will "be the judge" if the elders don't do as they say.

In the Israelite History, the phrase "in front of Yahweh" often means "in front of the treaty chest," and in the Persian-period layers of the Torah, the phrase often means "in front of the Meeting Tent." But neither the treaty chest nor the Meeting Tent play a role in the early material in Judges, and the phrase here must refer either to Yahweh's shrine at Mitzpah, or to the altar in front of his shrine there. It is worth noting that Mitzpah is east of the Yarden River, and for the authors of both the Josianic History and the Israelite History, it could not be "the place that Yahweh chooses."

41a Yiphtah sent envoys to the Ammonites' king...: This entire *parashah* alludes to the events of Numbers, and it is dependent on the accounts of these events given in both Numbers and Deuteronomy. The *parashah* is not necessary to the story of Yiphtah, and I believe it is an addition to the text from a Persian period edition of the book. The author of the *parashah* borrows language directly from the versions of Deuteronomy and Numbers known to him, and he alludes to the story of Mo'av's king Balaq Tzipporsson, which I argue in my translation of Numbers is an early Persian period addition to the text. If that argument is accepted, then this *parashah* in Judges must also date to the Persian period and cannot have been part of either the Josianic History or the exilic Israelite History.

Notes to P41

41b Yisra'el took my land... The lands between the Arnon, the Yabboq, and the Yarden: The Ammonites' king's reference to these lands may be confusing to the reader. For context, it is important to remember that in the account of the Yisra'elites' taking of the land east of the Yarden in Deut P1,4, it is the Amorites who occupy "the lands between the Arnon, the Yabboq, and the Yarden," whereas the Ammonites live to the east of these lands. By claiming that Yisra'el took his land and that this land consists of the area between the Arnon, the Yabboq, and the Yarden, the Ammonites' king is picking a fight with the Yisra'elites in order to claim the former lands of the Amorites as his own.

41c "Thus says Yiphtah: 'Yisra'el took neither Mo'av nor the Ammonites' country...: Yiphtah in his response reminds the Ammonites' king that the Yisra'elites did not take any of the Ammonites' land, but rather took land occupied by the Amorites. (In Deut P1,3, Yahweh tells Mosheh that the Yisra'elites must "skirt to the side of the Ammonites" and not "engage them in hostilities;" and so they did: we are told in Deut P1,4 that the Yisra'elites "didn't go near the Ammonites' land.")

41d they travelled in the desert wilderness as far as the Reed Sea, and then they went to Qadesh: The reference to the Reed Sea is an allusion to the story in Exodus P23 - P26; the reference to Qadesh is an allusion to Num P68 (the beginning of which is part of the oldest layer of Numbers).

41e When Yisra'el sent envoys to Edom's king...: This statement alludes to the story in Num P69,2.

41f Likewise, they sent envoys to Mo'av's king...: There is no story preserved in either Numbers or Deuteronomy that fits the reference to Mo'av here. It is unclear to me whether such a story ever existed. The king of Mo'av, Balaq Tzipporsson, is the subject of the story of Bil'am and Balaq in Numbers P72,1, but in that story Yisra'el does not send envoys or interact in any way with Balaq.

41g Then they resumed their travels... Yisra'el sent envoys to the Amorites' king Siyhon... the desert and the Yarden: The events in this entire paragraph refer to the itinerary in Num P71 and the story of Siyhon's defeat in Num P72.

41h the region north of the Arnon: Literally, "the region beyond the Arnon." In the itinerary described by the author, the Yisra'elites are coming from the south and have travelled to the east to go around Mo'av and make camp after crossing north of the Arnon. (The Arnon served as the northern border of Mo'av.)

41i between the Arnon and the Yabboq and between the desert and the Yarden: Yiphtah here defines the borders of the land taken by the Yisra'elites and which Mosheh later granted to the tribes of Re'uven and Gad. The Wadi Arnon is the southern border and the Wadi Yabboq the northern border; the Yarden serves as the western border and the desert as the eastern border. This description of the territory taken by the Yisra'elites closely mirrors the description of the land taken in Deut P1,4.

41j are you really going to be more successful than Mo'av's king Balaq Tzipporsson: Yiphtah here alludes to the story of Balaq and Bil'am in Num P72,1, in which Balaq is unsuccessful in convincing the famous diviner Bil'am to curse Yisra'el. In my translation of Numbers, I argued that the story of Balaq and Bil'am is not original to Numbers, but was added in the late sixth or early fifth century BCE. The fact that Yiphtah here alludes to the late story in Numbers offers strong support for understanding this *parashah* (P41) as a Persian period addition to Judges.

41k Did he in fact engage Yisra'el in battle, or did he actually go to war with them?: This is a rhetorical question. In the story in Num P72,1, Balaq did not go to war with Yisra'el, a fact which Yiphtah alludes to here. It is interesting to note, however, that Jos P54 (a relatively late Persian period addition to Joshua written by authors associated with the cult at Mount Gerizim) does make mention of a tradition in which Balaq went to war with Yisra'el.

41l For three hundred years: Yiphtah here uses a large round number; the number does not imply anything specific about the author's views on the chronology of the period between the occupation of the land and Yiphtah's time. In the chronology in Judges (which is the product of multiple compositional layers), 319 years pass between Yehoshua's death and Yiphtah's ascension as leader of Gil'ad.

Notes to P42

42a Yahweh's power filled Yiphtah...: This *parashah* and P44 belong together—they tell the story of Yiphtah's sacrifice of his only daughter to Yahweh in fulfillment of a vow. I believe these *parashot* are not original to the text, but are additions from the late Persian period or Hellenistic period. During this period, the books of the Torah and the Prophets had come to be viewed as authoritative in Yehud and in the diaspora communities. Because of their authoritative status, these books attracted numerous additional legends and stories that the leaders of Yahweh's cult and the stewards of the temple library understood to make important theological points, to be ancient, or simply to have great merit and to be worthy of preservation.

42b whoever is the one who opens the door and comes out of my house...that person will be given over to Yahweh: I have departed further than usual from the Hebrew to express the underlying idea naturally in English. Literally, "and it will happen the one coming out who exits from the doors of my house...he will belong to Yahweh."

43a Yiphtah crossed into the Ammonites' territory...: In the Josianic History, this *parashah* followed directly from P40. As I discuss in notes 41a and 42a above, I understand both P41 and P42 to be additions from later compositional stages.

Notes to P43

43b by the Yisra'elites: The author writes the phrase מפני בני ישראל ("from before the Yisra'elites"). When used with verbs describing military actions (such as "strike," "defeat," etc.), the prepositions מפני ("from before") and לפני ("in front of") indicate agency and are best translated as "by." I have commented on this use of these prepositions frequently in my other translations. See note 15m above.

44a Yiphtah arrived at his house in Mitzpah: Recall that Yiphtah does not live in Mitzpah—he has been driven away from there and resides in the land of Tov (see P39). As stated above in note 42a, I view both P42 and P44 as additions to the text. It is odd, however, that the author of this addition decided to relocate Yiphtah to Mitzpah. Perhaps the author assumed that when Yiphtah became Gil'ad's leader in P40, he would have moved back to his family home.

Notes to P44

44b You're not to blame, but you're why I'm in such agony: I have departed futher than usual from the Hebrew to express the idea in natural English. Literally, "You yourself are among those who cause me trouble."

44c to share stories: The meaning of the verb תנה, which only occurs twice in the Tanakh, is uncertain. BDB, p. 1072, proposes "recount" on the basis of the meaning of this verbal root in Syriac. I have based my translation on BDB's proposal.

44d **: The Leningrad Codex has a *parashah setumah* here.

45a The men of Ephrayim took up arms...: I view this *parashah* as the concluding story of the Josianic History's version of Judges. In this story, the Josianic historians illustrate the failure of the "champion" model, which is wholly dependent on the personal character of the champion. The conclusion to the Yiphtah material thus provides an appropriate set-up for the book of Samuel, in which the Josianic historians tell of how Yahweh agrees to replace the champion model with the institution of kingship and, most importantly, how Yahweh came to choose Dawid and his descendants as the leaders of all his people, both the northern and southern tribes.

Notes to P45

45b Why did you go to fight...without inviting us to go with you?: It is interesting to compare Yiphtah's response to the challenge here by the Ephrayimites with Gid'on's response to the challenge by the Ephrayimites in P24. Gid'on is the model of a great leader, and he handles the challenge with great skill and diplomacy. By contrast, Yiphtah reveals his rash nature in his response, and he provokes great destruction with it. Both stories offer lessons in leadership that would be appropriate as part of a king's education.

45c if I had summoned you, you wouldn't have saved me: I understand this sentence to be a conditional. Conditional sentences in Hebrew do not necessarily require a conditional particle such as אם ("if"). On conditional sentences without a conditional particle, see GKC § 159 *b-k*.

45d and even the Ammonites: Yiphtah's mention of the Ammonites here is jarring. If the text is not corrupt, Yiphtah is telling the Ephrayimites that he isn't afraid of their threat—he and his people like a good fight, and they should keep in mind that he has just defeated the Ammonites, who themselves are quite combative by nature.

45e you couldn't save me: Yiphtah uses the phrase אינך מושיע. The particle אין is often used in contexts where an English speaker would say something is "impossible," and that is the usage here. On this use of אין, see note 17c above.

45f And Yahweh did deliver them into my hands: This statement was likely in the source used by the Josianic historians. It is not by the Josianic historians themselves, who in the material they composed have sought to minimize Yahweh's support of Yiphtah. See the discussion in note 37d above.

45g Ephrayim's trash: I have departed from the literal meaning of the Hebrew to reflect that the statement is meant to be an insult. Literally, "Ephrayim's escapees"—that is, people who have been rejected by Ephrayim and who have thus sought a life elsewhere.

45h [*Now Gil'ad was located between Ephrayim and Menashsheh.*]: This sentence is a comment from the sixth compositional stage. The author of the comment is reminding the reader of the geography of the region. Gil'ad lies east of the Yarden River and is directly south of eastern Menashsheh; Gil'ad is also directly east of the territory of Ephrayim, which is located on west side of the Yarden River. Thus, Gil'ad is "between" Ephrayim and Menashsheh.

45i some "trash" fleeing Ephrayim: The language here repeats the phrase used in Ephrayim's insult of Gil'ad. Literally, "Ephrayim's escapees"—פליטי אפרים. The author uses the insulting language here ironically—the phrase is applied to genuine refugees from Ephrayim who are fleeing the conflict with Gil'ad, but the sentence is written from the perspective of the Gil'adites, who view Ephrayim as their enemy.

45j (because he wasn't able to speak the correct sound): That is, people from Ephrayim spoke a Hebrew dialect that did not have the sound that in linguistics is called the voiceless palato-alveolar fricative (or, in plain English, the "sh" sound). In its place, speakers of the Ephrayimite dialect of Hebrew used the voiceless alveolar sibilant (in plain English, the "s" sound).

45k somewhere in Gil'ad: The author does not know where Yiphtah is buried. A literal translation of the author's language is "in the towns of Gil'ad."

Notes to P46

46a Beyth Lehem: It is unclear if this is the Beyth Lehem in Yehudah, or a Beyth Lehem in some other tribal territory.

46b he married off to foreigners: My translation reflects my belief that the first word of the sentence must have fallen from the text due to the principle of haplography (a copying error in which a scribe omits a word or phrase identical to or resembling an adjacent word or phrase). I believe the word ובנותיו ("and his daughters") originally appeared before שלח החוצה; the appropriate translation with the insertion of the lost word would be "His daughters he married off to foreigners." It's worth noting that the phrase שלח החוצה is an idiom; its literal meaning is "he sent to the outside" (that is, outside the kin group within which marriages were normally arranged). We should presume that the author intended the reader to understand that Ivtzan made marriage alliances with powerful non-Yisra'elite families who lived outside Kena'an as a way to ensure Yisra'el was never threatened with an attack by foreigners.

48a in the territory of Ephrayim in the Amaleqite mountains: The adjective "Amaleqite" is nonsensical in this context, and the text may be in error. The Amaleqites were a desert people who lived beyond the southern border of Kena'an. It seems unlikely that a group of mountains in Ephrayim—far to the north of the Amaleqites' land—would be associated with this people.

Note to P48

49a The Yisra'elites once again did what Yahweh considered the worst thing...: I understand this *parashah* to be the conclusion of the Josianic History's version of the book of Judges. The *parashah* sets up the action for the early scenes of the book of Samuel, in which the priest and champion (and later, prophet) Shmu'el rescues the Yisra'elites from the Philishtines.

The stories about Shimshon (P50 - P58), Miykayehu and the Danites (P59 - P63), and the Lewite's concubine and the war with the Binyaminites (P64 - P74,2) were not part of the Josianic History but were added during the fourth and fifth compositional stages of the book.

Note to P49

50a There was a certain man...His wife was barren...: This *parashah* begins the lengthy birth narrative of the legendary Danite strongman Shimshon, which is found in P50 - P52. Following the birth narrative are the stories of his great exploits, which focus on his attacks on the Philishtines (P53 - P57) and which culminate in his spectacular death (P58). I believe that the Shimshon stories were not part of the earliest versions of Judges, but were added in the Persian period as part of the expansions to the book made in the fourth and fifth compositional stages. With the exception of P56, the Shimshon stories read almost entirely as a literary composition, although it is likely that in composing this material, the authors drew from old folk stories about the legendary strongman Shimshon. The author of the birth narrative was clearly well acquainted with the book of Samuel, and he has modelled parts of Shimshon's birth story on that of Shmu'el in Samuel. (He also modelled part of the birth story on the story of Yahweh's visit to Avraham and Sarah in Gen P19; see note 51,1a below.) In addition to the nearly identically constructed opening sentences in the birth narratives of Shimshon and Shmu'el, note that both boys are born to previously barren mothers and both are dedicated to Yahweh as *naziyr*s for their entire lives. Apart from the birth narratives, it is also worth noting that both are said to "champion" Yisra'el, and fight against the Philishtines, who are oppressing the Yisra'elites.

Notes to P50

We can only guess at the rationale for why the Shimson stories were composed and added to Judges. The fact that they read primarily as a literary composition suggests to me that they were composed specifically in order to be added to Judges. It is possible that prominent families of Danite descent were dissatisfied with the lack of material about their tribe found in Judges, and that they persuaded the priestly leadership in Mount Zion to commission the composition of material about the famous Danite strongman Samson for the purpose of including this in the book. But of course, this is wholly speculative, and there is no way to know what actually prompted the composition and addition of this material.

50b tribe: The author writes משפחה, which almost always denotes a subdivision of a tribe (שבט or מטה) and is often best translated as "clan." However, the term is sometimes used in a somewhat informal sense with the meaning of tribe, as here.

50c Don't let a razor touch his head: Note the parallel with the birth narrative of Shmu'el in the book of Samuel—in Sam P1, Hannah makes a vow to Yahweh that if he gives her a son, she will dedicate him to Yahweh's service for his entire life, "not allowing a razor to touch his head" (that is, he will be a *naziyr*). On the *naziyr*, see the note directly below.

50d *naziyr*: A *naziyr* was a person who makes a vow to Yahweh to keep the hair on his or her head unshorn for a certain period of time and to abstain from wine and beer and food made from grapes during that time. While the vow is in effect, the person is thought to be "dedicated" to Yahweh and must maintain a state of ritual purity with respect to the dead. Typically the vow was only for a limited period of time, but in the case of Shimshon and Shmu'el, the vow remained in effect for their entire lives. The most detailed picture of the *naziyr* is Num P28, which is a record of the cult rules that a *naziyr* must follow.

50e he's the one who will begin to free Yisra'el from the Philishtines' clutches: The author's choice of language—"begin to free" rather than simply "free"—is unusual. Unlike the other champions of Yisra'el, Shimshon doesn't save the Yisra'elites from the enemies oppressing them; rather, he simply initiates the fight back. The author's choice of language likely was influenced by his knowledge of the book of Samuel, where it is Shmu'el who is said to have vanquished the Philishtines (see the conclusion to Sam P13). (But then the wars with the Philishtines resume during the reigns of Sha'ul and Dawid, and it is Dawid who finally subjugates them [see Sam P82]).

Notes to P51

51a Guess what!?: In ancient Hebrew, the particle הנה, which is usually translated as "look, look here," can carry many different nuances, depending on the context in which it is used. One of its more interesting uses is in spoken language, in situations where the speaker wishes to call attention to a piece of news that is exciting or unexpected. In these instances, its use is identical to the English idiom "guess what?" For another example of הנה used in this way, see Gen P34, where Yoseph (somewhat obnoxiously) informs his brothers that he has had another dream.

51b my wife: A more literal translation is "this woman." This is a good example of the subtle departures one must make from literal renderings in order to produce natural-sounding English. In the situation here, it would be unnatural for an English speaker to refer to his or her spouse as "this woman" or "this man."

51c "Everything that I told your wife...: As above, the Hebrew reads "this woman," but I have translated as "your wife." It's worth noting here that Yahweh's emissary does not answer Manoah's questions about the boy.

51d —: The Leningrad Codex does not have a *parashah* break here.

Notes to P51,1

51,1a Please allow us to detain you...: The scene here—Yahweh's emissary, who is disguised as a human, visits a childless couple, tells them they will have son, and is offered a meal by the husband—is reminiscent of the story of Yahweh's visit to Avraham and Sarah in Gen P19, where Yahweh tells them that Sarah will bear a son. The author of the Shimshon narrative would certainly have been familiar with the book of Genesis, and it is likely that in his story here he has consciously imitated the story in Gen P19.

51,1b I won't eat any of your food...: Yahweh's emissary suggests to Manoah that rather than prepare the kid goat for a meal, he should offer it up as a whole offering to Yahweh.

51,1c we'd like to honor you: That is, make an offering to Yahweh on the man's behalf. To do that, Manoah needs to know his name.

51,1d Pil'iy: The Masoretes have vocalized the emissary's name as "Peliy" (פֶּלִי); however, I have translated the consonantal text (פלאי) in order to preserve the name's association with the Hebrew adjective for "amazing, incomprehensible, extraordinary." The name here is reminiscent of the epithet given to the future Davidic king in Isa 9.5, "Marvel of a Counselor," which also employs the root פלא.

51,1e **: The Leningrad Codex has a *parashah setumah* here.

52a they were being prepared with amazing skill: The Hebrew phrase ומפלא לעשות is elliptical. A literal translation would be something like "one was performing exceptionally in preparing." In the context of the cult, the verb עשה ("make, do") has a special technical meaning of "prepare an offering" (that is, slaughter the animal, drain the blood, and arrange its parts correctly on the altar), and that is clearly how the verb is being used here. With respect to the participle מפלא ("a person doing a thing in an extraordinary manner"), the subject may either be indefinite ("one") or it may refer to Yahweh's emissary. The most natural way to read the sentence, in my opinion, is to understand the subject as indefinite. Ancient Hebrew authors often used an active verb with an indefinite subject in place of the passive (on this phenomenon, see note 3e above), and I believe that is the case here. Although the individual preparing the offerings can only be Yahweh's emissary, the author has chosen not to make that explicit in the way he has composed this part of his narrative.

It is also worth noting here the author's pun. At the end of P51,1, we learn that the emissary's name is Pil'iy ("Amazing"), from the root פלא ("to be extraordinary, exceptional"), and the same root is used to describe the amazing skill with which the offerings are being prepared.

Notes to P52

52b vanished into the altar's flames: Literally, "rose up into the altar's flames." The image is of the emissary merging itself into the flames in a sort of natural physical act and rising into the sky in the form of smoke rising from the altar.

52c [Yahweh's emissary didn't show itself again to Manoah and his wife.]: This statement is clearly an addition to the text, likely made as part of the edits to the book's final compositional stage.

52d he wouldn't have earlier let us hear anything like this: That is, he wouldn't have had his emissary tell us that the boy will be a *naziyr* dedicated to God, nor that the boy would begin to free Yisra'el from the Philishtines' control. The phrase כעת ("like the time"), which I translate as "earlier," is difficult. It usually refers to a time in the future, not the past, and it is usually qualified by a word such as "tomorrow" (מחר) or "the spring" (חיה). It can be used, however, to refer to a past time, and that is what the context demands here. For another example of the phrase being used to refer to a time in the past, see Is 8.23.

52e The first time Yahweh's spirit struck him was at the place called Dan's Camp: The final sentence of this *parashah* reads as though it should introduce the following story, which is about the first time Yahweh's spirit struck Shimshon. However, the action in the following story takes place in Timnathah, not in Dan's Camp. I wonder whether there was originally an additional (brief) *parashah* set in Dan's Camp that has fallen out of the text.

Dan's Camp was a site near Forest Village in Yehudah. The etiology of the name Dan's Camp is given below in P63. In the book of Joshua, Forest Village is also known as Ba'al's Village (Jos P32 and Jos P36).

NOTES AND COMMENTS 103

Notes to P53

53a Shimshon went down to Timnathah: Timnathah (also known as Timnah) was a town on the northern border of Yehudah near Beyth Shemesh ("Sunville"). In the book of Joshua, it is listed as belonging to the tribe of Yehudah in P30, but as belonging to the tribe of Dan in P43. The author's choice of language reflects this geography: Shimshon lives in Tzor'ah in Dan, and travels south ("go down") to Timnathah, which lies on Yehudah's northern border and Dan's southern border.

53b Are you telling us there isn't one woman from all the Danite girls—or from anywhere in Yisra'el for that matter: I have departed from the literal meaning further than usual to capture the tone of the Hebrew, which is one of incredulity and anger, in the most natural way in English. Literally, "Isn't there among your kinspeople's daughters, or among my entire people, a woman [whom you can get for a wife]...."

53c those dickhead Philishtines: Ancient Hebrew authors commonly used the term ערל ("uncircumcised") as an ethnic slur against the Philishtines and other foreign peoples. I have tried to capture the pejorative sense of the term in my translation.

53d I really like her!: The author uses a Hebrew idiom. Literally, "She is straight in my eyes." The idiom is typically used to indicate that a thing is agreeable or pleasing to someone. Throughout the Shimshon stories, the author portrays his protagonist as driven almost entirely by his *id* and as simple-minded, emotionally immature, and lacking self-control. I have tried to capture some of that characterization here in my translation of the idiom.

53e (At that time, the Philishtines ruled Yisra'el.): The Leningrad Codex has an "open" blank space after this sentence to indicate the beginning of a new *parashah petuhah*.

53f But he didn't tell his father and mother what he had done: The author implies, but does not state explicitly, that Shimshon was some distance ahead of his parents at the time of his encounter with the lion—certainly far enough away that they wouldn't have heard or noticed the commotion from their son's encounter with the animal.

53g He returned some days later to get her: The narrative about bringing Shimshon's wife back home is very confused, as Shimshon does not in fact fetch his wife here; rather, his father goes to fetch her a few sentences later. It is likely, in my opinion, that there is a copyist's error in the text. The narrative logic would be sound if the verb phrase to "to get her" (לקחתה) was replaced with "to see her" (לראותה). One possible explanation for the error is that the scribe may have unconsciously thought of the verb לקח in relation to the woman because it had appeared three times in connection with her at the beginning of the *parashah*.

53h When they saw the festivities, they fetched thirty of their acquaintances, and they joined in the fun with him: The Hebrew is elliptical and ambiguous; as a result, it is very difficult to understand exactly what the author is trying to say. A literal rendering of the Hebrew is "When they saw it [or him], they summoned thirty friends, and they were with him." I have used the context of the party to attempt to understand the author's words. The first problem is that the pronoun "they" in the phrase "they saw" has no antecedent; based on context, I believe the pronoun refers to the wife's family. The second problem is that the second pronoun "him/it" (אותו) is ambiguous, and may refer back either to Shimshon or to the party. Again, based on context, I understand the pronoun to refer to the party. A third issue is how to understand the term מרעים, which may denote either a (close) friend or an acquaintance. I believe it is best to understand it in the latter sense, as later in the story these thirty fellows threaten Shimshon's wife, and it seems unlikely to me that family friends would act this way with her. Putting all this together, I understand the author to mean that when the bride's family saw Shimshon was holding a party in Timnathah (where he knew few people), they wanted to ensure the party was successful and quickly rounded up thirty acquaintances from town to attend. (We learn later that the thirty men are Philishtines, like Shimshon's fiancée and her family; see note 53k below.) In any case, however, it is very odd that the author was not explicit about the identity of "they" in the phrases "they saw" and "they fetched."

53i For three days… Then on the seventh day: Note the confusion in the narrative logic—the mention of "three days" doesn't make sense, as the guests have seven days to solve the riddle.

53j Did you all simply invite us here to take our money, or what?!: The use of the second person plural (קראתם) in addressing the wife and the threat to kill the wife's family in the previous sentence both support my proposal above in note 53h that it was the wife's family who invited the thirty fellows. The language used by the author is highly colloquial, as is appropriate for the situation, and I have translated with colloquial English.

53k these Philishtine fellows: Literally, "the sons of my people." Recall that the wife's people are Philishtines. This is the first clear indication we have that the men whom the wife's family invited to the wedding feast were fellow Philishtines.

53l but now I'm going to tell you?: The author depicts Shimshon as rude and inconsiderate in this scene with his wife; this is consistent with the depiction of him elsewhere as emotionally immature and as something of a hot-head.

53m She cried like this with him on each of the seven days: Note the break in narrative logic. Earlier the author implies that Shimshon's wife cried with him only on the seventh day, because it was only on that day that the locals threatened her. The author likely chose to portray Shimshon's wife as crying with him each day of the feast to create a heightened emotional impact in his narrative. The image of the wife crying on each of the seven days is more dramatic than her crying only on the last day of the feast. I have commented frequently in my other translations on the tendency of Hebrew authors to disregard narrative logic in order to achieve certain emotional effects in their story. For other examples of this phenomenon in Judges, see notes 9n and 19e above.

53n the Philishtine fellows: Literally, "the sons of her people." See note 53k above.

53o just before the sun was to set: Sunset marked the end of the day; thus sunset on the seventh day was the deadline for providing Shimshon with the answer to his riddle.

53p If you hadn't schemed with my heifer calf: Shimshon's speech contains a pun that cannot be captured in English. The base meaning of the verb חרש is to "to plow, cut," but it is often used in a pejorative sense with the meaning "to devise, scheme." Shimshon uses the word in the latter sense here, but he wishes to make a pun, so he refers to his wife as a "heifer calf."

Regarding the word עגלה: this denotes a heifer calf that has not yet been weaned—certainly not more than one year old. Ancient Hebrew did not distinguish between mature heifers (cattle that have not given birth) and cows (cattle that have given birth)—the term for both is פרה.

53q and so he went back home to his family: The Leningrad Codex has an "open" blank space after this sentence to indicate the beginning of a new *parashah petuhah*.

It's worth noting here the author's skill in portraying Shimshon's character through simple unadorned narration and letting readers draw their own conclusions. Throughout this *parashah* Shimshon consistently shows poor judgement and his volatile nature drives him to make poor decisions. In the party's aftermath, he is unable to let go of his rage, and in his anger at his wife, he rashly chooses to abandon her (at least for a short time) and return home to his family.

53r **: The Leningrad Codex does not have a *parashah* break here.

54a I thought you'd rejected her: The verb שׂנא has several special uses as legal terminology. In addition to the use discussed above in note 40b, the verb also can be used in the special legal sense of "reject [a spouse]," which is how the woman's father uses it here. A good example of this use of the verb can be seen in Deut 21,4, which treats the situation in which a man attempts to "reject" (שׂנא) his wife because he doubts her virginity. It is also noteworthy that the same verb is found in fifth century BCE Aramaic marriage documents from Elephantine in Egypt, where it is used as a condition allowing for divorce. See, for example, Ananiah's marriage to Tamet in B. Porten, *The Elephantine Papyri in English: Three Millennia of Cross-Cultural Continuity and Exchange* (New York 1996), pp. 208ff: "should Anani stand up in an assembly and say: 'I hate [שׂנא] Tamet my wife'. . . ."

A related legal usage of this verb is to denote that a wife has been disfavored by her husband (who now prefers another wife instead). See, for example, the story of Le'ah in Genesis (P27,3), as well as the law of the first-born in Deut P20,2 and the law against remarriage in Deut P21,22.

54b I wasn't to blame last time for what I did to the Philishtines: The meaning of the verbal construction that the author uses here—נקה מן ("to be free of blame for a thing")—is ambiguous. It is unclear if Shimshon is saying "I won't be held guilty this time for [what I'm going to do to] the Philishtines, but I'm going to do something bad to them" or if he is saying "I wasn't to blame last time for [what I did to] the Philishtines, but [now] I'm going to do something [really] bad to them." I have a preference for the latter option, but both options are entirely in keeping with Shimshon's character. In both options, it should be noted, Shimshon has become enraged at his Philishtine father-in-law for giving away his wife.

Note the contrast between the reasonableness of the father and the massive overreaction and destructiveness of Shimshon's behavior. The father was justified in thinking Shimshon had rejected his daughter, and he very reasonably offers to make amends by giving Shimshon his youngest—and apparently better—daughter. Shimshon, on the other hand, extracts revenge out of all proportion to the offense he has suffered: he destroys crops, vineyards and olive groves of people he does not know and who were not to blame for his problems. However, it is somewhat odd that Shimshon takes out his anger on the property of those who have done him no harm rather than on his father-in-law and his property.

54c said to them: It is unclear who Shimshon is addressing in his speech here, as there is no obvious antecedent to the pronoun. I think it is most likely that the author intended us to view Shimshon as addressing friends or family members back in his home town, but there is no way to be certain. This would require a very abrupt change of scene, and we do often see such abrupt changes of scene in Hebrew narrative. See for example the beginning of P56, when the Philishtine archons visit Deliylah and then the scene changes abruptly to a private moment between just Deliylah and Shimshon.

54d he placed one torch between every two tails: We should imagine that he uses rope to tie the two tails together and to tie the torch to the tails.

54e he burned all of it down: The author uses the grammatical construction מן...עד ("from... to"). This construction is used to express the concept of totality. See BDB, p. 581, def. 5b. I have reflected this nuance of the Hebrew in my translation with the phrase "all of it."

54f I'll be damned... if you do a thing like this and I don't take revenge: Shimshon's speech is in the form of an oath, but the language is colloquial, and so the Hebrew is somewhat difficult to make sense of. The phrase I have translated as "and I don't take revenge" is כי אם נקמתי—literally, "unless I take revenge." For כי אם followed by the perfect with the meaning "unless," see GKC § 163 c.

54g He killed them all: The Hebrew is elliptical: "them" refers to the Philishtines in Timnathah. Note how the cycle of violence in this *parashah* has spiraled out of control. Shimshon's father-in-law justifiably gives away Shimshon's daughter and offers to make amends. Shimshon's response is to destroy hundreds of grain fields, vineyards, and olive groves (but not to take any lives). The Philishtines then respond by killing Shimshon's father-in-law and wife. Shimshon in turn repays them by killing an untold number of Philishtines.

54h **: The Leningrad Codex has a *parashah setumah* here.

55a To do to him exactly as he did to us: That is, they plan to kill Shimshon to avenge his slaughter of their fellow Philishtines at Timnathah.

Notes to P55

55b "Exactly as they did to me," replied Shimshon, "I did back to them!": Shimshon is referring to the deaths of his father-in-law and his wife; he is saying that his murder of the Philishtines was to avenge their deaths. The tone of Shimshon's speech here comes across as quite obnoxious.

55c so I know you've not come to do me harm: The Hebrew here is informal and somewhat colloquial, as appropriate for spoken language. More literally, "otherwise [I'll think] you're going to harm me."

55d With an ass's jawbone—one heap, then two heaps: Shimshon is punning. In ancient Hebrew, the words for "ass" and "heap" are homonyms, pronounced and spelled identically (חמור).

55e He championed Yisra'el during Philishtine times for twenty years: I understand this sentence to be the conclusion to the original Shimshon material in P50-P55 and thus also the conclusion to the book of Judges in the form it had at some point in its fourth compositional stage.

56a to the Azzathites that Shimshon had come there: This clause lacks a verb, which appears to have fallen from the text. The verb is almost certainly וַיֻּגַּד ("it was reported"). With the verb added back in the text, the translation would be "When it was reported to the Azzathites that Shimshon had come there...."

Notes to P56

56b they surrounded his location and lay in wait all night long at the town gate: The narrative is confused. If they have surrounded his location (he's in a prostitute's house), then there is no reason to "lie in wait" at the town gate. Or is the reader to understand that there are two groups of Azzathites and the author simply hasn't expressed himself clearly?

56c he grabbed hold of the town gate's doors: The narrative logic of this *parashah* is broken. Presumably there is a gang waiting at the town gate for Shimshon, but they are nowhere to be seen as Shimshon breaks out of town by dismantling the gate. Does the author perhaps have in mind that there is more than one town gate in Azzah, and that Shimshon went to a gate where there was no gang waiting for him? But this seems implausible. The entire *parashah* is nonsensical, and, although its core may reflect some ancient tradition about the famous strongman Shimshon, I believe it is a very late addition to the text.

56d Then he put them on his shoulders and took them up to the top of the mountain facing Hevron: The conclusion of this brief *parashah* is as illogical as what has preceded it. The author gives no reason for Shimshon's actions. Why would no one in Azzah hear the commotion of the town gate being dismantled and sound the alarm? Why is no one pursuing Shimshon, given that there is at least one gang, and maybe two, lying in wait for him? And what is his purpose in carrying the doors and/or the door-posts of the town gate (which collectively must weigh two thousand pounds or more), some thirty miles to the east, and then climbing to the top of a mountain and depositing them there?

Notes to P57

57a Trick him: The author's language here repeats the language used in P53, when the thirty Philishtine fellows demand that Shimshon's wife "trick" (פתי) him to find the answer to his riddle. The author of the Deliylah story in P57 is writing at a later time than the author of P53, and he intentionally alludes to the earlier story in his choice of language.

It's worth noting here the parallels between the Deliylah story and the story of the wedding feast in P53. In both stories, Shimshon has secret information that his opponents/enemies desire to have; his opponents/enemies employ his betrothed/lover to get the information from him; Shimshon's betrothed/lover relies on her feminine wiles in repeated attempts to discover this information; Shimshon eventually relents and reveals the information to the betrothed/lover, who in turn gives the information to his opponents/enemies. The author of P57 clearly made a conscious effort to create these close parallels with P53, and in so doing he significantly elevated the literary quality of his story.

57b We'll each give you eleven hundred sheqels of silver: There were five Philishtine archons (each was the ruler of one of the major Philishtine towns), so in total they are offering Deliylah fifty-five hundred sheqels of silver. This is equivalent to more than sixty kilograms, or one hundred and thirty pounds, of silver. This is an enormous sum of money. By way of comparison, the priest in Jud P60 receives annual wages of ten sheqels per year plus room and board, and in Exod P37 a master whose manservant or maidservant is killed or maimed by an ox receives thirty sheqels of silver in compensation for the permanent loss of their labor.

57c Please tell me how you're so strong...: This is the first of three scenes in which Deliylah attempts to discover the source of Shimshon's strength. The scenes are fascinating for their portrayal of Shimshon and Deliylah and their relationship. To a modern reader, there appears to be a strong sexual undercurrent in the three scenes, although it is unclear to me whether the author intended the scenes to be read this way. In the first scene here, for example, Shimshon and Deliylah are alone and he allows her to tie him up. It doesn't take much imagination to see their interactions as playful and flirtatious banter, or even as a sexual game that involved playing out a bondage fantasy. Following this interpretation, Shimshon would understand Deliylah's call that the Philishtines are coming for him as just part of the sexual fantasy that they are acting out. (In this regard, it's worth noting that Shimshon in his naiveté never becomes aware in the Deliylah story that there really is a Philishtine ambush waiting for him in a back room.)

Deliylah is playing the game as part of her deception, whereas Shimshon sees the game as simple entertainment, possibly enjoying displaying his dominance and control over her, or—as suggested above—possibly seeing it as a sort of kinky foreplay. In the end, however, the lovers' game goes awry, for when Deliylah's deception doesn't go as planned, she turns to psychological abuse to get the secret from her lover.

57d If I was tied up: Literally, "If they tied me up," but the passive voice should be understood. Ancient Hebrew often expressed the passive with an active verb and an indefinite subject, and I believe that is the case here. For other examples of this phenomenon in Judges, see notes 3e, 8d, and 29a above.

57e cords of catgut: The Hebrew word is יתר. The term refers to strings or cords made from animal intestines, or what in English is called catgut. The process of making catgut cords requires drying them for two or more weeks. They only become strong after they are dried; thus, it is odd that Deliylah and the archons would think Shimshon could somehow be bound with catgut that hadn't yet been dried.

57f like a strand of flax snapping when exposed to a flame: In describing the snapping of the catgut cords, the author of P57 employs imagery similar to that used in P55 to describe Shimshon breaking his restraints ("like flax consumed in a fire"). I believe the author of P57 is deliberately alluding to P55 to connect his story more closely with the previous Shimshon stories.

57g new ropes: Note that "new ropes" (עבתים חדשׁים) are used to restrain Shimshon in P55. The author's choice of language here in P57 was likely influenced by the language in P55. This is one of several examples of the author of P57 seeking to achieve an elevated literary effect by creating connections between his story and the previous stories about Shimshon. See notes 57a and 57f directly above.

57h Tell me how you can be tied up!: Note that Deliylah's tone has changed. In the previous two times in her "game" with Shimshon, when she asks Shimshon to tell her how he can be tied up, she softens her language with the particle נא, which is often best translated "please." This third time she makes the request, however, she omits the particle and is more direct with Shimshon—she no longer finds their game as fun and her frustration with him is beginning to show.

57i Try weaving a net into the seven braids on my head: The meaning of the Hebrew is uncertain. The word מסכת occurs only in this passage in Judges. I take the word to be synonymous with מסכה ("woven stuff, web, covering") and translate as "net." The syntax of the sentence is also unusual: the author uses the verbal construction "weave a thing [the braids] with another thing [the netting]." I understand this to denote weaving the two things together, but the exact meaning of the construction is unclear.

57j she pressured him relentlessly: The verb that I translate as "pressured" is the *hiph'il* of צוק ("press, squeeze"). The author here has deliberately borrowed language from P53 in order to create a parallel with the story of the wedding party. In that story, Shimshon's wife "pressed [*hiph'il* of צוק] him so much" that he revealed the answer of the riddle to her. For other instances of the parallels between P53 and P57, see note 57a above.

57k pushed him: The Hebrew is obscure. The verb אלץ occurs only here. I follow BDB, p. 49, which proposes "urge," understanding the verb in parallel with הציקה (the third person feminine *hiph'il* perfect of צוק, "press, make tight").

57l she summoned a man: The clause is nonsensical. Like other ancient Hebrew authors, the author of this *parashah* writes in an elliptical style that often requires the reader to supply missing details. Usually the details can be easily inferred from context, but in this sentence it is not obvious what the missing detail is. I think it most likely that the author wished his readers to understand that she summoned one of the men hiding in the back room to bring her a razor. Alternatively, however, it may simply be that the text here is corrupt.

57m he didn't realize Yahweh had left him: The author presumably intends us to understand that Shimshon was disoriented upon waking up from his nap, and so didn't notice that his hair had been cut off.

Notes to P58

58a Then they called for him to stand between the pillars: I have departed slightly from the Hebrew to make clear to the reader what is going on in this scene. The Hebrew reads simply, "They made him stand between the pillars." The subject of the verb is not the Philishtine officials, but the people in the audience, who are calling out commands to Shimshon of things to do in order to entertain them.

58b the attendant who was holding his hand: Shimshon is blind, and so is being led around the arena by an attendant.

58c three thousand men and women were on the roof: The author does not give a clear description of the building, so we must guess at what he imagined it to be. It is unclear how people on the roof could watch Shimshon's sport unless the area above the arena was open to the sky. However, if that were the case, the roof would require many more than two pillars for support and they would be out of Shimshon's reach. The engineering of such a building supported by only two columns that are no more than four or five feet apart would defy the laws of physics. The impossibility of what the author describes shows that he didn't think clearly about the building's structure and its relation to Shimshon and the audience.

58d avenge myself...once and for all: The author's phrasing is a little unusual; literally, "avenge myself with a vengeance of one [final time]." For other instances of אחת (the feminine absolute form of "one") with the meaning "once and for all," BDB cites Ps 62.12 and Ps 89.36.

58e he extended his arms: The author uses the verb נטה. Among its many uses, it is often used specifically to describe the motion of a person extending his hand or arm. That is the usage here. The image is that of Shimshon extending his arms out, pushing against the two columns and causing each to topple over. There is no twisting or turning action intended, as BDB, p. 640, def. 3a seems to assume. It is somewhat odd that the author doesn't explicitly state that the columns toppled over.

58f His kinsmen: That is, members of the Danites' tribe who are not part of Shimshon's extended family.

58g He championed Yisra'el for twenty years: This sentence repeats the conclusion to P55. As discussed in the essay on Judges' composition history at the end of this book, I view the story of Shimshon and Deliylah and of Shimshon's death (P57 - P58) as a later addition to the Shimshon cycle. Originally, the Shimshon material consisted only of P50 - P55. While it may strike the modern reader as a little odd that the author of P57 - P58 did not remove the conclusion to P55, the biblical writers showed great respect for the work of their predecessors (whose work they were adding to) and it was rare for them to delete older material. This dynamic, I believe, explains many of the inconsistencies and oddities that appear in the narratives of the books of the Torah and Former Prophets.

59a There once was a man from the Ephrayim mountains...: This *parashah* begins the story of Miykayehu and the Danites, which is found in P59 - P63. The story, which I place in the late Persian period or early Hellenistic period, tells of the origin of the Danite priesthood and of the cult statue of Yahweh venerated in the Yahwistic shrine in the town of Dan. The story is somewhat odd, and it is not at all clear to me what the original rationale was for its inclusion in Judges. It is possible that the Persian-period or Hellenistic-period stewards of the book (who almost certainly lived in Yerushalem) added it simply because they thought it characterized so well the chaotic times prior to the establishment of the monarchy. Or perhaps influential families of Danite descent lobbied for its inclusion, similar to what they perhaps did for the Shimshon stories. But these are guesses, and there really is no way to know what prompted the composition of this story and its insertion into Judges.

Notes to P59

59b eleven hundred sheqels: It is possible that the mention of eleven hundred sheqels here was influenced by the mention of this number in the story of Shimshon and Deliylah, which I view as predating the story of Miykayehu and the Danites.

A standard sheqel was the equivalent of approximately 11.3 grams. Thus eleven hundred sheqels of silver amounted to nearly 12.5 kilograms or a little more than twenty-seven pounds. This is a very large sum of money; as mentioned above in note 29b, in the case law decisions in Exod P37, someone who accidentally causes the death or disability of a manservant or maidservant is required to pay only thirty sheqels in compensation to the master for the permanent loss of the servant's work. For a good discussion a weights and measures in the Tanakh, see the article "Weights & Measures" at the Jewish Virtual Library website.

59c ("*It's decided...for my son.*"): This sentence that I have placed in parentheses represents the thought of Miykayehu's mother; it does not appear to be a later addition to the text, but rather is the author's attempt to represent what the woman is thinking as she is speaking to her son.

59d to have an icon of the god cast for my son: Literally, "[given] from my hand for my son, for the making of an icon [פסל] and an icon [מסכה]." The author of this story in Judges somewhat unusually refers to a single icon by the phrase פסל ומסכה. Both פסל on its own and מסכה on its own denote a cult statue of a god, and the terms are used as synonyms by the authors in the Tanakh. Apart from this story in Judges, the two terms are used together in the singular (פסל ומסכה) only in Deut P24,3 and Nahum 1.14. In both those instances, the phrase is used as a collective noun that describes cult statues in general. The two terms are also used together in the plural (הפסלים והמסכות) twice, in 2 Chron 34.3,4, and in both instances, the phrase refers to multiple individual cult statues that are in Yahweh's temple.

Thus, the use of the phrase פסל ומסכה here in Judges to mean a single icon is very strange. Even stranger, later in the story, in P63, the author breaks up the phrase so that פסל and מסכה are separate items in a list (see note 63g below).

The root פסל refers to the act of hewing or carving and the root נסך refers to the act of pouring a liquid. Originally the term פסל must have denoted a carved image of a god, and the term מסכה (from the root נסך) must have denoted the image of a god cast in metal. However, the authors of Tanakh do not necessarily use the terms to distinguish between cast and carved images. In Is 40.19 and Is 44.10, for example, a פסל is said to be "cast" (נסך).

NOTES AND COMMENTS 111

One possibility worth mentioning is that the author of the story in P59 - P63 may in fact have viewed the פסל and the מסכה as separate items. There is a good deal of evidence from archaeology that small statues of gods used in the home were kept in small portable shrines. These portable shrines were typically made of clay, but some have been found that were made of carved stone. In this scenario, the author would have understood the מסכה as the statue of the god (cast in silver) and the פסל as the small portable shrine (carved in stone) that the statue was kept in. However, because there is no other evidence of the terms being used this way elsewhere in the Tanakh, I do not find this proposal very convincing. For a good discussion of these small shrine models (including numerous illustrations of models found in excavations), see S. Schroer, "The Iconography of the Shrine Models of Khirbet Qeiyafa," in S. Schroer and S. Münger (eds.), *Khirbet Qeiyafa in the Shephelah: Papers Presented at a Colloquium of the Swiss Society for Ancient Near Eastern Studies Held at the University of Bern, September 6, 2014* (Orbis Biblicus et Orientalis 282), Fribourg and Göttingen, 2017, pp. 137-158.

The story in P59 - P63 is an etiology for Yahweh's cult at the town of Dan in the far north. The author doesn't say what form this statue of Yahweh took. But given the story in 1 Kings 12 about Yarov'am (=Jeroboam) putting cult statues of Yahweh in the form of a bull calf in the temples at Bethel and Dan, we may presume that the author of the story of Miykayehu and the Danites intended the reader to think Miykayehu's icon was also in the form of a bull calf.

59e And now I'm giving it back to you: The Hebrew is confusing, as—quite unusually for Hebrew prose—there is no indication of a change of speaker. The content of the sentence suggests that Miykayehu is now the speaker, which is how I have translated it. It is possible that a phrase indicating the change of speaker has fallen out of the text. That said, there are instances in Hebrew prose (though rare) where a change of speaker is not indicated and the reader must infer the change of speaker from context.

59f two hundred sheqels: This is equivalent to 2.2 kilograms, or a little less than five pounds. Thus the reader should assume that the statue of the bull calf (if that's what it was) is quite small, less that a foot in length and less than half a foot in height. An icon of such a size would fit easily into the shrine models used in the home mentioned above in note 59c.

59g He cast the silver into an icon: Once again, the author here uses the phrase פסל ומסכה ("an icon and an icon") to refer to a single statue.

59h teraphim: *Teraphim* were small figurines of gods that were used in divination. They are mentioned near the end of Gen P27,3 (Rahel hides them in her camel's saddle cushion to keep them from her father) and in Sam P44 (Mikal uses them to make a dummy of Dawid on the bed, to make it appear that he is sleeping). Their connection to divination is mentioned in Sam P33,3 and in Ez 21.26. It is especially interesting to note that although *teraphim* are mentioned approvingly in Hos 3.4 as part of the "correct" cult practices in the northern kingdom, they were treated as abhorrent cult practices in the account of Yoshiyyahu's (=Josiah's) reforms in Kings (see 2 Kgs 23.24) and in a late Persian-period oracle in the book of Zekaryah (see Zch 10.2).

59i Back in those days, there was no king who ruled over Yisra'el—each man did as he thought was right: This sentence reads as a very late addition, made as part of the work during Judges' sixth compositional stage. The author of the addition has taken the concluding sentence of Judges in P75 (which I believe is from the fifth compositional stage) and applied it to the story of the foundation of Yahweh's cult in Dan. His purpose in inserting the comment here was presumably to help the reader understand the background for the highly unusual cult practices found in the story in P59 - P63.

60a I'm a Lewite: It should be noted that the young Lewite remains anonymous for the entire story, and we only learn his name at the conclusion of the story in P63 (see note 63r below). The anonymity of one of the main characters gives the story an ahistorical feel that is more appropriate for a fable. We see a similar approach to narrative in the story that follows in P64, in which the man, his concubine, and the concubine's father all remain anonymous.

Notes to P60

60b I'm currently travelling, staying awhile: The author uses an unusual verbal construction: the participle followed by the infinitive—in this case, הֹלֵךְ לָגוּר ("one who is travelling in order to stay awhile"). The exact nuance implied by this verbal construction is unclear, and I have translated to fit the context. A nearly identical construction—the *waw*-consecutive followed by the infinitive (וַיֵּלֶךְ ... לָגוּר)—appears earlier in the *parashah*, but that construction does not come across as unusual in the Hebrew because the verb and the infinitive are separated by several words.

60c advisor: The author here uses the term אב ("father") as an honorific. The usage is difficult to translate into English—the term implies something like a respected personal advisor or guru.

60d "Now I know," thought Miykah to himself, "that Yahweh is going to make things go well for me": This statement provides a good example of the author's literary skill. By portraying Miykah here as confident and trusting in Yahweh, he sets him up to be something of a tragic figure for whom the reader will later feel some sympathy. For, as we will learn near the story's conclusion, his confidence and trust in Yahweh is misplaced, and things do not at all "go well" for him.

60e **: The Leningrad Codex does not have a *parashah* break here.

61a Back in those days, there was no king who ruled over Yisra'el: Unlike the similar comment at the conclusion to P59 (see note 59i above), I believe this statement is original to the story—its purpose is simply to set the stage for the introduction of the Danites into the story.

Notes to P61

61b the Danites' tribe was looking for territory to occupy...: The sentence is at odds with the earliest version of the Israelite History, in which all twelve tribes receive an allotment from Yehoshua. Dan, which is the final tribe to receive an allotment, is given its territory in Jos P43. The author of the story of Miykayehu ignores this tradition, as he needs a rationale for why the Danites are looking for land. It is worth noting that Jos P43 does mention the Danites taking possession of Leshem in the far north; I treated this statement as a late addition to Joshua (see note 43b of my translation). The fact that the author of this addition to Judges does not refer to that passage about Leshem in Joshua may indicate that he was writing before the Leshem addition was made to Joshua. That said, however, both the author of this story and the author of the addition to Joshua were aware of and utilized a tradition about the Danites seizing land in the north.

61c **: The Leningrad Codex has a *parashah setumah* here.

NOTES AND COMMENTS 113

Notes to P62

62a The Danites sent five men... to explore the land and investigate it: This passage is interesting, as it demonstrates the significant departures from a literal rendering that one must sometimes make in order to produce a functionally equivalent, natural-sounding translation in English. In this instance, I have had to convert direct discourse to indirect discourse (English prefers indirect discourse in many places where Hebrew prefers direct discourse), and I have had to shift the order of the clauses in the sentence. A literal translation reads, "The Danites sent from their clan [used here as a synonym for tribe] five men from their entirety, some [of the most] capable men, from [the towns of] Tzor'ah and Eshta'ol, to explore the land and to investigate it. They said to them, 'Go, investigate the land.'"

62b they noticed the young Lewite's Yehudite accent: I have added the adjective "Yehudite" in translation to make clear to the reader that the Danites have noticed the Lewite is not from Ephrayim. They are curious what this "foreigner" is doing in Ephrayim, which is why they turn aside and speak to him in private.

62c Be on your way and don't worry... The mission you're going on has Yahweh's approval: The author here writes a very colloquial Hebrew, in imitation of spoken language. More literally, "Go in peace [i.e. go without worrying]... The road that you're travelling on is in front of Yahweh." I have translated with an equivalent in everyday spoken English.

Recall from the beginning of the *parashah* that the men's mission is to explore the land and investigate it (in order to find territory to occupy).

The young Lewite's response comes across as abrupt in the Hebrew, and it is possible that a short sentence or clause has fallen out of the text. We expect to read that the Lewite asked God about the Danites' mission before he informs them that their mission will succeed and bids them farewell. The addition of the short phrase וישאל באלהים ("he sought an oracle from God") is all that would be needed to make the narrative read smoothly in Hebrew.

Notes to P63

63a no one in the region being obnoxious about anything: Literally, "no one humiliating [another person] [with respect to] anything." The Hebrew is relatively clear and straightforward, in my opinion, and I see no reason to emend the text, as BDB, p. 484 proposes.

63b a model of restraint: Literally, "one possessing restraint." Here too, the Hebrew is relatively clear and straightforward in my opinion—the participle יֹרֵשׁ ("one possessing") modifies העם ("the people"), which appears back at the beginning of the sentence. I see no reason to emend the text as BDB, p. 783 proposes.

63c Travelling up into the hills, they made camp at Forest Village: The author uses the verb עלה ("go, go up, ascend") because the eastward journey from Dan into Yehudah involves moving to a higher elevation. I have added the phrase "up into the hills" to capture this nuance of the verb.

The book of Joshua mentions that Forest Village is on border between Yehudah and Binyamin and that the village is also called by two other names: Ba'alah and Ba'al's Village. See Jos P30, P32, and P36.

63d In light of the circumstances... the five men... addressed: The author here uses the verb ענה ("answer, respond") to indicate words spoken in response to a specific occasion or circumstances. To reflect this nuance, I have added the phrase "in light of the circumstances." On this use of the verb, see BDB, p. 773, def. 2a of the *qal*.

63e a sacred icon: This is the third instance in which the author uses the phrase פסל ומסכה ("an idol and an idol") to refer to a single cult statue. It's possible, although less likely, that he uses the terms together to refer to the statue of the god and the portable shrine that goes with it. See note 59d above.

63f in front of the gate: I believe the author intends the reader to understand that Miykah's property is surrounded by a wall, and that there is a gate in the wall controlling access to the property.

63g the icon, the priest's shoulder-cape, the *teraphim*, and the icon: The author here has broken up the phrase פסל ומסכה and refers first in his list to a פסל and then later in his list to a מסכה. But there is only one icon in the story. We should assume that there is an error here. Less likely, in my opinion, is that the author sees the two terms as somehow distinct—a portable shrine (the פסל) and the statue (מסכה) that goes in it. See note 59d above.

63h the icon of the priest's shoulder-cape, the *teraphim*, and the icon: The text is corrupt. Originally it likely read, "the icon, the priest's shoulder-cape, the *teraphim*, and the icon." On the duplicate mention of the icon, see note 63g directly above.

63i the priest cried to them: The narrative is somewhat confused. In the previous paragraph, the author states the priest remained standing at the gate with the six hundred armed men while the five Danite scouts entered Miykah's house and took the icon and other cult items. But the narrative here implies that the priest has followed the men into the house. Given the elliptical style of much Hebrew narrative, it is possible that the author didn't feel it necessary to state the priest waited at the gate for some time before then going to the house to check on what the men were up to. Alternatively, we can assume the author (or a later editor) has simply made an error in the narration.

63j the icon: Up until now, the author of the story of Miykah and the Danites has used the phrase פסל ומסכה to refer to the cult statue of Yahweh in Miykah's possession. However, here and for the remainder of the story, he uses the term פסל alone to refer to the cult statue.

63k putting the children and livestock and their most precious possessions in the front: Recall from earlier in the *parashah* that there are only 605 Danites travelling to Layish—the six hundred armed men and the five scouts. The author seems to have lost sight of the narrative, and he is now imagining the entire Danite tribe migrating north to Layish.

The statement that the children and livestock and precious possessions travelled in front, where they are unprotected is completely nonsensical. It is unclear what the author intended with this statement.

63l What's your problem?!: The exchange of words between Miykah and the Danites beginning here and continuing for the next five sentences is written in colloquial and idiomatic Hebrew. I understand this as the author's attempt to represent as accurately as possible the spoken language of his day, especially in situations where the language is emotionally charged. I have represented the dialog in idiomatic everyday English, but I do not comment on the places where I have departed from the Hebrew.

63m There was no one who could come to the town's rescue: The Hebrew reads simply אין מציל ("there is not one who is rescuing"). The particle אין ("there is not") often has the nuance of a thing being "impossible," and that is the nuance here.

63n *that is under Beyth-Rehov's control*: Literally, "that belongs to Beyth-Rehov." An equally plausible translation of the phrase is "that is next to Beyth-Rehov." The preposition ל is sometimes used alone to express locality, although this is rare; see BDB, p. 511, def. 2. The town of Beyth-Rehov is likely identical with the town of Aram Beyth-Rehov in Sam P83.

63o previously the town's name was Layish: In the tradition preserved in Joshua, the town's name was Leshem. See Jos P43. I understand the mention of Leshem in Joshua to be from that book's final compositional stage. It is unclear to me which name, Layish or Leshem, represents the older tradition.

63p The Danites set up the icon for their own use... They installed for their own use the icon...: The final two sentences of the *parashah* are variant endings of the story. I believe the second sentence is likely the original ending, and the first sentence is a later variant that has been inserted into the text alongside the original. One reason for thinking the first variant is not original is because it gives a name to the priest (Yehonathan Gershomsson Menashshehsson), who up until this point in the story has remained nameless.

63q the icon: See note 63j above.

63r Yehonathan Gershomsson Me^{n}ashshehsson... until the time of the land's exile: Gershom was the son of Mosheh, not Menashsheh. Originally, the consonantal text read "Yehonathan Gershomsson Moshehsson" (יהונתן בן־גרשם בן־משה). But because of the great reverence for Mosheh in Jewish tradition, the Masoretes inserted the raised letter *nun* into Mosheh's name and then vocalized the new name as "Menashsheh" in order to avoid any association between Mosheh and the objectionable cult practices at Dan. This change to the text likely dates to the fifth century CE or later—both the Septuagint translation of Judges (from the second or third century BCE) and the Vulgate translation of Judges (from the late fourth and early fifth centuries CE) read "son of Moses" here.

63s until the time of the land's exile: That is, until the fall of the northern kingdom in 722 BCE.

63t They installed... stood in Shiloh: As stated above, I believe that this sentence is the original conclusion to the story. Note that its chronology is at odds with the chronology given in the variant ending in the previous sentence, which states that the statue was in use until 722 BCE. By contrast, the original ending states that the statue was in use only during the period when there was a temple in Shiloh. In the traditions known to the Biblical authors, Shiloh was destroyed prior to the establishment of the monarchy under Sha'ul (see Jer 7.12,14 and Ps 78.60).

63u for the entire time that a temple to God stood in Shiloh: For stories about the temple in Shiloh, see Sam P1 - P7. The ancient readers of this story would have understood that this is a story about the origins of Yahweh's cult in Dan, and they would have been familiar with the fact the Yarov'am (Jeroboam) placed a statue of Yahweh in the form of a bull calf in the temple in Dan—the (presumably) grand successor to the small household cult statue of Yahweh that is the subject of our story here in P59 - P63.

Notes to P64

64a Back in the days when Yisra'el didn't have a king...: The final story in Judges is found in P64 - P74,2, and it is possibly the oddest piece of literature in all of the Tanakh. In my opinion, the story has little literary merit or redeeming qualities. Its main purpose is to justify the establishment of the monarchy by showing that the days when there was no king were violent and lawless. However, the approach the author takes is a disturbing one, as his primary strategy is to try to shock the reader with lurid details and events. The story is quite late, dating to the end of the Persian period or the Hellenistic period, and it was written by someone whose literary skills were, charitably speaking, uneven. The narrative itself is bizarre and contains many unrealistic elements, and is especially noteworthy for its strange misogyny. The larger story consists of three interconnected stories: in the first story (P64), a Lewite is travelling home after fetching his wayward concubine, and when he comes under threat, he shoves her into the hands of a gang who then brutally rape and murder her; in the second story (P65 - P71), the Yisra'elite tribes seek retribution for the concubine's murder by going to war with the tribe of Binyamin, resulting in the near annihilation of the Binyaminites; and in the third story (P72 -P74,2), the Yisra'elites feel compassion for the Binyaminites after slaughtering them and take it upon themselves to find wives for the survivors, which involves the abduction of the virgin women of Yaveysh Gil'ad and the slaughter of all the people there, followed by the abduction of yet more young women at a festival in Shiloh.

The author is writing about the distant past ("the days when Yisra'el didn't have a king"), and in order to make this setting feel authentic to the reader, he fills his story with elements reflecting what he knows—or thinks he knows—about the strange customs of that ancient time. A large part of his literary technique thus involves peppering his story with what to him were archaic terms and phrases. He borrows these terms primarily from Genesis, a book that he viewed as ancient, and he bases much of the story in P64 on the story of Lot, including reproducing dialog from that story nearly verbatim. The author's use of archaic terms very often rings false, as though he didn't have a good understanding of how these terms were used in the stories where they originally appeared, and these numerous false notes merely add to the strangeness of the overall story. I comment below on most places where I see the author using terms incorrectly, or where these terms strike an especially false note. Wherever possible, I have tried to capture the false-sounding language and its strangeness in translation.

With respect to the identity of the story's author, I think it is likely that he must have been someone very influential in Yehud, for otherwise it is difficult to see why the priestly leaders and the stewards of the temple library would agree to the inclusion of this bizarre story that goes on for far too long—it accounts for 102 of the book's 618 verses—and that is almost entirely lacking in literary merit. I also believe that the author could not have had a real role within Yahweh's cult, for as I discuss in the notes below, his use of language more than once betrays his ignorance of the system of offerings within the cult. It is tempting to think he might have had an important role in the provincial administration of Yehud in the late Persian period or early Hellenistic period, but of course, there is no way to know who he was or when he lived.

64b He acquired a concubine for himself: Here we see the author's first attempt at an archaism, and the first false note of the story. The author is familiar with the term פילגש ("concubine, secondary wife") from Genesis and also from the book of Samuel. However, his application of the term here in P64 doesn't really make sense. In Genesis and Samuel, the term describes a woman who is subordinate to the primary wife of a man—typically a man of wealth and/or power. Neither of these elements are present here. The Lewite does not have a primary wife, and because he is an itinerant (he "was living for a time" [גור] in Ephrayim), it seems doubtful that he would have had the means to support both a primary wife and a concubine.

64c But his concubine played the harlot on him: Here is the second false note in the story. The author uses the verbal construction זנה עליו ("to whore upon him"), which is nonsensical in this context. The author is familiar with the use of the verb זנה to mean "abandon, leave" from the prophetic books, where it is used to describe the Yisra'elites abandoning Yahweh for other gods. But the term is never used in this way to describe a woman abandoning her man, except in this one passage in Judges. Moreover, assuming there is no error in the text, the author has gotten the phrase wrong: he writes זנה עליו ("to whore upon him") when in fact to use the term זנה with the meaning of "abandon," the correct construction is actually זנה מעליו ("to whore away from him").

64d She had been there for a period of four months... to go visit her family: The Hebrew of these two sentences is ambiguous, and it is possible to translate the passage with two very different meanings. An alternative to how I have translated the passage is: "(When she left, she had been there for a period of four months.) Right away her man went after her, to sweet-talk her and get her to come back. With him were his valet and a pair of donkeys. She took him to visit her family." In this latter option, which I think is only slightly less plausible than how I have translated, the Lewite catches up to his woman quickly, but agrees to go visit her family with her rather than return immediately home.

I view these sentences as an oddity because I believe that an author who possessed better skills as a prose stylist would not have written them in such a way as to leave so much ambiguity about the meaning.

64e to sweet-talk her: The author uses the verb phrase דבר על לב ("to speak upon the heart"), which is an idiom that can have a range of meanings depending on context—"speak kindly to, comfort, console, flatter." See BDB, p. 181, def. 5. For another instance of the phrase specifically meaning "flatter, woo, sweet-talk," see the beginning of Gen P28,2 (Shekem wooing Diynah).

64f his valet: Here again, the author strikes a false note with an attempted archaism. The word נער is very common in ancient Hebrew and usually means "boy, young man." But in Genesis, Samuel, and other books set in the author's ancient past, the term has a number of specialized meanings—it can mean "valet, retainer, personal manservant," and in military contexts, it can mean "officer, adjutant." Here the author uses it to mean "valet," but his use of the term doesn't seem appropriate, as typically only wealthy and/or powerful men would have a personal valet, and there is no indication that our itinerant Lewite has either qualification.

64g made ready to go: On the verbal construction ויקם followed by the infinitive of a verb of motion ("he rose to go") with the meaning "make ready to go," see note 14d in my translation of Joshua. Note also, this same construction is used four sentences later with the same meaning: "when the man made preparations to leave."

64h "Fortify yourself with a little food... and then you all may be on your way!": The author has based the dialog in this scene on the dialog at the beginning of Gen P19, when Avraham is visited by Yahweh who is disguised as three men. Note the striking similarities in the dialog: סעד לבך פת־לחם ואחר תלכו here in Judges compared with וסעדו לבכם אחר תעברו in Genesis.

64i he relented: When the verb שוב ("go, return") appears alone with no other words following, it can have the meaning "change one's course of action," as here. On this use of שוב, see BDB, p. 997, def. 5e.

64j thine abode: Literally, "to your tent." This is another example of one of the author's archaisms that comes across in the text as strange and unnatural. The author is well aware that the nomadic characters of ancient times in the book Genesis lived in tents, and he is also aware of the formulaic phrases "to your tents" and "[each man] to his tent," which appear several times in the books of the Josianic and Israelite histories (especially Samuel and Kings), where they are part of the formula used to send home large groups of people or to describe their return home. But the use here in Judges doesn't fit either the situation of Genesis or the use in Samuel and Kings, and for that reason its presence in the text is jarring to the reader. I have tried to capture the author's unnatural archaism here by translating with archaic English language that is not natural for the context.

64k He had gone as far as the outskirts of Yevus (to wit, Yerushalem): The presence of the name Yevus is another example of the author's use of archaisms to imitate the elements of ancient stories known to him. The books of Genesis, Numbers, Deuteronomy, and Joshua all refer to the Yevusites as one of the native peoples of Kena'an, and the book of Samuel (P74,1) specifically mentions them as the dominant population in Yerushalem prior to its conquest by Dawid. Hence the town is sometimes referred to as "the Yevusites' town" (עיר היבוסי), which then was abbreviated to "the Yevusites' " (היבוסי) and then simply "Yevus" (יבוס). With respect to the narrative, it should be noted that Yerushalem is approximately six miles north of Beyth Lehem—equivalent to a journey of two or three hours on foot.

64l the daylight was quickly disappearing: Literally, "the day had very much declined." The verb form here is unusual. The text reads רד, which I and many other scholars interpret as a defective form of the third-person masculine singular perfect form of ירד. It is also possible that the text is simply in error, as GKC § 19 *i* suggests.

64m where there aren't any Yisra'elites: The Hebrew is difficult. The most natural way to express this idea in ancient Hebrew is אשר אין שם איש מבני ישראל. The author has departed in several ways from this, either because his literary skills are uneven, or—perhaps more likely—because he is attempting to represent colloquial speech. Note the following departures from "normal" Hebrew in the text: he has used the negative particle לא ("not") in place of the expected particle אין ("there aren't"); he has used הֵנָּה ("to here, hither") in place of שָׁם ("there"); and he has omitted אִישׁ ("a man"), which although would be natural to include, is strictly speaking not required here.

64n We'll continue on to Giv'ah: Giv'ah was four or five miles north of Yerushalem, or roughly one-and-a-half hours on foot.

64o we're getting close to one of the places: The Hebrew is awkwardly expressed, and one wonders if is this another indication of the author's subpar skills as a prose stylist. Presumably "one of the places" is a reference to the different options for where to spend the night, but prior to this statement the Lewite has only mentioned Giv'ah as their destination.

64p Ramah: Ramah is another four or five miles north of Giv'ah. The mention of Ramah is perhaps the author's way of characterizing the Lewite as overly focused on making as much distance as possible for the day without due consideration to the practicalities of travel or the physical safety of the group.

64q the town plaza: The author of this *parashah* has modeled the scene at the town plaza and the following narrative of the Lewite's stay in Giv'ah on the story of Lot and the two envoys of Yahweh in Gen P19.

It's worth noting here that walled towns in the ancient near East typically had a large open space, or plaza, inside one or more of the town gates. The plaza was a public space where most of the town's commercial and legal business was conducted. Note, for example, that Avraham negotiates the purchase of a grave for Sarah at the town plaza in Gen P23. Note also that Shekem in Gen P28,2 addresses his townspeople at the town gate to gain their assent in making a marriage alliance with Ya'aqov's family. Ancient readers would have understood the townspeople in that story to be assembled in the plaza, and not in the area outside the town wall.

The recently excavated site of Khirbet Qeiyafa, which was located in the territory of Yehudah and which dates to the tenth-century BCE, gives us a good idea of the size of these plazas and of their relationship with the gate and the surrounding town. Khirbet Qeiyafa had two plazas: the plaza at the town's western gate was rectangular in shape and roughly thirty meters by fifteen meters in size; and the plaza at the town's southern gate was "L-shaped," with each leg of the "L" being roughly twenty meters long and ten meters wide. For diagrams of the plazas and the surrounding areas, see figure 16 of Y. Garfinkel, "Khirbet Qeiyafa in the Shephelah: Data and Interpretations," in S. Schroer and S. Münger (eds.), *Khirbet Qeiyafa in the Shephelah: Papers Presented at a Colloquium of the Swiss Society for Ancient Near Eastern Studies Held at the University of Bern, September 6, 2014* (Orbis Biblicus et Orientalis 282), Fribourg and Göttingen, 2017.

64r This man was from the Ephrayim mountain region: It's worth noting that the old man is from the same region as where the Lewite was living. The author may have intended the reader to understand this as the reason for his hospitality.

64s From a distance, he espied: The author here uses an idiom "lift the eyes and see" (נשא עינים ויראה). This is likely another example of his use of an archaism. The construction is relatively common in the ancient literature known to him (and less common in later literature), and most importantly, the construction occurs at the beginning of Gen P19—the *parashah* in Genesis that the author used as the model for much of his story. I have tried to capture the old-fashioned and not-quite-natural tone of the language with the verb "espy."

64t I'm going to visit Yahweh's shrine: The author most likely has in mind Yahweh's shrine in Shiloh, as biblical tradition viewed this as the most important of Yahweh's shrines during the pre-monarchic period. Moreover, Shiloh is located in the Ephrayim mountains, close to the Lewite's destination. The author's readers would understand that the Lewite intended to visit the shrine to make a thanksgiving offering for the return of his concubine.

64u He gave the donkeys some hay while they washed their feet: The host feeding the visitors' donkeys while the guests wash their feet is a common trope in the ancient literature known to the author. That said, the language here is quite similar to the language of a similar scene in Gen P37, when Yoseph's brothers make a return trip to Egypt to buy more grain from Yoseph; it is conceivable that our author has borrowed the language here from that *parashah* in Genesis.

64v we're going to have our way with him: The men use a common Hebrew euphemism for sexual intercourse—literally, "so that we might know him [sexually]." I have translated with an English euphemism for forced sexual intercourse to reflect the context.

64w The man who owned the house went outside...: The narrative here and the old man's speech to the scoundrels are modeled very closely on the story of Lot in Gen P19. There is a near verbatim correspondence in numerous places in the text. Note the following: (1) ויצא אליהם האיש בעל הבית (Gen P19) and ויצא אליהם לוט הפתחה here; (2) אל־נא אחי תרעו (Gen P19) and אל־אחי אל־תרעו נא here; and the lengthy parallel (3) הוצאה־נא אתהן אליכם ועשו להן כטוב בעיניכם רק לאנשים האל אל־תעשו דבר (Gen P19) and אוציאה־נא אותם וענו אותם ועשו להם כטוב בעיניכם ולאיש הזה לא תעשו דבר here. In this last example, it's also worth noting the clear superiority of the Hebrew from Gen P19; especially glaring in the parallel passage in Judges is the use of the third masculine plural pronoun in reference to the two females (the old man's daughter and the concubine).

64x my teenage daughter and his concubine...Rape and abuse them: The man's offer of his daughter and his guest's concubine is shocking and doesn't ring true for ancient Near Eastern cultures. It is important for the reader to remember that the author has set the story in what for him is the ancient past, a time of unusual social practices when "each man did whatever he felt like"—things that would be inconceivable in the author's own day. Two women—the old man's daughter and the concubine—are mentioned here because in the story in Gen P19, Lot offers two of his daughters to the men of Sedom.

This scene captures the essence of the strange misogyny in the story. The old man, who is otherwise presented in a positive light, begs the town scoundrels not to do "such an immoral thing" to the man who is his guest, but apparently it is fine in the old man's eyes for the scoundrels to do that same "immoral thing" to his own daughter and to the guest's concubine.

64y Rape and abuse them: This phrase is absent in the parallel passage in Gen P19. The author's intent in adding the phrase was certainly to make the scene even more shocking to the reader. He takes a similar approach in the following scenes, where he uses especially lurid language to shock the reader—the men "ruthlessly abused her all night long" (ויתעללו בה כל הלילה) and then later the Lewite "butchered her limb by limb" (וינתחה לעצמיה). While I think it is clear that the author wished to make the case for kingship by portraying the lawlessness of society in the premonarchic times, his argument in my opinion is not at all effective, as the details in his story are so revolting that they distract readers from appreciating his larger message.

64z the man grabbed hold of his concubine and brought her outside to them: The Hebrew is ambiguous, but "the man" here is almost certainly the Lewite and not the old man.

64aa Her master rose in the morning...: It is important not to overlook the extremely unrealistic nature of the narrative in this story. The author does not base his narrative on his understanding of human nature, but rather relies on stock language and images to move the narrative forward, even if that means the language is profoundly at odds with normal human behavior. This sentence provides a good example of this. The author characterizes the man as showing no concern or worry for his concubine—he rises in the morning after a restful night and leaves the house to resume his journey, as though he has entirely forgotten about his concubine and the fact that he had sent her out the previous night to be abused and raped by a gang of worthless scoundrels.

64ab But there was no response: Note the elliptical style, which is characteristic of Hebrew narrative. The author doesn't state that the Lewite's concubine is dead, but relies on readers to deduce that from the clues in the narrative. Hebrew authors often utilized an elliptical style at key points in their narrative for literary effect, when they wished to achieve a heightened emotional impact.

64ac He sent the pieces of her into every part of Yisra'el: The Lewite's actions here recall Sam P22, when Sha'ul dismembers two oxen and sends their parts by messenger throughout the territory of Yisra'el to summon the Yisra'elites to assist in the fight against the Ammonites. I believe the author of this story in Judges has modeled this scene on the story in Samuel. But one's reaction to reading about the butchering of a human being is very different than one's reaction to reading about the butchering of an ox. Thus the butchering here rings a strange and false note, whereas the butchering in Samuel is perfectly understandable in the context.

64ad he would say to them: The Hebrew is somewhat ambiguous. I understand the pronoun "he" to refer back to the Lewite who has butchered his concubine, not the person who saw one of the butchered pieces. That the Lewite is somehow present and commenting about his own butchery to people to whom he sent his concubine's body parts simply adds to the overall bizarreness of the story.

64ae Nothing like this has ever happened or been seen...: The author makes use of a common literary trope used by ancient Hebrew authors—"such and such a thing has never happened/been seen since such and such a time." The trope is often stated in relation to the exodus from Egypt, as here. The purpose of the trope is to heighten the emotional impact on the reader through exaggeration.

64af Consider her closely: Another example of the author's fondness for adding perverse details that sound a false note and serve only to offend readers. In the sentence here, the Lewite is asking the Yisra'elites to take a close look at one of the concubine's body parts, and then give "advice" on a course of action.

Notes to P65

65a from all ends of the land—from Dan to Be'er Sheva to Gil'ad: The author here uses the construction מִן ... עַד ("from... to"), which is a common way in Hebrew of expressing totality. Dan is the northernmost part of the Yisra'elites' land, Be'er Sheva the southernmost part, and Gil'ad the easternmost part. Thus "from Dan to Be'er Sheva to Gil'ad" denotes the entirety of the Yisra'elites' land. To capture the meaning of the grammatical construction used by the author, I have added the phrase "from all ends of the land," which is not present in the Hebrew.

65b the community convened: The author has borrowed this phrase from Persian period material in the book of Joshua. See in particular the end of Jos P50 (where the Yisra'elites convene at Yahweh's shrine in Shiloh to prepare for war) and also the beginning of Jos P35. In the author's day (ca. late fourth century or third century BCE), all the material in Joshua and in the books of the Torah would have been viewed as ancient. It is likely, in my opinion, that the author used this language here in order to give this brief *parashah* an ancient feel, as he did with P64.

65c Mitzpah: Mitzpah, which means "Lookout Place," was a common place name. In the story of Yiphtah in P38-P45, Mitzpah appears several times as the name of a town in the Gil'ad region. And from Sam P13, we know there was a Mitzpah in Binyamin. I agree with BDB, p. 860, which suggests that the Mitzpah here was in Binyamin. The Mitzpah here has a shrine to Yahweh, and this fits neatly with Sam P13, which states that Sha'ul presented whole offerings to Yahweh in Mitzpah in Binyamin. Moreover, the first sentence of P66 makes most sense if we understand Mitzpah here to be located in Binyamin. It would also be logical for the Yisra'elites to gather in Binyamin, as this would allow them more effectively to confront and punish the criminals, who were from Binyamin.

65d along with four hundred thousand infantrymen armed with swords: The mention of the four hundred thousand infantrymen strikes another false note, as the phrase comes out of the blue and does not make sense in the context. The author perhaps has recalled passages in Numbers and Joshua mentioning thousands of warriors, and has thought to add the detail about the infantry in imitation of them in order to give this *parashah* the feel of an ancient work. The phrase איש שלף חרב ("men armed with swords") is relatively common, appearing in Jud P25 (where I translate as "soldiers"), in Samuel, Kings, and Chronicles. The author would be aware of this phrase from those works, and has likely borrowed it from them; notably, however, his use of the phrase reads quite awkwardly due to redundancy with the term for "infantry" (איש רגלי).

66a intending to kill me. Then they raped my concubine: It's worth noting that in recounting the events leading to concubine's death, the Lewite omits the key detail that he himself forced her to go outside to the men who raped and murdered her.

Notes to P66

66b abode: Literally, "tent." The author repeats the archaism that he used in P64. See note 64j above.

66c Here's what we're going to do: cast lots for who will attack it...: The story of the Lewite concubine's death and its aftermath in P64 - P74,2 is full of strange and often unnecessary details that reflect the author's attempt to give his story the feel of the ancient stories known to him from the books of the Torah and the Former Prophets. He has liberally borrowed language, imagery, and details from those ancient stories, but—as his literary skills are very uneven—he often employs the things he has borrowed in ways that don't make sense within the narrative. The passage here is a good example of that. The author states that lots will be used to determine who will attack Giv'ah, but then in the following sentence he implies that the lots instead determined who would provision the troops, not who would attack. And then later in the story—in P68—rather than using lots, the Yisra'elites seek an oracle from Yahweh to determine who will attack first.

66d as appropriate for the act of depravity which they committed in Yisra'el: The phrasing of the Hebrew—ככל־הנבלה אשר עשה בישראל (literally, "in accord with the entirety of the depraved act which he committed in Yisra'el")—is very awkward, but I believe the meaning is clear. The point the author is making is that the plan for punishing Giv'ah—that is, to organize a well-supported military attack on them—is a proportionate response given the extreme depravity of the crime. The author may have modeled his language on phrasing known to him in the books of the Torah and the Prophets: the phrase עשה נבלה בישראל ("he committed a depraved act in Yisra'el") and variations of it occur in Gen P28,2, Deut P21,5, Jos P13,2 and Jer 29.23.

67a all Binyamin's tribes: The author's use of the plural "tribes" (שבטים) here instead of the singular "tribe" is strange, and strikes yet another false note. It is unclear to me what the author had in mind with the use of the plural term. There is an instance in Num P23 of שבט being used to denote a subunit of a tribe, but I do not believe that is what the author of our story in Judges intended here in P67. (For שבט denoting a tribal subunit, see note 23a in my translation of Numbers.)

Notes to P67

67b and thoroughly cleanse such wrongdoing from Yisra'el: The author has borrowed formulaic language from Deuteronomy, and my translation here repeats the way I translate this formula in my book on Deuteronomy. The phrase in Deuteronomy has two variants: בער הרע מקרבך ("thoroughly cleanse wrongdoing from your community") and בער הרע מישראל ("thoroughly cleanse wrongdoing from Yisra'el"). The two phrases appear in Deuteronomy nine times: in P13; P17,4; P18; P19,2; P20,3; P21,5; P21,6; P21,7; and P21,24.

67c there were seven hundred valiant men who were left-handed: The detail is strange and incongruous. The author may have modeled this detail about being left-handed on the story of Ehud the Binyaminite in P12. Again, his purpose was likely to give his story the feel of ancient stories known to his audience, but the arbitrary way in which he inserts these details serves only to heighten the strangeness of his story.

67d each one of them could sling a stone...: Another strange and unnecessary detail. In this instance, the author may have modeled this detail on the story of Dawid and Golyath in Sam P39 - P40,7.

Notes to P68

68a the Yisra'elites mustered four hundred thousand armed men: The author is confused—he seems to have forgotten his statement back in P65 that there were four hundred thousand infantrymen already armed and assembled among the Yisra'elites.

68b sought an oracle from God. "Who should go first...: The author has modeled this passage on Judges P1, which to him is an ancient text. Note in both instances, the oracle informs the Yisra'elites that Yehudah should go first.

68c and established a position against Giv'ah: The Leningrad Codex has an "open" blank space after this clause to indicate the beginning of a new *parashah petuhah*.

68d organizing their battle lines: The author likely has borrowed this language from the story of Dawid and Golyath in Sam P37.

68e The forces [*the Yisra'elites*] regrouped: I understand the phrase in brackets to be a fake gloss by the author of this story, made in order to give his narrative the appearance of the ancient stories in the Torah and Former Prophets, which by the author's time (ca. late fourth century or third century BCE) were peppered with clarifying comments and glosses made by later editors. For other examples of fake comments by our author, see notes 69c, 73f, and 74,1a below.

68f The Yisra'elites then went to Beyth-El: I have added the phrase "to Beyth-El," which is absent in the Hebrew. Ancient Hebrew usage does not require an explicit mention of the destination, as the location is implied by context. However, in this situation, natural English usage does require an explicit statement of the destination.

68g in front of Yahweh: That is, in front of the shrine/temple at Beyth-El. Petitions to the god are made in front of the structure or building where the god's presence (or cult statue) resides.

68h our kinsman Binyamin: Literally, "my kinsman the Binyaminites." Ancient Hebrew was quite flexible with regard to use of singular and plural; because of this, I often treat places in the text where there is disagreement in number as "normal," and translate as though there are no grammatical problems present. While the disagreement here is more unusual than is typically seen with these sorts of disagreements, I do not believe the text is in error and thus translate as if there is no grammatical problem.

Notes to P69

69a The Yisra'elites approached the Binyaminites on the second day: The author has confused his chronology. It is now the third day, not the second day. On the second day the Yisra'elites reestablished their battle lines and then travelled to Beyth-El, where they bewail their situation until evening before seeking an oracle from Yahweh.

69b welfare offerings: The mention of welfare offerings is incongruous, as this is not a situation in which welfare offerings would be presented to Yahweh. Welfare offerings were typically made during occasions of celebration—either celebrations of the community or celebrations of individual families. The author's mention of welfare offerings, in my opinion, betrays an ignorance of the sacrificial cult and of the occasions for which different types of offerings are required to be presented to Yahweh. This is a clear indication that the author had no formal role within the cult, but earned his living in some other capacity. The phrase "whole offerings and welfare offerings" is a relatively common one, and I believe that the author simply wrote the customary phrase without understanding that it did not actually apply to the situation he was describing.

69c [*Now God's treaty chest...in front of it as priest.*]: At first glance, this sentence reads as a late addition to the text because it interrupts the direct speech that we expect after the request for an oracle. However, I believe there is good reason for viewing this sentence as original. The author of the story in P64 - P74,2 is writing at the end of the Persian period or in the early Hellenistic period. At the time he was writing, the stories in the ancient books he was imitating had already received numerous clarifying comments and glosses. I believe the comment here about the treaty chest is not a late addition, but rather the author's attempt to imitate the comments and glosses that by his day appeared frequently in the books of the Torah and Prophets. The mentions of the treaty chest (the only place it is mentioned in Judges) and of Phiynehas come out of the blue and add nothing to the story. The author is aware of their association with Shiloh through his familiarity with the opening *parashot* of the book of Samuel, and through his addition, he now associates both the treaty chest and Phiynehas with Beyth-El. He has inserted this "fake" comment to make his story appear like the ancient stories in the books of the Torah and Former Prophets, into which later editors had inserted comments and glosses at numerous places. Our author, like others of his time, would have viewed these comments and glosses as giving greater authority to the stories in which they appeared, for they demonstrated that the stories were worthy of close study by later generations. Thus, by adding such comments and glosses, our author sought to enhance the authority of his own story.

69d our kinsman Binyamin: See note 68g above.

69e Yisra'el then set ambushes all around Giv'ah: This sentence sets the scene for the final day of battle in P70 - 71. The author has modeled his description of the final day of battle on Jos P14 - P15, which is the story of the Yisra'elites' conquest of the town of Ay, and which involves setting ambushes and drawing the inhabitants away from town so that the ambush forces can seize the undefended town.

70a All the Yisra'elites then stood up...: The narrative in the final sentences of this *parashah* is confusing and difficult to follow. There are extraneous details—the hiding places of the regular Yisra'elite troops and the locations of Ba'al Tamar and Geva—that serve only to muddle things in the reader's mind. The author is writing in imitation of the detailed description of the battle over Ay in the book of Joshua, but the details he adds achieve nothing except to weaken his story and make it less effective.

70b Geva: I believe the author intended the reader to understand that the Geva here is a different town than Giv'ah, where this *parashah* takes place. Both names are attested in the Tanakh as names of towns in the tribal territory of Binyamin. The names are common words—both mean "hill"—and it certainly seems possible that two towns in relatively close proximity could have had such similar names. Thus there is no reason, in my opinion, to emend the text here to read Giv'ah, as BDB, p. 148, suggests.

Notes to P71

70c they didn't know: The pronoun "they" refers back to the Binyaminites, not the Yisra'elites. In this instance, the ambiguity in the Hebrew may be due to the fact that the author is not a particularly competent writer. For that reason, I have left the ambiguity in the translation.

71a Then Yahweh let Binyamin be routed by Yisra'el: The author uses a common Hebrew idiom, the nuance of which is often missed by translators. The idiom involves the verb נגף ("to strike down, defeat") and the preposition לפני ("in front of"). Typically the verb is in the passive and the preposition in this phrasing implies agency—"to be struck down by" and not "to be struck down in front of." But the idiom also occurs with the active form of the verb, with the preposition still implying agency. For other examples of the *qal* of נגף followed by לפני meaning "let [someone] be routed by [another]," see Sam P8; see also 2 Chr 13.15 and 2 Chr 14.11. BDB, p. 619, recognizes this usage of the idiom.

71b twenty-five thousand one hundred men: Recall from P67 that the Binyaminites mobilized a total of twenty-six thousand seven hundred men. The clause mentioning the loss of twenty-five thousand one hundred is a summary of the total losses during the day—the numbers of casualties are detailed later in the *parashah*, but the totals add to twenty-five thousand, not twenty-five thousand one hundred. See note 71j below.

71c warriors one and all: The author repeats the odd phrasing that he first used at the beginning of P69. The author uses this unnecessary phrase as a sort of refrain in several places in the *parashah*—a good example of his penchant for unnecessary detail that strikes a false note with the reader.

71d The ambush forces quickly went into action...: The passage here and in the following paragraph describing the action of the ambush forces, their attack on Giv'ah, the column of smoke, and the resulting confusion of the Binyaminites is based entirely on the story of the Yisra'elites' capture of Ay in Jos P14 - P15.

71e Wilderness Road: The author has borrowed the name of the road from the passage in Jos P14.

71f in the midst of it all: An example of the author's awkward prose style, which peppers the narrative with stock phrases and language borrowed from ancient stories. The phrase here is unnecessary and is nonsensical within the context.

71g the forces who had emerged from the towns: This is a reference to the ambush forces, which have left Giv'ah after slaughtering its citizens and which have now joined the battle. It is unclear to me whether the plural "towns" is a mistake on the part of the author or a later scribe, or is an example of the author's ham-fisted style, which often ignores narrative logic.

71h They surrounded the Binyaminites and then gave chase: This clause provides good examples of the author's lack of attention to narrative logic and his awkward prose. With regard to narrative logic, if the Binyaminites are surrounded, how is it that the Yisra'elites then give chase to them? With respect to the prose style, the author oddly uses the *hiph'il* of רדף ("cause to chase") when in fact he means simply "chase," which would require the standard *qal* form of the verb and which would read much more smoothly in Hebrew.

71i The remaining Binyaminites turned and fled to the wilderness: This is another good example of the author's disregard of narrative logic. The wilderness lies to the east of Giv'ah, and the Yisra'elite forces at this point in the narrative are directly to the east of Giv'ah, between the Binyaminite forces and the wilderness. Narrative logic would suggest the Binyaminites would flee to the west, away from the Yisra'elites.

71j The total number... who fell in battle... was twenty-five thousand: Note the slight inconsistency with the opening sentence of this *parashah*, which states that twenty-five thousand one hundred Binyaminite soldiers were killed by the Yisra'elites.

71k Six hundred men turned and fled to the wilderness: The author's math doesn't add up. We know from P67 that the Binyaminites mustered twenty-six thousand seven hundred soldiers. We are told here in P71 that twenty-five thousand one hundred (or just twenty-five thousand) of these soldiers fell in battle. Thus, the remaining soldiers should number sixteen hundred (or seventeen hundred), not six hundred.

71l slaughtered them all—people in the towns, livestock, and anything else that was found: The author has likely based the details of the slaughter on the accounts in Joshua of the ban devotion (חרם) of the towns in Kena'an, in which all people and animals are slaughtered and the towns are burned to the ground. Oddly, however, the author does not mention the ban devotion in his description of the slaughter. (On the ban devotion, see the discussion in my introductory note to the book of Joshua.)

71m all the towns they happened upon: The Hebrew is awkwardly phrased. Literally, "all the towns that were encountered."

72a (Now the Yisra'elites had sworn at Mitzpah...: The author must have had in mind that the Yisra'elites swore this oath when they met at Mitzpah back in P65 and P66.

Notes to P72

72b in front of God: That is, in front of the god's shrine or temple. See note 68f above.

72c built an altar there and then offered up whole offerings and welfare offerings: This sentence is a good example of the incompetence of the author of the story in P64 - P74,2. Recall that in P69, the Yisra'elites offer up whole offerings and welfare offerings in Beyth-El. From that, we can conclude there is already an altar to Yahweh there, and thus there would be no need to build an altar. But the author knows of numerous stories from the books of the Torah and Joshua in which the protagonist builds an altar and then makes offerings to Yahweh, and so he wishes to include such an event in his story as a way to give the story the feel of ancient literature. Achieving this literary effect was clearly more important to him than any concern for consistency between the narrative in P69 and the narrative here in P72. It is also worth noting one further sign of the author's incompetence in this *parashah*: his mention of welfare offerings betrays his ignorance of the working of the cult. As discussed above in note 69b, welfare offerings are associated with occasions of celebration, not occasions of mourning. The author has included mention of them here because he is familiar with the phrase "whole offerings and welfare offerings" in the ancient stories known to him. It simply does not occur to him that the context in which he mentions welfare offerings is nonsensical.

73a Who's the one out of all Yisra'el's tribes who didn't come to the assembly at Yahweh's shrine?: Because of the author's incompetent narrative technique, it is extremely difficult for the reader to understand where the action in this *parashah* takes place. It is possible to read the *parashah* as set in Mitzpah, as set in Beyth-El, or as set in Shiloh. In the latter two cases, the references to Mitzpah in this *parashah* would refer to the assembly at that location held in P65 - P66. After going back and

Notes to P73

forth between these three options, I think it most likely that the author intended the action in P73 to be set in Beyth-El. My translation reflects this understanding. The translation would be slightly different if we understand P73 to be set in Mitzpah.

73b was subject to a severe curse that he be put to death: The detail about the curse comes out of the blue and strikes the reader as strange—there was no mention of such a curse in the account of the assembly at Mitzpah in P65 - P66. In any case, I believe the language here is another example of the author seeking to add details that he thinks will make his story seem ancient.

73c (For the Yisra'elites had changed their mind... any of our daughters for wives.): The author has written these two sentences as background context for the reader, to explain why the Yisra'elites are suddenly asking who didn't appear at Mitzpah. His narrative technique here is a little odd—it would have been more effective to begin the *parashah* with a statement for the rationale of the Yisra'elites' actions, but, as we have seen in the previous *parashot*, the author of this concluding story in Judges displays very uneven story-telling skills.

With respect to the translation here, the *niph'al* of the verb נחם has a range of meanings, including "change one's mind." Other equally plausible translations are "the Yisra'elites felt sorry for their kinsman Binyamin" and "the Yisra'elites regretted what had happened to their kinsman Binyamin." For another example of the *niph'al* of נחם with the meaning "change one's mind," see the final sentence of Exod P52.

73d the camp: Here we see another element of ancient stories that the author has included in his own story. The stories in the books of the Torah and in Joshua speak of the Yisra'elites staying in a camp (מחנה) in their wilderness wanderings and also during the conquest of Kena'an before they had settled in any towns. The author is familiar with this term from those stories, and he wishes to include it in his story to make his story feel similar to other stories about the distant past.

73e Yaveysh Gil'ad: It is unclear to me why the author has chosen Yaveysh Gil'ad for the punishment that follows. The town is mentioned several times in the book of Samuel and is associated with the figure of Sha'ul. In Sam P22 - P22,1, Sha'ul rescues Yaveysh Gil'ad from the threat posed by Nahash the Ammonite; in Sam P65, the inhabitants of Yaveysh Gil'ad recover the corpses of Sha'ul and his three sons from the Philishtines and give them a proper burial; in Sam P69,1, Dawid expresses his gratitude to the citizens of Yaveysh Gil'ad for burying Sha'ul; and in Sam P101,4, Dawid collects the remains of Sha'ul and Yehonathan from Yaveysh Gil'ad and has them interred in the family grave in Binyamin.

73f [*to the assembly*]: At first glance, this phrase appears to be an addition to the text. However, I believe that it is original. As I discuss above in note 69c, at the time that the author of P64 - P74,2 is writing (the end of the Persian period or the early Hellenistic period), the ancient stories in the Torah and the Prophets had already received numerous clarifying comments and glosses; the author of this story in Judges has inserted the gloss here about "the assembly" in imitation of the comments and glosses that he is familiar with in the ancient stories that served as the model for his story. A clear indication that the gloss here is "fake" is that it is misplaced—genuine glosses are customarily placed immediately after the word or phrase that they explain. Our author wished to gloss the phrase "to the camp," to indicate to the reader that "to the camp" meant "to the assembly." However, he has placed the gloss after "Yaveysh Gil'ad" rather than after "to the camp," which is its proper location.

73g the community: The appearance of the word "community" (עדה) comes out of the blue. This term is especially common in material in Exodus and Numbers dating to the Persian period. I believe that this is an instance of the author borrowing a term found in what to him were ancient stories in order to dress up his own story and give it an ancient feel. He also uses this term in P65, as discussed in note 65b above.

73h you must make a ban devotion of: The author mentions the ban devotion (חרם) because he is familiar with the concept from the stories in the book of Joshua, and—once again—he wishes to give his story the tone and feel of other stories about the distant past that are known to him. But, as with the many other archaisms that the author has sprinkled throughout his story, the mention of the ban devotion here is jarring and strikes a false note. The author misunderstands what the ban devotion is used for, and he has thus misapplied it in his story. The ban devotion is mentioned in multiple places in Deuteronomy and Joshua; from those passages, we know that the ban devotion is applied only to those individuals (or towns) that are actively hostile to Yahweh and that promote worship of other gods. Yaveysh Gil'ad is guilty of no such crime. Moreover, the author doesn't appear to understand that the ban devotion requires the slaughter of all the inhabitants of a town; in his account of the ban devotion of Yaveysh Gil'ad, all the virgin women are spared. For more on the ban devotion, see my discussion of it in the introductory comments to my translation of Joshua.

73i Shiloh: The appearance of Shiloh is unexpected, and the abrupt shift of the action from Beyth-El to Shiloh is jarring. I understand this to be another attempt by the author to dress up his story with elements he has borrowed from stories about the ancient past. With the mention of Shiloh, the author has now included in his story the location of three famous ancient shrines to Yahweh—Shiloh, Beyth-El, and Mitzpah.

73j **: The Leningrad Codex has a *parashah setumah* here.

74a the numbers they found were insufficient: The Hebrew is awkwardly expressed, and the exact meaning is unclear. A literal translation is "but they did not find for them so." BDB, p. 593, def. 4 and BDB, p. 485, def. 1a suggest a meaning that fits the context, which I largely follow, but it is nonetheless the case that this passage's usage of both כן ("so, thusly") and מצא ("find, happen to be") is somewhat unusual. It is possible that the text is corrupt—the Hebrew would read smoothly if כן ("thusly") were changed to כדי מספרם ("according to the sufficiency of their number"). Regarding the "insufficiency" of numbers, recall that there are six hundred Binyaminite men who survived and that there are four hundred young women from Yaveysh Gil'ad, so there is a shortfall of two hundred women.

Notes to P74

74b But Binyamin does have in its possession some escapees: Literally, "Binyamin does have a patrimony of escapees." The phrasing used is very odd. The author has peppered his story with terms—in this instance, ירשה ("property, land owned, patrimony") and פליטה ("[group of] escapees")—from ancient stories in a way that barely makes sense. It is strange that the author mentions the escapees, because wives for four hundred of them have already been found. The passage here is another example of what I take to be the author's less than competent storytelling.

74c (For the Yisra'elites had sworn a curse on anyone who would give a woman to Binyamin.): This curse is also mentioned at the beginning of P72. See note 72a above.

74,1a [*which is north of Beyth-El... and south of Levonah*]: I believe that this comment is not a later addition to the text, but rather is original. It is the fourth example of the author of the stories in P64 - P74,2 adding a "fake" clarifying comment in imitation of the clarifying comments and glosses that he was familiar with in the ancient stories that he used as the model for his own story. See notes 68d, 69c and 73f above.

Notes to P74,1

NOTES AND COMMENTS 129

74,1b Keep a close watch: when you notice: Translation of וראיתם והנה אם. The particle אם ("if") sometimes has the force of "when," as here. For other examples of this special use of the particle, see BDB, p. 50, def. 1.b.(4). The use of the particle הנה here is also interesting. In this instance, it introduces what the Binymaminites should look for. To capture this nuance, I have translated the particle with a verb phrase ("you notice") and placed a colon after "keep a close watch."

74,1c for none of us acquired a wife in the war: It is unclear what the author is driving at here—the statement is completely irrelevant to the situation at hand. It is possible that the text is corrupt. If the letter *nun* is removed from the verb לקחנו, the text would read "for none of them [i.e. none of the Binyaminites] acquired a wife in the war," which is still awkward but at least fits the context a little better.

74,1d for you wouldn't have given women to them when you would be the ones in the wrong: It is difficult to extract a meaning from the Hebrew that fits the context. My translation is a little tortured, but it reflects the idea that the men of Shiloh wouldn't have chosen to give their daughters to the Binyaminites as wives because of the oath taken by the Yisra'elites that was mentioned at the beginning of P72 and again at the end of P74.

74,1e —: In the Aleppo Codex, this *parashah* break occurs in the last line of the column. The author of the consonantal text, Shlomo ben Buya'a, initially wrote the letter *nun* in the line, which is used to indicate that the last line of a column is blank and which would imply that a *parashah petuhah* begins on the first line of the next column. But immediately following the *nun*, ben Buya'a has instead begun the new *parashah*. It is clear that he must have realized there is a *parashah setumah* here and not a *parashah petuhah*; however, it is odd that he left the *nun* in the text rather than erasing it.

Notes to P74,2

74,2a The Binyaminites did exactly that...: This short *parashah* is written in a particularly ham-fisted way, with formulaic phrases borrowed from what the author believed were ancient texts and then strung together into a text that is clumsy and repetitive.

74,2b the requisite number of women: That is, exactly two hundred women, which represents the difference between the six hundred surviving Binyaminite men and the four hundred young women who were spared in the ban devotion of Yaveysh Gil'ad.

74,2c each man departed there for his own property: The author has likely modeled the somewhat unusual language here—איש לנחלתו ("each man to his own property")—on the conclusion to Jos P56, where the same phrase is used.

74,2d **: The Leningrad Codex does not have a *parashah* break here.

Notes to P75

75a In those days...: I believe that P75 was added as the conclusion to the book of Judges as part of the editorial work done in the fifth compositional stage, when the stories about the Danites' relocation to Layish (P59 - P63) and about the murder of the Lewites' concubine and the resulting war with the Binyaminites (P64 - P74,2) were added. The *parashah* serves to summarize the main message of Judges that the editors of the fifth stage wished the reader to take away from the book: without a king to enforce a single set of laws and rules for the Yisra'elites and to unify them as a people, each person acted as he or she saw fit. The result, as the stories in Judges show, was a period of chaos and anarchy in which the Yisra'elites forsook their god and repeatedly suffered violence and oppression at the hands of the neighboring peoples. The summary in P75—and the book of Judges as a whole—thus appropriately sets the stage for the book of Samuel, which is the story of Yahweh's decision to allow his people to be ruled by a king, followed by the establishment of the Davidic dynasty and Yahweh's selection of Yerushalem as the site of his future temple and altar ("the place that he will choose").

75b Total sentences in the book: As a means to help safeguard the integrity of the text, at the end of each book of the Tanakh, the Masoretes included a short note (considered part of the *Masorah magna*) that totalled up the number of sentences for that book. I have reproduced their note for Judges here.

The composition history of Judges

When I began this project of translating the Torah and the Former Prophets, I didn't intend to spend a great deal of energy thinking about the composition history of these books. Very quickly, however, I realized that to be successful in expressing the books' ideas and thoughts in a natural modern-day English, I would need to connect on an emotional and personal level with their authors and, insofar as it is possible, understand the authors on their own terms. In translating this and other books, I have found that in order to make that emotional connection with the authors, I first had to form opinions about who they were, who their audience was, and especially what motivated them to write. What follows then is a summary of my views, developed over the course of this translation, about the circumstances behind the composition of Judges and about the motivations of its authors in writing what they did.

**

As a preliminary to examining the composition history of Judges, it is important to keep in mind that the scholarly effort to reconstruct the composition history of the books of the Torah and the Former Prophets is an entirely speculative endeavor. This is primarily because there are very few external controls available to us that can serve as productive anchors for the analysis. For Judges, as well as for the other books of the Former Prophets and the books of the Torah, the manuscripts from Qumran and ancient authors' references to the Septuagint are our only true external controls. The main thing that we learn from these two controls is that between the third and first centuries BCE, the books had grown into a form very close to their form today.[1] But with very

---

[1] With respect to Judges, the most useful external control are fragments of three manuscripts of Judges found at Qumran—1Q6 (or 1Q Judges), 4Q49 (or 4Q Judges^a), and 4Q50 (or 4Q Judges^b). From the fragments of Judges found there, we can determine that a version of the book relatively close to the one we have today was in circulation by the first century BCE. In addition, it is worth mentioning that there is a fragment of a fourth manuscript of Judges—referred to as XJudges—that dates to the first century CE and is of uncertain provenance. On XJudges, see E. Eshel, H. Eshel, and M. Broshi, "A New Fragment of XJudges," *Dead Sea Discoveries*, Vol. 14, No. 3 (2007), pp. 354-358.

few exceptions, external controls provide us with little information about when these books were first composed or about the existence of different literary layers within the books.

In addition to the small number of external controls, very often there are internal controls—that is, links or references to a book found elsewhere in the Tanakh—that scholars can use to inform their understanding of a book's composition history. These internal controls take a variety of forms, but most commonly they are vocabulary and language that two books have in common, or they are explicit references made in one book to the characters and events of another book. While these internal controls can be very useful in informing a theory of composition history, they are almost always highly problematic, for they are typically open to interpretation and can be used to support any number of theories about a book's composition. For example, in my introductory comments, I used references found in the book of Samuel to specific "champions" (Jerubaal, Bedan, and Jepththah) as an internal control to inform my ideas about what stories in Judges were part of the pre-exilic version of the book. While I believe this is a plausible way to understand these references in Samuel, there are other ways to understand these references that are equally plausible and that would not necessarily provide us with any information about an early version of Judges.

As discussed in my introductory note, my approach to Judges' composition history follows my understanding of the growth and development of the work that most scholars call the Deuteronomistic History (but which I have divided into the Josianic History and the Israelite History). Within Judges, I identify six broad compositional stages spanning a period from perhaps as early as the eleventh century BCE to the second century BCE. While this six-stage framework helps make sense of the messiness and the many contradictions and inconsistencies in the text, it should be emphasized that the nearly continual writing, rewriting, supplementing and revising of the book over a period of centuries means that it is not always possible to separate with confidence the changes and additions made during one stage from those made in preceding or succeeding stages. With that caveat in mind, I present in detail below my views on the composition history of Judges. As stated above, these views are highly conjectural—they are only one way of looking at the history of Judges, and they are very much influenced by my own starting assumptions about the histories of ancient Israel and Judah; scholars with a different set of starting assumptions will come to a very different view of the book's history.

**

The book of Judges in its current form presents itself as a more or less connected narrative. However, as numerous scholars have argued (and as I argue in the introduction), there is good reason to think that many of the stories in it had an independent life prior to its existence as a connected narrative. These old stories, which are about the ancient heroes of the northern tribes and which likely circulated both in written form and orally, served as the primary source material for the earliest full version of the book. It is these old stories in their independent form, prior to their being brought together, that I treat as the book's first compositional stage. In essence, this is a "pre-compositional" stage, because in this stage the stories about the individual leaders were not yet joined into a single narrative.[2] In their original form, these stories would have been simple accounts of the hero's exploits, and they would have lacked the broader narrative frame based on the cyclical "apostasy–foreign oppression–rescue by a champion" structure. These stories by and large have their roots in ancient tribal memories of actual individuals. We should presume that the stories would have evolved and been embellished over the centuries before being integrated into Judges. As I will argue below, most of these stories were inserted into Judges as part of the second compositional stage, but at least one of the stories was not added until much later, as part of the work during the fifth compositional stage. Thus, we may think about this first "pre-compositional" stage as relatively fluid and as stretching over a very long period of time, from as early as the eleventh century BCE to as late as the fourth century BCE, when I believe the last of these ancient hero stories was integrated into Judges.

The primary benefit of collecting the source material together like this and viewing it as a "compositional stage" is that it helps the reader understand more clearly the composition techniques of the biblical authors. Moreover, looking at the material in this way helps us draw a sharper line between what was original source material and what was

---

[2] The German scholar Wolfgang Richter proposed that the earliest literary layer of Judges consisted of a "Book of Saviors"—a collection of stories about the great heroes Ehud, Yael, and Gideon. While my views on the early material in Judges have a number of similarities to Richter's proposal, I do not see a good reason to understand these stories as integrated into a single work at such an early time, primarily because there is no plausible "setting in life" that I can find for such a work. The details for Richter's proposal for a Book of Saviors, which is still popular among many scholars today, can be found in his books *Traditionsgeschichtliche Untersuchungen zum Richterbuch*, Bonner Biblische Beiträge 18, Bonn: 1963 and *Die Bearbeitung des 'Retterbuches' in der deuteronomistischen Epoche*, Bonner Biblische Beiträge 21, Bonn: 1964.

composed by later authors and editors. The material that I attribute to this earliest compositional stage is as follows:

—Core of P12. This *parashah* tells the story of the champion Ehud Gerasson, from the tribe of Benjamin. It details his daring assassination of Moab's king Eglon. In its early independent form, the story would have lacked the present narrative frame, and it likely also lacked the subsequent account of the Israelites' attack on Moab after Eglon's death.

—Core of P16. This *parashah* records the Song of Deborah, which celebrates the northern tribes' victory over Sisera's army and Yael's murder of Sisera after he had fled the scene of battle. The song is full of archaic grammatical forms and language; along with many scholars, I believe that the song represents the oldest material in the entire Tanakh and that it may date to the tenth or even the eleventh century BCE.

—Core of P19-P26. These *parashot* tell of the exploits of Gideon Yoashsson against the Midianites, as well as the stories of Gideon's "call" and of his testing Yahweh in order to receive proof that he will be victorious. The material in these *parashot* is quite diverse and there were likely multiple traditions about Gideon at this stage that were only loosely connected with one another. I identify ten stories about Gideon in this early material: Gideon's call (P19-P20); why Gideon is called Yerubbaal (P20,1); Gideon's test of Yahweh with the wool (P20,2); the selection of the three hundred warriors (P20,1-P21,3); the Midianite's dream (P22); the attack of the jars and torches (P23 and the first part of P24); the argument with the Ephraimites (middle section of P24); the treachery of Sukkoth and Penu'el (end of P24 and middle section of P25); the execution of Zevah and Tzalmuna (end of P25); and the gift of the spoils (P26).

—Core of P39-P40; core of P43; core of P45. These *parashot* represent what I believe is the oldest material about Jephthah, a hero from the region of Gilead. The material about Jephthah is less diverse and more cohesive than the stories about Gideon. I identify three early stories in the material about Jephthah: the disinheritance of Jephthah (P39); Jephthah's return to Gilead (P40); and Jepththah's war with Ephraim (P45). In addition, although the brief treatment of Jephthah's defeat of the Ammonites in P43 doesn't qualify as a story, I believe the details in that *parashah* represent old material. I view the story of Jephthah's vow and sacrifice of his daughter (P42 and P44) as a literary composition of the fifth compositional stage, and I view the account of his communication with the Ammonite king (P41) as a product of the book's fourth compositional stage.

—Core of P56. This *parashah* contains elements of an old folk story about the legendary strongman Samson of the tribe of Dan. I have included it here as part of the first compositional stage in order to highlight its background as a folk story. That said, however, this particular story about Samson (not to mention the other stories about him) is unlike the other old folk traditions that I attribute to the first compositional stage, which are about great military heroes of the northern tribes. Samson, by contrast, is not a military leader, but rather a strongman who acts on his own and who is unable to lead others or attract followers.

**

I believe that the earliest written version of Judges—the version that first connected stories of the ancient northern tribal heroes into a single narrative—was composed during the 630s BCE as part of what I call the Josianic History. It is the body of work that went into creating this original version of Judges that I treat as the book's second compositional stage. As discussed in the introduction, I believe that the authors of the Josianic History were from northern families that had come to Judah in the late eighth century after the Assyrian conquest of the northern kingdom. These families had some role in one of Yahweh's cults in the north, and they may have been closely allied with the prophet Hosea and his circle. Moreover, when they came to Judah, they likely brought ancient cult rule books with them which contained the rules for the practice of their version of Yahwism—rule books that would later form the basis for the book of Deuteronomy.[3] Once settled in Judah, these families would almost certainly have been opposed to the practices within Yahweh's cult in Jerusalem, and they would have been treated as unwelcome outsiders by the leaders of the Jerusalem cult. However, by the mid-seventh century BCE, some individuals from these families must have managed to secure positions within the royal court. While this is wholly speculative, it is conceivable that they may have been involved in the palace conspiracy to assassinate Amon and to replace him with his eight-year-old son Josiah.[4] Whether or not they were involved in the conspiracy, it seems very likely that they must have won influence with Josiah's mother, Jedidah Adayahsdaughter, who would have served as regent for her

---

[3] On the role of cult rule books within the northern cults, see the introduction to my translation of Leviticus.

[4] See 2 Kings 21.19-26 for the account of Amon's reign. The account of Josiah's reign begins in 2 Kings 22; his mother is named in 2 Kings 22.1.

young boy in the initial years of his reign. This, I believe, is the most plausible scenario explaining the cult reforms and expansionist political policies of Josiah's reign, the composition of the earliest version of the book of Deuteronomy and its connections to those cult reforms, and the composition of a "Josianic History"—the earliest versions of Judges, Samuel, and Kings—to justify the Davidic dynasty's claim on the lands of the former northern kingdom.[5]

The version of Judges that was part of the Josianic History was much shorter and less substantial than the versions of Samuel and Kings that it was (quite loosely) connected to. I believe this version of Judges consisted of the stories of Ehud, Deborah and Baraq, Gideon, and Jephthah plus a brief account of the champion Othniel; the authors of the second stage joined all this material through the creation of a cyclical narrative framework. This cyclical structure had two purposes. First, it enabled them to connect the stories without needing to concern themselves with continuity of characters or events. Second, and most importantly, the cyclical structure was a means to demonstrate their main theme, which was that the loose organization of the tribes and the actions of the great tribal leaders were insufficient to prevent the people from regularly forsaking Yahweh and doing "the worst thing"— that is, giving service to the gods of the surrounding peoples. This theme prepares the reader for one of the principal arguments of the Josianic History: that the governance and protection of the people is best accomplished through the rule of a king who himself is loyal to Yahweh and who follows the laws and precepts that Yahweh has established for him and his people. The other theme that the authors of the second stage expressed through their narrative framework was the idea of a unified people called "Israel" that encompassed both

---

5   I speculate that the earliest versions of the books of Judges, Samuel, and Kings may have been composed in the 630s BCE as part of the educational curriculum of the young king Josiah. In this scenario, we may imagine members of these northern families winning influence with the queen mother Jedidah and convincing her to delegate responsibility for the king's education to them. These families used stories about great northern tribal heroes of old to educate (and to entertain) the boy-king, and especially to instruct him in the difference between a great leader (Gideon) and a poor leader (Jephthah). The stories of David (a great leader) and Saul (a poor leader) were likely used in a similar fashion in the king's education. Then later, as Josiah began implementing his ambitious political policies and cult reforms in the 620s, these authors would have expanded and revised Samuel and Kings (but not necessarily Judges) in order to provide justification for the king's actions with a broad audience that included the Judean elite. For some additional thoughts on the initial composition of the books of Judges, Samuel, and Kings as part of the king's education, see note 23 of my introductory essay.

the northern tribes and the southern tribes. It is important to note, however, that there is no evidence that the authors of the second stage thought in terms of there being twelve tribes. Their version of Judges mentions only ten tribes: Ephraim, Manasseh, Benjamin, Zebulon, Asher, Issakar, Naphtali, and the tribe of Gilead[6]—all of which are in the north—and Judah and Reuben in the south. The tribes of Gad, Dan, Simon, and Levi are absent from the narrative of the Josianic History.

The material that I attribute to the second compositional stage is as follows:

—P9, excluding the final paragraph. This *parashah* summarizes the principal themes of Judges and states the cyclical narrative structure of the stories that follow. It is important to note that in this *parashah* the terms "Israel" and "Israelites" refer to the unity of all the tribes as a single people. This is an important concept for the authors of the Josianic History, as it is needed to help justify the Davidic dynasty's claim on the north, which is a key theme of the early version of Samuel and which formed the basis of Josiah's expansionist political policy. The opening of the *parashah* does not read as the beginning of a new book, and I believe that the authors of the third stage (that is, the authors of the Israelite History) likely removed the introductory sentence or sentences from this *parashah* when they connected Judges to the newly composed book of Joshua.

—P11. This *parashah* provides a brief account of the champion Othniel Qenazsson. The *parashah* is almost entirely a composition of the authors of the second stage—the narrative frame and the dates come from them; the names are likely the only parts of the *parashah* that have a basis in oral tradition. It is interesting that Othniel's tribal affiliation is not mentioned. In the book of Joshua, he is from the tribe of Judah, but it is an open question as to whether the Josianic historians (the authors of Judges' second stage) knew of a tradition about where Othniel was from. If the Josianic historians were aware of Othni'el's connection to Judah, it is quite possible that they may have included a story about him in their narrative in order to have some southern representation in their version of the book, which otherwise concerned only the tribal heroes from the north.

—Insertion of P12 plus addition of the narrative frame. This *parashah* tells the story of Ehud Gerasson, a hero from the tribe of Benjamin

---

6   In the work that I call the Israelite History, which I understand to be a sixth century expansion of the Josianic History, the tribe of Gilead has been replaced by the tribe of Gad and the eastern clans of Manasseh.

who assassinated Eglon, the king of Moab. The authors of the second stage appear to have left the original story known to them (whether in oral or written form) mostly untouched. They have clearly added the narrative frame at the beginning of the *parashah* and the concluding sentence, both of which presume a unified people "Israel" that is not present in the story itself. I believe it also likely that the account at the end of the *parashah* about the Israelites as a unified force attacking Moab and capturing the fords of the Jordan was not based on an old tradition but was composed by the authors of the second stage.

—P14-P15; insertion of P16. These *parashot* tell the story of the Israelites' defeat of the army of Hatzor's king Yavin and of the murder of his general Sisera by Yael.[7] The authors' source for their story is the Song of Deborah and Baraq, which must have been a famous ancient song in their own day and which they have incorporated into their book as P16. In order to integrate the song into their narrative, they composed P14 and P15, which consist almost entirely of a prose summary of the song and a narrative frame connecting the prose summary to the larger narrative of Judges. Neither the stanza at the song's beginning about Yahweh marching to war nor the stanza in the middle of the song about Gilead, Dan, Asher, Zebulon, and Naphtali appear to be original, although the language of both stanzas appears to be of a similar age to that of the song. I believe that the authors of the sixth stage (whose work overlapped with the fourth and fifth stages during the Persian and Hellenistic periods) added these stanzas to address two problems in the original song: the lack of Yahweh's involvement in the actual battle, and the omission of Gilead, Dan, and Asher from a battle involving all the northern tribes.

—P16,1. The Josianic historians composed this *parashah* as the conclusion to the story of Israelites' defeat of the king of Hatzor and the murder of Sisera and to fit that story into their cyclical narrative frame.

—P17. This *parashah*, which the authors of the second stage composed to introduce the Gideon stories in P19-P26, provides a good example of the Josianic historians' composition technique: the authors have joined some elements from oral tradition (the livestock raids and pillaging of Midian, Amaleq, and Qedem) with things they had personal experience of (the remains of old signal towers and forts in the mountains) and then placed the resulting story within their cyclical

---

7   There is also an account of the defeat of Yavin and his army in Jos P22-P23. In that account, Yael, Deborah, and Baraq are absent, and Joshua is solely responsible for leading the Israelites to victory. See note 14a above for a discussion of how the two accounts relate to one another.

narrative frame.

—Insertion of the old stories in P19-P26, plus edits to P20, P20,2, P24, and P26. The stories of the tribal hero and champion Gideon Yoashsson of the tribe of Manasseh are found in P19-P26. The authors of the second stage knew of numerous stories about Gideon, most of which were originally not connected to one another. In this second stage, the authors have connected these stories together into a single narrative by adding framing sentences at various places in their account; but otherwise in these *parashot*, they made few other changes to their source material. The sentences that the Josianic historians added are often easy to identify because they speak of "the Israelites" rather than individual tribes or they impose the cyclical narrative structure on the underlying stories. The Josianic historians' main edits to the Gideon stories are as follows: they added the final sentence of P20; they added the first sentence to P20,2; they possibly made some additions in the first half of P24, where the story transitions from the attack on the Midianites' by the three hundred men to the pursuit of Midian involving multiple tribes; and in P26, they added the final sentence and the preceding parenthetical comment about the priest's vest that Gideon made, and they likely also added the passage at the beginning of the *parashah* where Gideon rejects the offer of kingship.

—P36 and the first half of P37. The Josianic historians composed this material as the introduction to the Jephthah stories. In this material, they place the Jephthah stories within their cyclical narrative framework. The Jephthah stories play in important role in the scheme of the Josianic historians: to them, Jephthah demonstrates the inadequacy of the "champion" model, and thus the stories about him serve to lay the groundwork for the establishment of the monarchy in the book of Samuel. As discussed in note 37d above, in the old stories about Jephthah from the first compositional stage, Yahweh actively supports Jephthah and "delivers" the Ammonites into his hands. This poses a problem for the Josianic historians' scheme regarding the failure of the champion model; they solve this problem through the composition of the first half of P37, in which Yahweh expresses his frustration with the Israelites and refuses to "rescue" them again.

—Composition of P38, insertion of P39-P40, insertion of P43 with edits, and insertion of and conclusion to P45. These *parashot* represent the account of Jephthah as it existed in the second compositional stage. The authors of this stage composed P38 to provide the setting for the old tribal traditions about Jephthah that are preserved in P39-P40, P43, and P45. The Josianic historians have made no edits to the old material with the exception of the concluding sentence to P43, which they added to overlay their "all Israel" theme onto Jephthah's victory. The conclusion of the story of Jephthah in P45 highlights the problems with the "champion" model—it is overly dependent on the individual who serves as champion, there is no natural successor to take the champion's place after his death, and there is no structure or set of requirements to ensure that the individual is an effective and just leader. Thus, the Jephthah stories may be understood to lay the groundwork for the necessity of kingship and of a set of laws for the king to follow, which is one of the key themes of the Josianic History.

—P49. This brief *parashah*—just a single sentence—represents the original conclusion to Judges. The book concludes with the beginning of another cycle of apostasy–oppression–rescue; the oppressors this time are the Philistines, and the *parashah* thus serves to prepare the reader for the events of the book of Samuel, which would have directly followed this *parashah* in the "official" version of the Josianic History that was promulgated in the 620s BCE to the Judean elite.

**

I attribute the work on the third compositional stage of Judges to the authors of what I call the Israelite History. I understand the Israelite History, which I believe was composed in the first half of the sixth century BCE, to be primarily a reinterpretation and expansion of the older Josianic History. The authors' purpose in creating this new history was to explain and come to terms with the traumatic events of the 590s and 580s BCE, when the Babylonian king Nebuchadnezzar and his army destroyed the temple in Jerusalem, exiled the Judean king, and made Judah a vassal state. The authors of the Josianic History, as I have argued above, were from northern refugee families and were treated as "outsiders" by the Jerusalem cult officials. The authors of the Israelite History, by contrast, were most likely of Judean background, and they were "insiders" associated with the leaders the Jerusalem cult and the former royal court. In the five or six decades between the composition of the two histories, the northerners succeeding in transforming the Jerusalem cult in accord with the principles of Deuteronomy. As a result, by the time work began on the Israelite History, its authors—a collection of individuals from the royal court of Judah and from Yahweh's cult in Jerusalem—had been fully "converted" to the practice of the cult according to Deuteronomic principles. Yet, because these individuals' families were mostly from the south and not the north, their perspective on many issues was different than the authors of the Josianic history.

The authors of the Israelite History expanded the Josianic History—which consisted of the earliest versions of Judges, Samuel, and Kings—

into a comprehensive historical chronicle that covered the time from the origin of Yahweh's relationship with his people to the destruction of the temple and the exile of the leading Judeans to Babylonia. The creation of this new history was a very large undertaking: I believe it involved the composition of the earliest version of Exodus-Numbers (then a single book); the composition of the earliest version of Joshua; the expansion of Deuteronomy and the addition of a narrative frame connecting it both to Exodus-Numbers and to Joshua; the replacement of the original beginning of Judges with a new *parashah* (P8) to connect it to Joshua; and additions and expansions to Samuel and Kings in support of the history's larger themes and to bring the chronicle up to the current day.[8] Most notably, these authors transformed Yahweh's binding agreement with the Davidic king (which was a key theme of the Josianic History) into a treaty between Yahweh and his people. The introduction of this novel concept of a treaty between Yahweh and his people involved the integration of the exodus, wilderness, and conquest traditions via the composition of the books of Exodus-Numbers and Joshua, and it prompted the authors to transform the ancient concept of Yahweh's "battle chest" (which plays a prominent role in the book of Samuel) into "the treaty chest" (ארון הברית), where both the ten commandments and the Torah scroll written by Moses were stored.[9]

With respect to Judges, I believe the authors of the Israelite History made only a small number of edits, as there is little evidence of their hand in the book. They likely were satisfied with the Josianic historians' overarching theme in Judges—that the people regularly forsook Yahweh for the local gods, despite his rescuing them time and again from their foreign oppressors—and consequently, they must have felt that there was little need to make significant changes or introduce new themes. It is surprising to me, however, that the Israelite History's authors incorporated into Judges only a single reference to Yahweh's treaty with the Israelites (see the end of P9), and that they did not see fit to make any references to the Israelites' obligations to Yahweh under those treaties, nor make mention of the treaty chest. One might speculate that the authors were preoccupied with the larger tasks of writing Exodus-Numbers and Joshua and expanding Deuteronomy and so devoted much less of their attention to Judges, but there is really no

---

8   The Josianic History likely ended with the summation of Josiah's greatness in 2 Kings 23.25.
9   See Deut P30.

way to know the reason they made so few changes to Judges.[10]

The material in Judges that I attribute to the third compositional stage is as follows:

—Composition of P8 and removal of the original beginning to Judges. In order to connect the newly composed book of Joshua to the book of Judges, the authors of the Israelite History removed Judges' original beginning (likely only a couple sentences) and composed the account of Joshua's death in P8 to serve as a new beginning to the book. In the original Israelite History, this *parashah* would have followed directly from Joshua's farewell speech in P53, which was the original conclusion to Joshua.

—Additions to P9. The authors of the third stage have made four additions to this very important *parashah*. Three of the additions are minor and are discussed above in notes 9f, 9h, and 9l. The fourth addition, which consists of two sentences near the end of the *parashah*, is quite significant. In this addition, the authors of the third stage connect the apostasy–oppression–rescue theme to Yahweh's treaty with the Israelites. Specifically, the addition makes clear that the Israelites' inability to uphold the treaty obligations is what leads Yahweh to allow foreigners to invade the Israelites' land and oppress them. It is worth noting here that this addition represents the sole mention of Yahweh's treaty with the Israelites in the version of Judges that existed in the third compositional stage.

**

During the Persian period and the first two centuries of the Hellenistic period, the book of Judges nearly tripled in size. The book during these years was likely an important text within the temple library in Jerusalem, and the cult officials, leaders, and scribes who were the

---

10   During my work on Judges, as I was developing my thoughts about the book's background and composition history, I reread both Samuel and Kings. In rereading those two books, I was struck by the small amount of material in either book that I felt could clearly be assigned to the authors of the Israelite History. Just as these authors made relatively few changes to Judges, so I believe they made few changes to Samuel and Kings—apart from bringing the historical narrative down to their own present day, they appear to have left the Josianic History's version of those two books largely intact. This is an issue I hope to explore in detail in the future, when I tackle Kings and when I update my translation of Samuel.

library's stewards made many additions and expansions to Judges and the other books in their library.[11] I have somewhat arbitrarily divided the expansions made to Judges during the Persian and Hellenistic periods into two compositional stages: a fourth stage of "early" expansions dating from roughly 550 BCE to 425 BCE, and a fifth stage of "late" expansions dating from roughly 425 BCE to 150 BCE. It is not possible to date this material with any real precision; my assignment of material to either the fourth or fifth stage represents simply my most reasonable guess as to where this material best fits based on my views about the composition history of the other books of the Former Prophets and of the Torah, and based on what we know of the evolution of the Yahwistic religion and the emergence of Judaism during the Persian and Hellenistic periods.

The expansions to Judges that I assign to the fourth stage were quite diverse, and were motivated by many different reasons—as we might expect given the long period of time covered by this stage. I identify four main types of expansions that the authors of Judges made to their book during this fourth compositional stage:[12] (1) they added old traditions and stories that they believed to be authoritative and that they wished to preserve and/or that would enhance the authority of their book; (2) they added material to correct what they saw as factual problems in material from an earlier compositional stage; (3) they composed new material introducing themes that were important to them but that were new to the book; and (4) they added comments and brief passages that corrected the theology of the older material and that made it consistent with the theology of their own day.

The material that I attribute to the fourth compositional stage is as follows:

—P13. This *parashah* provides the very brief account of Shamgar, about whom all that the authors of the fourth stage knew was that he

---

[11] I believe that nearly all the editorial work on the books of the Torah and Joshua during the Persian period and the first half of the Hellenistic period was the result of collaboration between the leadership of Yahweh's cult at Mount Gerizim and the leadership of his cult in Jerusalem. But for Judges, Samuel, Kings, and the major and minor prophets, the cult leadership in Jerusalem was responsible for all changes and expansions. On the partnership between the priesthoods in Mount Gerizim and Jerusalem and their editorial activity on the books of the Torah and Joshua, see my discussions of the composition histories of Exodus, Numbers, Leviticus, and Joshua in my translations of those books.

[12] The Persian-period edits and expansions made to Judges were consistent with the types of edits and expansions made during these years to the other books of the Former Prophets and also, to a certain extent, to the books of the Torah.

killed six hundred Philistines with a cattle-prod.[13] They have added this *parashah* immediately before the story of Sisera's murder in P14-P16 because of the mention of Shamgar in the Song of Deborah. The addition of P13 is an example of the first type of expansion listed above—the addition of old traditions and stories that the authors wished to preserve in an effort to create a more comprehensive and authoritative account of Israel's history.

—P27-P33. These *parashot* recount the story of Abimelek, who ruled as king in Shekem for three years before suffering a gruesome death. The story does not fit well with the principal themes of either the Josianic History or the Israelite History, which is the primary reason that I have assigned it to the fourth compositional stage. In the story, which reads as an entirely literary composition not based on any old traditions, the authors portray Abimelek as an opportunist and murderer who will stop at nothing to gain power, and the citizens of Shekem as his accomplices. The authors' main message is a simple one, and they state it clearly in the beginning of P30 and then again in the conclusion to P33: that in the end, those guilty of murder will be killed by Yahweh in retribution, as is required to satisfy their blood-guilt. Especially interesting, however, is that in addition to this main storyline, the Abimelek story contains much material concerning the god Baal Berith that I believe served as an oblique polemic against the cult of the god Bethel and/or the cult of El (Shaddai).[14] During the Persian period, many of Yahweh's devotees in the diaspora equated the god Bethel with Yahweh, and, equally important, the Jacob material in Genesis equates Yahweh with both Bethel and El Shaddai. I speculate that the polemic against Baal Berith in these *parashot* most likely reflects the discomfort felt by the leaders within Yahweh's cult at Mount Zion regarding the popularity of the god Bethel and the equation of this god and El Shaddai with Yahweh in the Samarian book of Genesis, which had only recently been added to the temple library and connected to the books of the proto-Torah. In particular, the inclusion of the material about Baal Berith in the Abimelek story, including the destruction of his *tzeriah* (an enormous structure within his shrine) and the immolation of his followers, may have served to express the rejection of Bethel (and/or El Shaddai) by the leaders of Yahweh's cult at Mount Zion.

---

13 I believe the authors of the Samson stories, who wrote as part of the fourth and fifth stages, may have used Shamgar as the model for their story of Samson slaughtering the Philistines with the jawbone of an ass.

14 See the discussion above in note 28a.

—P34-P35. These two *parashot* are brief accounts of the champions Tola Puahsson and Jair the Gileadite, and they almost certainly represent old material known to the authors of the fourth stage that they wished to preserve in order to make their history more comprehensive. The reference to Abimelek in P34 is odd, as it seems to view Abimelek in a positive light. One possible explanation of this oddity is that the authors of the fourth stage may have felt obligated to present him as a "champion" of Israel in order to fit his story into the overall narrative framework of the book.

—P41. This *parashah* recounts Jephthah's attempt to dissuade the Ammonites' king from attacking the Israelites. The centerpiece of the *parashah* is a lengthy message from Jepththah in which he summarizes the Israelites' wilderness wanderings and their battles with Heshbon's king Sihon to argue that the land east of the Jordan rightfully belongs to the Israelites. It is unclear to me why the authors of the fourth stage decided to compose this *parashah* and insert it into the Jephthah stories. Possibly they wished to present Jephthah in a more positive light, as without this *parashah* he is not portrayed positively in the stories about him. But there is really no way to be certain about why they chose to add this material here. (On the date of this *parashah*, which is dependent on Persian period additions to the Torah, see note 41a above.)

—P46-P48. These three *parashot* provide brief accounts of the ancient heroes Ivtzan of Beth Lehem, Elon the Zebulonite, and Abdon Hillelsson. As with the addition about Shamgar in P13 and the additions about Tola and Jair in P34-P35, the authors of the fourth stage likely included the accounts of these three heroes out of a desire to make their history more comprehensive and to enhance its authority.

—P50-P52. At some point during the first half of the Persian period, I speculate that there must have been a dissatisfaction among prominent individuals or families of Danite background in what they perceived as the under-representation of their tribe in the book of Judges. To address this, they must have persuaded the stewards of the book of Judges to expand the book with stories about the ancient Danite strongman Samson. However, in the old folk stories about Samson, he was not a very sympthetic figure. Thus to make him "acceptable" and to present him in a more positive light, the authors of the fourth stage composed a lengthy birth narrative for him, which is found in P50-P52. These *parashot* serve as the introduction to the individual stories about Samson's life and present him as a *"naziyr* dedicated to God" who has been specially chosen by Yahweh to "begin to free" Israel from the Philistines. In composing Samson's birth narrative, the author used parts of Samuel's birth narrative in Sam P1 and parts of

Isaac's birth narrative in Gen P19 as models.

—P53-P55. These *parashot* are literary compositions by the principal author of the fourth compositional stage's material about Samson. For the stories in these *parashot*, the author has taken bits and pieces from four old folk stories about Samson—the story of his killing the lion, the story of his murder of thirty citizens of Ashqelon, the story of the foxes, and the story of the spring in Lehi. To these, he has added the story of the slaughter with an ass's jawbone, which was originally about Shamgar (see P13), but which he has recast as about Samson, and he has composed out of whole cloth the story of his betrothal and wedding feast. Impressively, the author has almost seamlessly woven all this disparate material together and he has created a unified narrative of considerable literary sophistication. By the end of the fourth compositional stage, the book of Judges would have concluded with the statement in P55 that Samson "championed Yisra'el during Philistine times for twenty years."

**

As discussed above, I have somewhat arbitrarily divided expansions made to Judges after the Israelite History as "early" and "late," assigning the former additions to the fourth compositional stage and the latter additions to the fifth compositional stage. In my view, this fifth stage began around 425 BCE and lasted well into the second century, after which the book received only minor changes and edits.[15] The additions to Judges in the fifth stage were even more extensive than those of the fourth stage, and the motivations for adding this material were slightly different. I identify five types of additions made by the authors of the fifth stage: (1) they created a new beginning to the book that added complexity to the conquest narrative of Joshua and that more appropriately set the stage for the chaotic period described in

---

15 My starting date for the fifth compositional stage is based on a comparison of this material with material from Joshua and Leviticus. The material from Judges' fifth compositional stage presents the conquest of Canaan as a partial one, with native Canaanite peoples remaining in various pockets of the land. We also see this view expressed in Persian period expansions to Joshua. However, I argued in my translation of Leviticus that sometime in the early fourth century BCE, the idea came into vogue among certain segments within Yahweh's cult that the occupation of the land was entirely peaceful. I have thus chosen a starting date of ca. 425 BCE for Judges' fifth compositional stage to explain the addition of the material about the occupation at the beginning of the book, as this material reflects the Persian period view found in Joshua and also likely predates the views about the occupation found in Leviticus.

the stories that followed; (2) they added material emphasizing certain theological points that were important to them but that were not explicit in the older material; (3) they expanded the stories of individual champions with the composition of new material and the insertion of old traditions; (4) they added stories about events in ancient times that are unrelated to the larger narrative concerns of Judges, but that serve as explanations (or "origin stories") for unusual current and past practices; and (5) they composed new stories to highlight the problematic nature of the period when "there was no king who ruled over Israel and each man did as he thought best." On the whole, the material from the fifth compositional stage is much more poorly integrated into the narrative of Judges than material from the fourth compositional stage. The authors of the fourth compositional stage were one to two centuries removed from the Josianic History and the Israelite History, and their understanding of the book was still partly influenced by themes of those two works. By contrast, the authors of the fifth stage were writing two to three centuries after the authors of the Josianic History and the Israelite History—their worldview was entirely different, and their understanding of the book and their purpose in adding new stories to it were consequently very different as well.

The material that I attribute to the fifth compositional stage is as follows:

—P1, first half of P2, all of P3 - P5,4. These *parashot* reflect old tribal traditions about the occupation of their territory and their conflicts with the native Canaanite peoples. The authors of the fifth stage added this material to express a more nuanced view of the settlement of Canaan than that presented in the book of Joshua. The authors of the earliest version of Joshua, which I associate with the original composition of the Israelite History, present the conquest of Canaan in terms of the "ban devotion," in which the Israelites slaughter all the inhabitants of the land—including women, children, and the elderly. In this version of Joshua, only the inhabitants of Gibeon, who trick the Israelites into making a peace treaty, are spared. As I discuss in the notes to my translation of Joshua, the authors of the Persian period viewed the description of the land's settlement found in the earliest layer of Joshua as highly problematic, in part because it was so obviously at odds with old stories about the Israelites interacting with the native Canaanites in the period after they occupied the land. As a result, the Persian-period authors of Joshua made a number of changes to Joshua to reflect this more nuanced picture of the occupation. I believe it likely that some of these same individuals were responsible for composing a new beginning to Judges here in P1 - P5,4, which also expressed this more nuanced picture of the occupation of the land. This more complicated picture of the occupation also served as a more appropriate set-up for the following stories in Judges, which depict a chaotic and lawless time at odds with the monolithic picture of the occupation of the land in the earliest layer of Joshua.

—Second half of P2. At a different time than the addition of P1-P5,4, the authors of the fifth stage added to P2 the material about Kaleb's giving his daughter Aksah to Othniel. This material also appears in Jos P30, but I believe the material in Judges represents the original version. See the discussion about this material in note 2d above.

—P6-P7. These two brief *parashot*, which are not at all integrated into the larger narrative of Judges, provide an etiology for how the place called Cryers got its name. The author of these *parashot* seeks to explain the inconsistency between the old material in Joshua, where the local people have been entirely eradicated, and the traditions found in later versions of Joshua and Judges, in which some local peoples remain in the land. The author of P6-P7 explains their presence as due to the Israelites' violation of their treaty with Yahweh. The author uses Deuteronomic language, but these *parashot* cannot have been part of the third stage of Judges (the Israelite History), as the authors of that stage assume that the local peoples were killed off entirely. I believe that the material in P6-P7 was added later than P1-P5,4, although both are part of the fifth compositional stage.

—End of P9. The authors of the fifth stage have added the two sentences at the end of the *parashah*; in them, they state that the reason Yahweh didn't drive out all the native peoples from Canaan was so that he might use them to test the Israelites and see whether they would follow his precepts.

—P10, excluding the end. This *parashah* was likely added at a different time than either P1-P5,4 or P6-P7. The addition in P10, like P1-P5,4, is concerned with correcting Joshua and presenting a more nuanced view of the occupation of the land. The authors of this *parashah* provide the reason why there were "nations" still living in Canaan after the Israelites' took possession of the land: Yahweh allowed them to remain as a way to test whether the Israelites would obey his commandments that were given to them by Moses.

—The end of P10. I understand the comment at the end of this *parashah*, which states that the Israelites lived among the local peoples and intermarried with them, to be an addition from the fifth stage, but added at a later time than the rest of P10. The authors' goal in inserting this comment was to provide context explaining why it was that the Israelites gave service to other gods (the principal crime of the Israelites in the book of Judges). It is worth noting here how this comment reflects the Persian period view of the occupation as gradual, with many native peoples remaining in the land.

—P18. This *parashah* appears in the introduction to the Gideon stories. The point of the *parashah* is to remind the reader of Yahweh's freeing the Israelites from their servitude in Egypt and of the Israelites' disobedience. This addition, like P6-P7, is not at all integrated into the larger narrative. Like those *parashot*, it seems to have been added only to highlight a theological point the author felt was missing from Judges. This *parashah* may have been one of the last pieces of material added to the book of Judges. As discussed above in note 18a, this *parashah* is missing from one of the manuscripts of Judges found at Qumran (4Q Judg^a), suggesting that it may have been added to the text in the second century, or even the first century, BCE.

—Second half of P37 plus additions to first half of P37. The first half of P37 appears to be corrupt in multiple places; while it is not possible to recover the original version of this material, I believe that the authors of the fifth compositional stage inserted the mention of the Ammonites and Philistines at the beginning of the *parashah*. The authors of the fifth stage were also responsible for the addition of the second half of P37; in this addition, they integrated Yahweh more deeply into the story of Jephthah, likely because they were unaware of the rationale of the original authors (the Josianic historians) for minimizing Yahweh's involvement in Jephthah's time as "champion."

—P42 and P44. These two *parashot* are the account of Jephthah's sacrifice of his daughter in fulfillment of a vow to Yahweh; they provide an etiology for an old folk custom that was known to the author but likely no longer practiced. The insertion of this story about human sacrifice reflects the interest of the authors of the fifth stage in showing the objectionable practices and lawlessness of society prior to the establishment of the monarchy—an interest that also prompted the lengthy additions in P59-P63 and P64-P74,2.

—Insertion of and edits to P56. This brief *parashah* tells the story of Samson's dismantling of the town gate at Gaza to escape the Philistines. The *parashah* is unlike the other Samson material in Judges, lacking dialogue and the sophisticated literary elements found in the other Samson stories. For that reason, I believe this *parashah* partially preserves the remains of an old folk story; the authors of the fifth stage inserted it into the text to complement the stories about Samson added in the fourth compositional stage. Given that this *parashah* likely would never have served as an "ending" to the book and given the lack of literary sophistication found in this *parashah*, it seems most probable to me that it was added after P57-P58.

—P57-P58. These two *parashot* are the story of Samson and Delilah. The story reads as an entirely literary composition, although it may draw on an old folk story about Samson's death. The author of the story shows great literary skill and has introduced into his story numerous connections with the older Samson narrative from the fourth compositional stage in P50-P55. One of the "editions" of Judges that existed early in the fifth compositional stage likely would have concluded with P58. The final sentence of P58 is clumsily tacked on; it was clearly added in an attempt to make the narrative frame of the Samson stories consistent with the narrative frames of the stories of the other champions in Judges.

—P59-P63. The authors of the fifth compositional stage added the story of the origin of the Danite priesthood and the origin of the image of Yahweh used in the shrine in Dan. The authors don't specify what form the image had, so it is unclear if we should view this as an alternative origin story to the one in Kings that attributes the foundation of the shrine in Dan and the image of the bull calf there to the Israelite king Jeroboam. There is no obvious rationale for why the authors of the fifth stage added this story to Judges. There was much material added to the books of the Torah during the Persian period that seems to have been prompted by a desire that the record of traditions be "complete," and the same rationale may perhaps explain the addition of the material about Dan here in Judges. That is to say, the authors of the fifth compositional stage wished to enhance the authority of Judges by ensuring it represented a complete record of the traditions about Israel during the pre-monarchic times, including traditions known to them about Yahweh's cult at Dan.

—P64-P74,2. These *parashot* tell the story of the Benjaminites' rape of the concubine of a Levite man, the resulting war between the Israelite tribes and the tribe of Benjamin, and the problem of finding wives for the six hundred Benjaminites who escaped the slaughter of their tribe. The story reads entirely as a literary creation of the late Persian period or of the first half of the Hellenistic period, and it does not appear to have any connection to old folk traditions. As discussed in the notes to these *parashot*, the author crafted his story by borrowing extensively from elements of stories in Genesis, Joshua, and Samuel; his goal was to create what he hoped readers would perceive as an "ancient" story. Unfortunately, because of his relatively poor literary skills, what resulted from his efforts was a mostly incoherent hodgepodge. The composition and insertion of this bizarre and disturbing story was likely motivated by the desire of the authors of the fifth stage to demonstrate in a vivid way the objectionable practices and lawlessness that characterized society prior to the establishment of the monarchy. Given both the extremely poor literary quality of this story and its excessive length (it takes up one-sixth of the entire book), it is surprising to me that the priestly leadership agreed to its inclusion into Judges. The story reads as the composition of someone on a "power trip" who refused to accept the changes for improvement suggested by others involved in the creation of new material for the fifth compositional stage; as mentioned above in note 64a, I suspect the author might have been someone very influential and powerful, whose full control over this material was impossible for the priestly leaders to deny.

—P75. This short *parashah* concludes the book of Judges in its final form. It sums up the views of the authors of the fifth stage, and was likely added to the book when the story about the origin of the Danites' shrine to Yahweh was added. A similar sentence appears in the story about the Danites at the beginning of P61; I believe that sentence was composed by the same individual as the author of P75. (By contrast, the comment at the end of P59, which repeats the sentence here in P75 verbatim, is likely an addition from the sixth stage.)

**

In the sixth compositional stage of Judges, the authors largely limited themselves to editorial work—adding glosses and comments to clarify obscure terms and passages, to resolve inconsistencies, to correct errors, and to make certain theological points more explicit. This stage spanned a very long period and overlapped in part with the fourth and fifth and possibly even the third stage.[16] However, most of the activity in this stage was likely contemporaneous with the fifth stage, taking place in the fourth through the second centuries BCE. In these centuries, the books of the Torah, the Prophets, the Psalms and the other books of the Writings first began circulating outside the cult libraries in Jerusalem and Mount Gerizim and began to be read and studied in the diaspora communities. It was during these years that the institution of what ultimately became the synagogue began to emerge from the religious practices of Yahweh's devotees,[17] the majority of whom lived

---

16 Some of the authors of the sixth compositional stage likely also contributed to the fourth and fifth stages. I separate out their work on what I call sixth stage from their work on the fourth and fifth stages because the nature of the work that I attribute to the sixth stage is quite different, being primarily editorial in nature and not at all concerned with the addition of old traditions or the composition of new stories about premonarchic times.

17 For an excellent discussion of the origins of the synagogue, see L. Levine, *The Ancient Synagogue: The First Thousand Years* (New Haven: Yale University Press,

far from Jerusalem and Mount Gerizim. As study and reading of the books of the Torah and the Prophets and some of the Writings became a regular part of the religious practices of Yahweh's devotees, it seems certain that questions would have arisen about confusing matters in the text or about what appeared to be omissions in the text—and it also seems certain that these questions would have been brought back to the priestly leaders in either Jerusalem (in the case of the books of the Torah, Prophets, and Writings) or Mount Gerizim (in the case of the books of the Torah alone), and that the priestly leaders would have felt some responsibility to clear up these confusions and to address the various omissions. Obviously, the scenario I have painted here is hypothetical, but I believe that some scenario such as this explains the circumstances surrounding the sixth compositional stage of Judges.

To Judges' sixth compositional stage, I assign nearly all the material in the book that in my translation appears within brackets and much of the material that appears within parentheses. This material is as follows:

—Edits to P2, P3, P4, and P5,4. The editors of the sixth compositional stage have added a number of explanatory comments to the *parashot* at the beginning of Judges. These comments, all of which I translate in brackets or in parentheses, provide readers with information about the former names of towns (P2 and P4), clarify references that might confuse readers (P3), and remind readers of family relationships (P3) and geographical boundaries (P5,4).

—Edits to P9 and P10. The editors of the sixth stage have added a brief comment in P9 to emphasize that Yahweh's punishment of the Israelites for their apostasy was in fulfillment of the oath he made to them in Deut P31 (the Song of Moses). In P10, they have added a comment that corrects a statement by a previous author: they state that the reason Yahweh left some of the neighboring nations alone was not to test Israel, but rather to teach them the ways of war. This comment is later corrected by a different editor, who clarifies that it is only the ways of war "which they didn't know previously."

—Edit to P11. In this *parashah*, the editors of the sixth stage have added a clause informing the reader that Othniel Qenazsson was a "much younger" kinsman of Kaleb, thus harmonizing the reference to him here with the reference to him in P2.

2000), pp. 19-41. The earliest firm evidence for synagogues in the diaspora comes from Egyptian inscriptions dating to the third century BCE; on these, see Levine, *The Ancient Synagogue*, pp. 75f.

—Edit to P12. The editors of the sixth stage have added one short comment to clarify that the phrase "your enemies" near the end of the *parashah* refers to Moab.

—Edits to P15. In this *parashah*, the editors of the sixth stage have added a brief comment clarifying where Deborah's Palm is located. They have also added a parenthetical comment explaining how it happened that someone from Qayin (which is located south of Judah) came to live in the northern territory of Naphtali.

—Additions and edits to P16. I believe the editors of the sixth stage made a number of additions and edits to the Song of Deborah over the course of the Persian and Hellenistic periods. First, they added fragments of other ancient songs known to them in two places in order to address two problems in the original song. To address Yahweh's lack of involvement in the battle, they have added the second stanza (the first line of which is "When you, Yahweh, march from Se'iyr"). And to address the omission of Gilead, Dan, and Asher from a battle involving the other northern and transjordanian tribes, they have added the twelfth stanza (the first line of which is "Across the Yarden, Gil'ad stays put"). The material from the second stanza appears to come from a single song, whereas the material in the twelfth stanza is disjointed and likely was drawn from three or more separate songs. Apart from adding these two stanzas, the authors of the sixth stage have also inserted three comments in the song: near the song's beginning, they inserted a comment to clarify that "Yahweh's approach" takes place at Sinai; in the description of the battle, they glossed "chieftains" as belonging to Yahweh's people; and at the end of the song, they added a wish that all those who love Yahweh remain strong.

—Edit to P22. The editors of the sixth stage have added a comment about the vast size of the camp of Midian, Amaleq, and the Qedemites. The comment is based on language from P17. See note 22b above.

—Glosses to P27 and P28. In these *parashot*, the editors of the sixth stage have added a brief comment reminding readers that Ophrah was the ancestor of the Ezrites (P27) and that Yerubbaal and Gideon are the same person (P28).

—Comments to P35. The editors of the sixth stage have added a clarifying comment that Jair's sons owned the jackasses that they rode, and they have inserted the statement about Jair's Hamlets, likely due to the influence of the mentions of Jair's Hamlets in Joshua, Numbers, and Deuteronomy.

—Edit to P36. I believe the editors of the sixth stage added a mention of the Philistines to include them with the Ammonites as the oppressors of Israel. This addition may have been prompted by the mention of the Philistines' gods earlier in the *parashah*, or possibly by the mention of the Philistines together with the Ammonites in P37.

—Correction to P38. In this *parashah* the editors of the sixth stage clarify that it was Gilead's chieftains, not the Israelite forces, who proposed that the man who starts the fight against the Ammonites should serve as leader of Gilead.

—Edit to P45. Here the editors of the sixth stage have added a comment clarifying the geographical relationship of Gilead to the tribal territories of Manasseh and Ephraim.

—Comment to P52. The editors of the sixth stage have added a brief comment stating that after Yahweh's emissary vanished, it never showed itself again to Manoah and his wife.

—End of P59. The final sentence of this *parashah* is likely from the hand of the editors of the sixth stage, who borrowed the language from P75 and inserted it here to provide the reader with context for understanding the unusual cult practices of Miykah, which were adopted by the Levite priest who founded the cult at Dan.

—Comments to P63; addition to P63. The editors of the sixth stage added three comments to this *parashah*: a brief comment about why Forest Village is also known as "Dan's Camp;" a gloss that the men in battle gear were Danites; and a comment stating the exact location of Laish. The editors have also added a sentence at the conclusion of the *parashah* that preserves a variant ending to the story; in the variant ending, the shrine at Dan was in operation until the fall of the northern kingdom (722 BCE) rather than until the destruction of Shiloh (ca. 1000 BCE). The variant ending also informs the reader of the Levite's name—Jonathan Gershomsson Mosesson. (Note that at a much later date, Mosesson was changed to Manassehsson; see note 63q above.)

Schema for the composition history of Judges

First Stage [Tribal Hero Stories] (ca. 1100 – ca. 500 BCE)	Second Stage [Josianic History] (635 – 620 BCE)	Third Stage [Israelite History] (ca. 590 – ca. 550 BCE)	Fourth Stage [Early Expansions] (ca. 550 – ca. 425 BCE)	Fifth Stage [Late Expansions] (ca. 425 – ca. 150 BCE)	Sixth Stage [Canonical Scripture] (ca. 550 – ca. 100 BCE)
				P1 – P5,4 and P6 – P7	Edits to P2, P3, P4, and P5,4
		P8			
	P9 excluding end	Additions to P9		End of P9	Edits to P9
				P10 excluding end; end of P10	Edits to P10
	P11				P11 edit
P12 core	Insertion of P12 plus narrative frame				Edit to P12
			P13		
	P14 – P15				
					Edits to P15
P16 core	Insertion of P16				Additions and edits to P16
	P16,1 – P17				
				P18	
Core of P19 – P26	Insertion of and edits to P19 – P26				
					Edit to P22
			P27 – P33		Glosses to P27 and P28
			P34 – P35		Comments to P35
	All of P36; first half of P37; all of P38			Second half of P37 plus additions to first half of P37	Edit to P36; correction to P38
P39 – P40 core	Insertion of P39 – P40				
			P41	P42	

First Stage [Tribal Hero Stories] (ca. 1100 – ca. 500 BCE)	Second Stage [Josianic History] (635 – 620 BCE)	Third Stage [Israelite History] (ca. 590 – ca. 550 BCE)	Fourth Stage [Early Expansions] (ca. 550 – ca. 425 BCE)	Fifth Stage [Late Expansions] (ca. 425 – ca. 150 BCE)	Sixth Stage [Canonical Scripture] (ca. 550 – ca. 100 BCE)
P43 core	Insertion of P43 plus conclusion to P43			P44	
P45 core	Insertion of P45 plus conclusion to P45				Edit to P45
			P46 – P48		
	P49		P50 – P52; P53 – P55		Comment to P52
P56 core				Insertion of and edits to P56; composition of P57 – P58	
				P59 – P63	End of P59; comments to P63; addition to P63
				P64 – P74,2	
				P75	

Appendix

The Song of Deborah and the display of songs in the Masoretic tradition

The standard format of the Aleppo Codex, the Leningrad Codex, and the other important early Masoretic manuscripts is to display the Hebrew text in three columns to the page. The Masoretes used the three-column format for the "historical" books and other narrative works, for the prophetic literature, and for many songs.[1] But for two of the wisdom books—Job and Proverbs—and for the book of Psalms, as well as for songs that had special importance, the Masoretes did not utilize the three-column format and instead arranged the page in two columns or in a single column. The books of Psalms and Job, for example, are displayed on pages with two columns of text, while the Song of Moses (Deut P31) and the Song of the Sea (Exodus P26) are displayed on pages with just a single column.

With respect to writing out songs, the Masoretes' decision to employ one- and two-column pages was likely motivated by a desire to display the songs in a way that reflected their structure, which is based on what in poetry is called a bicolon. Simply defined, a bicolon is a pair of lines in which the second line repeats or elaborates the ideas and imagery expressed in the first line.[2] For the most important songs—the songs on pages with just a single column of text—the Masoretes made a special effort to highlight the bicolon-based structure of the song by placing a "closed" blank space between the first line and second line of each bicolon.[3] For these songs, each bicolon typically occupies a single line of text, with a new bicolon beginning on a new line, and blank spaces in the text used only to separate the two halves

---

1   The Song of Songs, for example, is displayed in the Aleppo Codex and the Leningrad Codex in three columns to the page, and looks no different on the page than prose text.
2   Although ancient Hebrew lyrics are overwhelmingly composed of bicolons, many songs also contain one or more tricolons—that is, units of three lines in which the second two repeat and/or elaborate the topic of the first line.
3   The "closed" blank space separating the two lines of a bicolon in songs is equivalent in form to the "closed" blank space used to mark the *parashah setumah* in prose texts.

of a bicolon. While the presence of tricolons often made it impossible to maintain the principle of one line per bicolon, the scribe for the consonantal text of the Aleppo Codex, Shlomo ben Buya'a, made a great deal of effort to adhere to this principle for the Song of Moses and for David's Song of Thanksgiving (Samuel P104).[4]

The first twenty-one lines of the Song of Moses in the Aleppo Codex.

However, for the Psalms and for Job and Proverbs (each of which was displayed in two columns to the page), it was not possible for ben Buya'a and other scribes to maintain the principle of one bicolon to the line, as the columns on the page were too narrow to display the text of an entire bicolon. For these books, the Masoretes instead adopted the practice of one "closed" blank space in each line of text.[5] This was in principle identical to the format used for songs displayed on single-column pages, but it resulted in blank spaces appearing in the

---

[4] By contrast, the scribe for the consonantal text of the Leningrad Codex, Shmu'el ben Ya'aqov, barely adhered at all to this principle for the Song of Moses. Instead, he arranged the blank spaces for that song in a way that created a visually pleasing "zig-zag" pattern.

[5] But note that in the figure of Psalm 13 on the following page, there is an "open" blank space after the heading (similar to the "open" blank space that marks a *parashah petuhah*) to indicate that the heading is not considered part of the psalm.

text almost at random—sometimes at the end of a colon, sometimes at the end of a bicolon, and sometimes in the middle of a colon—and the blank spaces did not line up visually.

For two songs in the Tanakh, the Masoretes used a special method of display that alternated between lines with a single "closed" blank space and lines with two "closed" blank spaces. In this method of display, which was used for the Song of the Sea (Exodus P26) and the Song of Deborah (Judges P16), the Masoretes placed a "closed" blank space after each and every colon, regardless of whether it was the first or second colon of a bicolon. This method of display results in what to the modern eye looks like a checkerboard pattern. The unique display of these songs is very old and was likely developed sometime in the Talmudic Period (70 - 640 CE). We know this because in the Exodus fragments found at Qumran (ca. first century BCE), the Song of the Sea is not displayed in this special format, whereas in the Ashkar-Gilson manuscript (a rare example of a "proto-Masoretic" manuscript that scholars date to between the seventh and eighth centuries CE), the Song of the Sea is displayed in this pattern.[6]

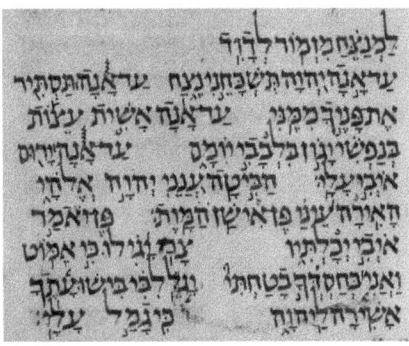

Psalm 13 in the Aleppo Codex.

A selection of nine lines from the Song of Deborah in the Aleppo Codex.

In fact, there is some evidence to suggest that during the Talmudic Period, all major songs in the Tanakh's prose books—the Song of the Sea, the Song of Moses, the Song of Deborah, David's Song of Thanksgiving, and David's Song of Praise (1 Chr 16)—may have been

---

6   See P. Sanders, "The Ashkar-Gilson Manuscript: Remnant of a Proto-Masoretic Model Scroll of the Torah," *Journal of Hebrew Scriptures* 14 (2014), article 7.

arranged in this "checkerboard" pattern. This evidence comes from the Tractate Megillah, which describes the layout of songs in the Tanakh as follows:[7]

כָּל הַשִּׁירוֹת כּוּלָּן נִכְתָּבוֹת אָרִיחַ עַל גַּבֵּי לְבֵנָה וּלְבֵינָה עַל גַּבֵּי אָרִיחַ חוּץ מִשִּׁירָה זוֹ וּמַלְכֵי כְנַעַן שֶׁאָרִיחַ עַל גַּבֵּי אָרִיחַ וּלְבֵינָה עַל גַּבֵּי לְבֵינָה

All the songs [in the Tanakh] are written as a half-brick above a whole brick and a whole brick above a half-brick, except this song [Esther 9.7ff] and the Kings of Canaan [Jos P24 - P24,31], which are [written as] a half-brick above a half-brick and a whole brick above a whole brick.[8]

Traditionally, the "whole brick" has been understood to refer to a line (or partial line) of a song, and the "half-brick" to refer to the "closed" blank space in the middle of a line of a song. Thus "a half-brick over a whole brick and whole brick over a half-brick" describes a song in which a blank space appears over each song line, and a song line appears over each blank space. This is exactly the display of the Song of Deborah and the Song of Sea in the Aleppo and Leningrad codexes. By contrast, in the method of display that the Tractate Megillah says is the exception—"a half-brick over a half-brick and a whole brick over a whole brick"—each song line appears above another song line and each blank space appears above another blank space. This is how the Song of Moses is displayed in the Aleppo Codex and Leningrad Codex.

If the above evidence for the display of songs during the Talmudic Period can be trusted, then when the Masoretes began standardizing the text in the eighth and ninth centuries CE, they must have decided to simplify the display of songs by abandoning the complex "checkerboard" method of display that alternated between lines with one "closed" blank space and lines with two "closed" blank spaces. Instead, they adopted the simpler method of one "closed" blank space per line for all major songs in the prose books, and they retained the checkerboard display only for the Song of the Sea and the Song of Deborah.

**

---

7   See *b. Meg.* 16b.
8   Esther 9.7ff and Jos P24 - P24,31 are in fact lists; they were likely treated as songs because the use of *parashot setumot* to separate the short items they contained made them appear offset from the surrounding material, similar to the display of genuine songs.

The checkerboard pattern of display for songs must have been quite challenging for scribes to execute. We can see this most clearly in the Leningrad Codex's display of the Song of Deborah. Shmu'el ben Ya'aqov, who wrote the entire codex including its *Masorah*, adhered very closely to the principle of placing a "closed" blank space after each colon in the first half of the song; however, by the second half of the song, the demands of alternating between lines with one blank space and lines with two blank spaces proved too difficult, and in this half of the song, he frequently resorted to inserting blank spaces into the middle of colons in order to maintain the alternation between lines with one blank space and lines with two blank spaces. The struggles of ben Ya'aqov in writing down the Song of Deborah thus allow us to appreciate all the more the achievement of ben Buya'a in the Aleppo Codex. In the Song of Deborah, he adhered almost exactly to the principle of a "closed" blank space after each colon; in only three instances is it obvious that he omitted a blank space after a colon, and never did he insert a blank space in the middle of a colon.

Because of the unique display of the Song of Deborah in the Masoretic text, and because of the special care the Masoretes took to write this song, I thought readers might find it interesting to see an English version of the song arranged in the way the Masoretes wrote it. Thus I have reproduced my translation of the song below, but I display the lines as they are displayed in the Aleppo Codex, with the English text of each colon occupying the same location in the song that the colon occupies in the Hebrew text. Because I was unable to expand the width of the text block as the Masoretic scribes did when they shifted to a single-column format for the page, I have instead shrunk the font size so that more letters fit into each line of text. I should also note that the introduction to the song, which I did not represent as part of the song in my translation of Judges above, is written as though it is part of the song in the Aleppo Codex and the other Masoretic manuscripts. Similarly, the text in the body of my translation that I identify as P16,1 (because it is clearly not part of the original song) is in fact shown as part of the song in the Masoretic manuscripts.

**

On that day, Devorah and Baraq Aviyno'amsson sang 'When in Yisra'el commanders commanded when men joined up for war (give praise to Yahweh!).' "Listen here, kings and viziers, and to me turn your ears. A song I shall sing, a song to Yahweh plucking the lyre for Yahweh, god of Yisra'el! [*When you, Yahweh, march from* Se'iyr *when from Edom's fields you stride forth* the earth *shudders and shakes, the sky bursts and spurts   clouds let loose great floods of water.   Mountains judder and quake at Yahweh's approach   (that is, Siynai) yes, at the approach of Yahweh, god of Yisra'el!]*   Back in the days of Shamgar Anathsson   yes, back in Ya'el's time, highways had vanished   and wayfarers traveled tortuous roads.   Country folk had disappeared from Yisra'el, vanished   til Devorah appeared, til a great mother rose in Yisra'el!   God chose new things: food was bought and sold   but neither shields were seen, nor lances   among the forty thousand living in Yisra'el.   Sing of the plans of Yisra'el's commanders   of men joining up for war (give praise to Yahweh!),   of men astride tawny jenny-asses   sitting atop saddle-blankets, and traveling down the road!   Arrows whizzed twixt watering holes   (where later were recounted Yahweh's victories   the victories of Yisra'el's country folk).   Then Yahweh's forces swooped, attacking the gates!   'Get up, Devorah, get going!   Get up, get going and recite this song!   Quickly, Baraq! Take captive your captives, Aviyno'amsson!'   'But then arrived a fugitive, a noble [*Yahweh's   people*] a valiant one among warriors, seeking refuge with me   someone from Ephrayim, with ancestors in   Amaleq.'   'After you, Binyamin! Right there with your troops!'   From Makiyr the generals marched down   from Zevulun those wielding the officer's baton.   Yissakar's commanders took position with Devorah   as Yissakar, so too Baraq, deployed into the valley on foot.   Meanwhile in Re'uven's brigades, leaders planned their attack.   'Why do you sit amongst desolate encampments   listening to the bleatings of goats   while for Re'uven's brigades, great men mull over their plans?'   [*Across the Yarden, Gil'ad stays put.   As for Dan, why does he tarry back by the ships?   Or Asher, why does he stay at the edge of the sea,   settling in where he disembarked?   Zevulun—a people belittling life to the point of death.   And Naphtaliy—up in the heights of the countryside.*]   Kings arrived, they entered battle   'twas then the kings of Kena'an waged war   at Ta'nak, alongside Megiddo's watercourses   while plunder of silver they forswore.   Swooping down from the sky, they attacked   yes, from their tracks the stars at Siysera struck.   The Wadi Qiyshon swept them away   that most ancient of wadis, the Wadi Qiyshon   its mighty stream stamping them under.   Then the horses' hooves hammered down   their warriors charging at a furious gallop.   [*'Damn Meroz!' Yahweh's envoy cried. 'Its denizens be damned!   For they came not to Yahweh's aid   went not with the valiant to Yahweh's support!'*]   Most bless'd of women: Ya'el Hever-the-Qeynites-wife   most bless'd of women living in tents!   He asked for water, she gave him milk   yes, she proffered clotted cream in the finest of bowls!   She reaches with her hand for a tent spike   with her right hand, grasps a workman's hammer.   She hammers Siysera, she obliterates his head   smashing and slicing through his temple!   At her feet he crumpled, fell and lay   at her feet he crumpled and fell!   Where he crumpled, there he fell—destroyed!   Siysera's mother gazed out the window, squealed thru the lattice: 'Why is his chariot so bashful about arriving?   Why the hoof-beats of his chariotry still slow to sound?'   Her ladies-at-court shrewdly responded   (to herself she too posed an answer):   'Surely they found and are divvying the spoils   a lass, maybe two lasses for each of the men!   For Siysera, great piles of finely dyed cloth   yes, great piles of intricate finery   intricate weavings brilliantly dyed, borne on captives' backs!'   Thus may all your enemies, O Yahweh, perish!" [*And those who love him be strong as the rising sun!*]   And so the land was tranquil for forty years.

www.ingramcontent.com/pod-product-compliance
Lightning Source LLC
LaVergne TN
LVHW061331060426
835512LV00013B/2605